David

Material Worlds
Simon J. Bronner, Series Editor

DESIGNING the
CENTENNIAL

*A History
of the 1876
International
Exhibition
in Philadelphia*

BRUNO GIBERTI

THE UNIVERSITY PRESS
OF KENTUCKY

Publication of this volume was made possible in part by a grant from the National Endowment for the Humanities.

Editorial and Sales Offices: The University Press of Kentucky
663 South Limestone Street, Lexington, Kentucky 40508-4008
www.kentuckypress.com

The Library of Congress has cataloged the hardcover edition as follows:
Giberti, Bruno.
    Designing the centennial : a history of the 1876 International Exhibition in Philadelphia / Bruno Giberti.
    p.   cm. — (Material worlds)
    Includes bibliographical references and index.
    ISBN-10: 0-8131-2231-7
    1, Centennial Exhibition (1876 : Philadelphia, Pa.) I. Title. II. Series.
T825.B1 G53 2002
907.473—dc21   2001004580
ISBN-13: 978-0-8131-2231-1 (cloth : alk. paper)
ISBN-13: 978-0-8131-9213-0 (pbk. : alk. paper)

Chapter 5 appeared previously as "The American System of Awards: Order and Anxiety at the U.S. Centennial Exhibition." *American Studies in Scandinavia 31,* no. 1 (1999), 1–23.

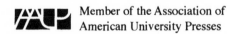

To my mother, the teacher,

and my father, the carpenter

The classification of an exhibition may be said to be its organic life, the basis of its growth, the frame-work or skeleton from which it takes its shape and character. The groups and classes are like crystalizing points, drawing to themselves like objects. The elaborated system stimulates and directs effort and is the basis of organization of the work of collecting, arranging, and examining the objects. The classification is intended not only as an expression in general and in detail of what the exhibition is to be, and as the guide for the arrangement or placing of the objects, but it should be at the same time a guide to the exhibition, useful alike to the exhibitors, the jury and the public. The system, whatever it may be, characterizes the whole exhibition, pervades its literature, and is the basis of the descriptions, the catalogues, and the reports. It has no ephemeral influence, but modifies virtually and for all time the results of the undertaking. It is therefore of first importance to secure a well-devised system.

—William P. Blake,
"Report to the United States Centennial Commission"

CONTENTS

PREFACE

This book began as a very different kind of project. My original intention was to study the history of nineteenth-century British design reform, particularly the impact of the 1851 Great Exhibition in London, which served as a wake-up call to the artists, critics, and bureaucrats who formed the backbone of the reform movement. I was dissuaded from pursuing this topic by a dearth of resources, and by the amount of existing scholarship in this area. In looking for a subject closer to home, I settled on the United States Centennial Exhibition, held in 1876 in Philadelphia, as a parallel experience for American reformers. Here I quickly became distracted by another, more fundamental part of the exhibition's story, which was the organizers' apparent obsession with order. This manifested itself first in the creation of a complicated system of classification, and then in an attempt to impose this structure on the rest of the exhibition, with the intention of creating a transparently organized, classified landscape of commodities.

The organizers of the Centennial—by this I mean the commissioners, administrators, and professional designers who were collectively responsible for the shape of the exhibition—were not alone in this preoccupation; they shared it with the organizers of other exhibitions. In fact, the Centennial typifies a whole generation of early world's fairs, which began with the Great Exhibition and ended with the 1933 International Exposition in Chicago, where the managers self-consciously rejected the existing tradition of competitive display. In contrast to a later generation of world's fairs, which focused more and more on the circulation of images, the early fairs celebrated the production and consumption of goods, which were collected in great number and displayed with a puzzling directness. It was not enough to have a representative sample of things, the collection of the exhibition had to include as many examples of as many things as possible, made in every part of the world. How these things were organized, how they were housed, how they were arranged, how they were displayed, and, finally, how they were judged as commodities—these were all issues facing the organizers of world's fairs and their kindred institutions, like the bazaar, the museum, and the department store. These were issues constituting an array of design problems—order, architecture, installation, display, evaluation—which form the subject and structure of this book.

Under the influence of the 1867 Exposition universelle in Paris, the organizers of the Centennial devised a dual system of classification and installation, which located each object in two ways: by country and by type. The exhibition was meant to be transparent, systematic, and tabular—transparent in the sense that the order was legible in the arrangement of displays; systematic or scientific in the sense that the classification was supposed to be a taxonomy of goods; tabular in the sense that the dual system naturally suggested a grid, which the organizers attempted to build in the real space of the fair.

Surprisingly, at this late date, the organizers of the Centennial were still conceiving the exhibition in terms appropriate to the Enlightenment. But as they came to know their project and their audience, the organizers gradually adopted a more modern stance. This shift was clearly evident in the ways that people looked at the exhibition, and in the ways, both large and small, that the exhibition was constructed as a space for different kinds of looking—both the focused gaze and the distracted glance. These were symptomatic of the two visual regimes, the Cartesian and what I am calling the contextual, which have dominated Modernity—the first in its early phase (the Enlightenment), and the second during the nineteenth and twentieth centuries. The first was represented physically by the vitrine, a traditional form of display, which situated the artifact in the abstract space of a closed glass box and thus provided a clear separation between subject and object. The second was represented by more progressive forms like the mannequin and the model room, which resituated the artifact in the putative context of the body or the domestic environment and thus promoted a subjective engagement with the object.

In the architecture of the exhibition, we see the organizers negotiating a threshold between two ways of building, between the representational form of traditional masonry monuments, and the rationalized space and structure of utilitarian frames in iron (and later in steel). The architecture of the exhibition was arguably a triumph of rationalization, although the situation is complicated by the fact that some of the engineers responsible for the design of the Centennial also had aspirations toward architecture. Certain judges fought a rear-guard action against this process of rationalization, which was represented by the whole system of the exhibition and particularly by the so-called American System of Awards. The organizers devised this as an alternative to what they considered the anonymous and irresponsible system of juries and prizes that had characterized previous fairs.

In devising the preceding argument, I have been more than a little influenced by the work of Michel Foucault, especially his account of epistemic change in *The Order of Things* (see chap. 1). I have also been influenced by other works of cultural studies, particularly Martin Jay's *Downcast Eyes* (1993) and Jonathan Crary's *Techniques of the Observer* (1990), which together provide a parallel account of the transformation of modern visuality, that is, culturally determined vision. Finally, Burton Benedict's important essay "The Anthropology of World's Fairs" served as a kind of précis for my own examination of the Centennial.

While I am an architectural historian, this book is obviously not a study of buildings alone, although buildings played an important part in the overall design of the exhibition. I can claim no great debt to a work of architectural history, with the possible exception of Dell Upton's *Holy Things and Profane: Anglican Parish Churches in Colonial Virginia* (1986). This showed me how to study material culture in the context of architecture (or was it the other way around?) with the intention of recovering the mind, the motive, the mentality of the people in question.

In my own mind, material culture has always been the subject of this book, although not in the conventional sense. *Designing the Centennial* is not a study of *things* per se—an impossible task, given the encyclopedic scope of a world's fair—but of *ideas about things,* as expressed in the design of a fair, and a group of related institutions. I have tried to understand the intentions of the people who shaped the exhibition in Philadelphia, which were different, and arguably less modern, than the intentions of the people who went to see it. In doing this, I had to resort to some very general explanations, drawn from outside my own discipline, to interpret the particular situation of the Centennial. This may trouble some historians, who are still wary of "theory." In my defense, I can only cite the words of an anthropologist, who explained his presence at a meeting of architectural historians by saying, "I borrowed what I needed to explain what I found."

I can still remember the day I was sitting in the dimly lit office of Dell Upton, then at the University of California, Berkeley; I was trying to explain the nature of my project. I think I'm doing *this,* I said, and he responded, Aren't you really doing *that?* I am grateful to Dell for turning me around with a question when I was still backing into the subject of this book. Margaretta Lovell and Galen Cranz of the University of California also had an encouraging influence.

In doing the research, I worked in several locations: at the Berkeley libraries; in Philadelphia, at the Athenaeum, the Free Library, and the Historical Society of Pennsylvania; in Washington, at the Library of Congress and the libraries of the Smithsonian Institution. I am grateful to the staff in all these places, but I would especially like to thank Elizabeth Byrne of the Environmental Design Library at UC Berkeley and Joseph Benford of the Free Library's Print and Picture Collection for their personal attention and support.

I am grateful for the support of my own institution, California Polytechnic State University at San Luis Obispo, which included a generous grant to produce the illustrations for this book. I am also grateful to the Architecture Department for allowing me to spend two years at an off-campus program in Alexandria, Virginia, where I was nearer my material, and particularly to my two colleagues, Professors Serim Denel and Christopher Yip, for filling in during my absence.

On a more personal level, I would like to thank my good friend and colleague Mark Brack of Drexel University, Philadelphia, for reading parts of this manuscript, and for continuing to entertain me with his perverse view of academic life—make that life in general. Finally, I must thank my dear friend and companion, Kent Malcolm Macdonald, for also having read the manuscript—several times, as he just reminded me. But especially for reminding me, at a low moment, that I had to write this for myself.

1

THE ORDER OF
THE EXHIBITION

Natural history is nothing more than the nomination of the visible.
—Michel Foucault, *The Order of Things*

From the middle of the nineteenth century to the beginning of the twentieth, the first step in the design of any international exhibition was to classify the goods that would be on display. This was a formative act that influenced every other aspect of the exhibition's design—the organization of the catalogue, the plan of the site and buildings, the arrangement of displays, and the comparison of goods.

One could argue that this classificatory imperative was neither new nor unique. The international exhibition was a vast collection of things, and every collection, whatever its size, implies some form of order. The objects must be arranged to form a meaningful assemblage; that is what distinguishes them from a mere accumulation of things.[1] What was it, then, that made the exhibition distinctive as a collection? Certainly its great size and transient nature, the fact that all these objects were brought together for only a short time and then dispersed. But also the presumption that the order of the collection would be made concrete, that the mental structure of the classification would be revealed in the physical structure of buildings and displays. This was an assumption on the part of the organizers that the exhibition shared with other institutions of knowledge, with zoos and botanical gardens, with libraries and museums. But the size and complexity of the fair made it a demonstrably different kind of design problem. As a collection, it did not consist of just one kind of thing—animals or plants; books or paintings or mechanical models—but of every thing made in every part of the world.

In this sense, the exhibition fulfilled an ideal of universal knowledge, which we associate with Denis Diderot and Jean Le Rond d'Alembert's *Encyclopédie* (1751–72). As the first modern work of its type, the *Encyclopédie* was not only alphabetized but also illustrated. The plates depicted the object in three different contexts: by itself, in production, and in use. As Roland Barthes has put it, "The object is thus accounted for in all its categories: sometimes it *is*, sometimes it is *made*, sometimes it even *makes*."[2] The exhibition retained this emphasis on the object but replaced the plates and text of the encyclopedia with an obsessive display of the thing itself, accompanied by an absolute minimum of explanation. This was consistent with the idea of the object lesson, that principle of nineteenth-century education whereby people were presumed to learn best by looking at things.

As a collection, the international exhibition was also distinctive in the sense that it was so thoroughly institutionalized. It was a corporate endeavor in which the "systematic" practices of the professional and the bureaucracy replaced the personal, idiosyncratic efforts of the amateur and the individual. As a result, the planning of the exhibition was deliberate, detailed, and well documented, and the official records provide us with the rare spectacle of a group of people engaged in the conscious project of ordering the world through the analogy of a world's fair. This was certainly true in the case of the 1876 United States Centennial Exhibition, which was held in Philadelphia under the aegis of the United States Centennial Commission.

Order was a founding preoccupation of this bureaucracy. As engineer Henry Pettit, one of the organizers of the exhibition, recalled, "During the earlier sessions of the United States Centennial Commission in 1872 and 1873, perhaps no one subject attracted more serious attention than that of providing the best method for the classification and arrangement of exhibits."[3] The commission quickly decided on a dual system, one that was "both geographical and systematic." This meant that every object was to be located at the intersection of two fields, one national and the other typological. The result was a taxonomy of things, a reflection of the natural order that had been one of the principal achievements of early modern science.

It is evident that the organizers of the Centennial Exhibition were motivated by some very old fashioned ideas about the world, ideas that put them at odds with both their project and their audience. But it is also evident that the organizers were obsessed with history, and they scarcely made a move without examining it in the light of precedent. Although industrial fairs were as old as the industrial revolution itself—the Austrians may have held the first in Vienna in 1754—comprehensive, international exhibitions were still a relatively recent invention. Only eight had taken place by the time the commission began to meet in Philadelphia in 1872. (The British ran a series of partial exhibitions from 1871 to 1874.) Of these eight, the organizers of the Centennial were primarily interested in the three largest and most successful: the 1851 Great Exhibition in London, the 1867 Exposition universelle in Paris, and the 1873 Weltausstellung in Vienna.

The most important antecedents of these fairs were the many national expositions held by the French between 1798 and 1849. Here we can see all the important features of an international exhibition: the development of elaborate systems of classification and concomitant systems of juries and awards, the publication of lengthy reports and catalogs, and the attempted imposition of bureaucratic forms of control. To these we should add the construction of temporary exhibition halls, such as the portico and Temple of Industry at the 1798 exposition. This was the first of eleven fairs, which took place under every type of government and in a variety of locations— the Champs-de-Mars (1798), the courtyard of the Louvre (1801, 1802), the esplanade of the Invalides (1806), inside the palace of the Louvre itself (1819, 1823, 1827), the place de la Concorde (1834), and the Champs-Élysées (1839, 1844, 1849).[4] Each one was bigger than the last, their numbers mounting from a modest 110 exhibitors in 1798 to a whopping 4,532 in 1849—a certain measure of the growing importance of manufacturing in French life.[5]

According to the jury report of the 1834 fair, these expositions were inspiring other countries to do the same, with one conspicuous exception:

> Almost all, in Europe, have wanted to follow this brilliant example, even those who seem the least progressive. Austria and Spain, the Piedmont and Portugal, the Two Sicilies and the Netherlands, Prussia and Bavaria, [the Napoleonic kingdom of] Holland and Denmark, Sweden and Russia have established national expositions. . . . England alone in Europe believes herself too rich and too superior to resort to such stimuli. She disparages, she disdains these efforts; she pretends to close her eyes, but she looks long and hard at attempts whose aim is to diminish the inequality of national industries; and, as a result, to erase the supremacy of one over the others.[6]

Why did the British not follow the French example? In addition to a longstanding rivalry, and a traditional distrust of things European, there are two good reasons. First, as the leading industrial nation with a well-developed commercial empire, the British simply had less incentive to follow the example of their competitors across the Channel.[7] Second, in an attempt to secure their preeminent position, the British had pursued a policy of industrial secrecy, which would have discouraged the exhibition of new products, at least to foreigners.[8] Nevertheless, the British had their own modest but well-established tradition of competitive display in the Society of Arts exhibitions. These had begun—first for art, then for industry—shortly after the founding of the society in 1754. They had continued in some fashion into the 1840s, when certain members of the society began to consider the challenge of sponsoring a national fair.[9]

London, 1851

When the British finally got around to organizing a major fair, they trumped the French tradition by vastly expanding its premise. They held the world's first international exhibition in London's Hyde Park, in a single remarkable building that quickly became known as the Crystal Palace (fig. 1-1). The idea of the exhibition seems to have been the joint product of Prince Albert, the consort of Queen Victoria, and that consummate bureaucrat and design

1-1. "The Great Exhibition." 1851, London (John Tallis, *Tallis's History and Description of the Crystal Palace* [London: John Tallis, 1851], vol. 1, n.p., Library of Congress).

reformer, Henry Cole. In 1849, Cole and English architect Digby Wyatt had visited the last and largest of the French national fairs in Paris and had submitted a report that is supposed to have served as the basis for the 1851 Great Exhibition.[10]

As president of the royal commission in charge of the exhibition, Albert proposed to divide the displays into four broad sections: "the first comprising the raw materials which nature supplies to the industry of man; the second, the machinery by which man works upon those materials; the third, the manufactured articles which he produces; and the fourth representing the art which he employs to impress them with the stamp of beauty." This last section was frequently abbreviated as "fine arts," but in fact it was supposed to be limited to the arts as applied to manufactures.[11] In an imperfect attempt to maintain the industrial focus of the exhibition, painting was excluded as something not dependent on material conditions; sculpture was included as something in between art and craft or industry. Even this limited construction allowed for a drastic change from the French tradition in which art and industry were displayed in entirely separate contexts—art at the annual Paris Salon and industry at the national expositions.

The commissioners of the Great Exhibition accepted Albert's plan in principle, although it was clearly very rudimentary. They established seven Committees of Sections, including prominent men in various fields, which assumed the task of elaborating his plan into a series of more detailed lists of things admitted into the exhibition. Even these inventories proved to be inadequate, so Lyon Playfair, the chemist in charge of the juries, prepared a more developed system of thirty classes.[12] Subdivided into as many as three levels of smaller groups, the classes were supposed to be a development of Albert's four sections. These had implied a certain equality between areas, but what is immediately apparent about Playfair's system is the dominance of manufactures, with nineteen classes (63 percent of the total), over the other areas; the relative lack of importance of machinery and raw materials, with six (20 percent) and four (13 percent) classes, respectively; and the almost complete insignificance of the arts, with one class (3 percent). These proportions were similar if less extreme in the juries, where the number of the members was supposed to reflect the number of goods on display—raw materials with 30 members (9 percent of the total), machinery with 93 (29 percent), manufactures with 180 (57 percent), and fine arts with 15 (5 percent). The jury reports warned readers not to draw any conclusions from these numbers, yet it is hard not to see them as a sign of the relative importance of manufactures in an industrial economy.[13]

The order of this exhibition was not supposed to be arbitrary; the organizers had considered the French approach too abstract and had asked "eminent men of science, and manufacturers in all branches" to assist in the creation of a system reflecting the reality of "commercial experience." As pragmatic as this may have been in theory, the classification was not successfully applied to the installation of the exhibition. The organizers had hoped for a "scientific" arrangement of displays—objects arranged according to type, without regard to country or place of origin. But the difficulty, if not the impossibility, of predicting the size of foreign exhibits made it necessary to adopt a more practical geographic arrangement. The transept of the Crystal Palace divided the building into two parts; Britain and its colonies exhibited in the western half, while foreign countries mounted their displays in the east. The precise location of these countries was supposed to be determined by latitude to form a map of the world, but the actual plan of the exhibition was more confused (fig. 1-2). By necessity, each country was left to its own devices in the installation of its own exhibit, although the catalogue claimed that the displays were generally arranged according to Albert's four headings—machinery on the north side of the building, raw materials on the south, art and manufactures in the middle. Over and above this very rudimentary scheme, the structural frame of the Crystal Palace promoted a "system" of courts in which displays were arranged by country,

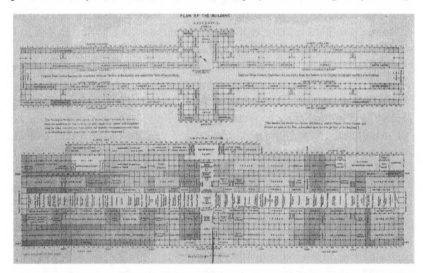

1-2. "Plan of the Building." 1851 Great Exhibition in London (Great Exhibition, *Official Descriptive and Illustrative Catalogue*, n.p., Library of Congress). *Enlarged plate appears on page 229 of the appendix.*

British district, or class of object.[14] In the end, the installation of the Great Exhibition shows the same conflict and compromise between the abstract space of knowledge and the real space of the building, as mediated by logistical problems, that characterized later fairs.

PARIS, 1855 AND 1867

Given their long history of industrial fairs, it is surprising that the French did not take up the challenge of the Great Exhibition until 1855, when they held their first Exposition universelle in the Champs Élysées in Paris (fig. 1-3). The exposition took place in a group of buildings, rather than a single, comprehensive structure like the Crystal Palace. The main building was a new, permanent exhibition hall called the Palais de l'Industrie. This was connected to an annex, the Galerie du Quai, by way of an existing structure, the Rotunde du Panorama. As the size of the exhibition became more apparent, the organizers added three other temporary buildings for the display of agriculture, carriages, and cheap things *(articles de bon marché)*. Finally, after some controversy, they built the Palais des Beaux-Arts, also temporary, on a nearby site.[15]

The Palais des Beaux-Arts signified a fundamental difference between

1-3. Overview of the 1855 Exposition universelle in Paris (Exposition universelle, 1889 [Paris], *Exposition universelle internationale de 1889 à Paris* [Paris: Imprimerie nationale, 1891–92], vol. 1, n.p., Smithsonian Institution Libraries).

this fair and its British predecessor. The French had been troubled by the ambiguous position of the arts at the Great Exhibition—the exclusion of painting because it did not serve an industrial function; the inclusion of sculpture, but in motley surroundings that compromised its status as art.[16] As a result, the 1855 fair included all the arts, but as a virtually separate exhibition, with its own rules, its own section of the organizing commission, and its own building. This allowed the French to claim that their fair was the first truly *universal* exposition, important for reasons of national prestige, while maintaining a boundary between art and industry, a concern of French artists.[17]

Appropriately, then, the order of the 1855 fair consisted of two great categories: products of industry and works of art. These were divided into eight major groups:

- Industrial pursuits related to the extraction or production of raw materials
- Industrial pursuits related to the employment of mechanical power (machinery)
- Manufactures based on the employment of physical and chemical agents or connected with the sciences and instruction
- Industrial pursuits related to the learned professions
- Manufactures of mineral products (metals)
- Woven fabrics
- Decorative furniture and upholstery, millinery, industrial design, printing, and music
- Fine arts

The groups were divided into thirty classes, which were further subdivided into a variable number of sections.[18] If this system recalls the thirty classes of the Great Exhibition, it is because the organizers of the 1855 fair wanted to profit from the experience of their predecessors.[19] In fact, the organizers devised a fundamentally different kind of order. Only half of the classes were comparable; the four sections of the Great Exhibition corresponded only roughly to the eight groups of the Exposition universelle, with manufactures in London broken down into five smaller groups in Paris, to produce a more evenly branching system. Finally, and perhaps most important, the 1855 fair represented a peculiarly French attempt to define a larger and more inclusive order while still maintaining the boundary between art and industry.

The Exposition universelle was similar to the Great Exhibition in one important sense: the classification was typological, while the installation was supposed to be geographic. However, the physical division of the exhibition into six separate buildings, each devoted to some broad area of material culture, meant that the national exhibits were fragmented. At the same time, Henry Cole complained that the "local arrangement," such as it was, made it difficult to compare goods of the same type, as they were separated into national exhibits. Furthermore, the inherent conflict between the principles of typology and geography meant that the classification could not serve as an index or guide to the exhibition. Worse still, the presence of lattice-like connections between branches of the classification made it possible to locate a single thing in several different places.[20] The same complaint was made by another source, which described the classification as "a series of elaborate contradictions."[21]

Other than the introduction of all the fine arts, the most important legacy of the 1855 exposition was the final report of Prince Joseph-Charles-Paul-Bonaparte Napoléon, the president of the exposition and the nephew of the emperor, Napoléon III. In the report, the prince considered the form of such fairs in the future. First, he insisted that they should be serious, educational institutions, not a spectacle offered up for the visitor's curiosity. Second, he suggested that they should be universal only in the sense that they appealed to everyone; they should be partial in the sense that they pertained to a limited sector of the material world—for instance, the fine arts, agriculture and raw materials, machinery, manufactures, or domestic economy. A partial exposition would make it easier to address the problem of space and structure, which had become so critical in Paris. It would also be more educational because it provided a more discreet set of object lessons. "In the presence of infinite diversity," he observed, "however good the classification one adopts, the visitors sees poorly and remembers with difficulty."[22]

According to the prince, the universal exposition was still valid as a record of progress for an entire age, but such a fair should be held on an infrequent basis, say, every fifty years, and then only in a very large industrial center like London or Paris. In this case, the question of building is so important, the prince maintained, that material arrangements rise to the level of a methodological question; they have to be an aid to study. The structures have to be not only vast but also easily expandable, since the size of the exhibition is always difficult to predict. Forget about fixed boundaries, he argued; settle on very light structures, temporary and adapted to the needs of the moment. These would make it possible to give the exhibition the unitary character that is so essential to productive study.[23]

The prince went on to observe that the arrangement of fairs had almost always been geographic. This had been exhausting for visitors who had to hunt down the scattered products. The solution he proposed was a dual system of classification *and* installation: "I am thinking of a structure that, transversally, will offer the objects arranged by nationality and that, longitudinally, will present them disposed according to type of good, in three great divisions"—raw materials, machinery, and various sorts of manufactures. The resulting exhibition would take the form of a giant table of knowledge, a spatial and epistemological grid in which each display is simultaneously located by country and by class. By crossing this grid in one direction, visitors could compare all the goods of a single country; by crossing in the other, they could compare all the goods of a single class.[24]

The British seem to have taken at least the first part of the prince's message to heart with a series of partial world's fairs held in London, beginning in 1862. The French clung to the idea of the universal exposition, but they did adopt a dual system in 1867 at their second world's fair in Paris. Returning to the example of the Great Exhibition, the organizers erected a single, large, "elliptical" hall in the middle of the Champs-de-Mars (fig. 1-4). Covering thirty-nine acres and measuring a mile in circumference, this enormous structure served as the main building and contained most of the displays.[25]

1-4. "Vue officielle a vol d'oiseau de l'Exposition universelle de 1867," by Eugéne Ciceri and Philippe Benoist ([Paris: Lemercier; Berlin: Goupil; New York: Knoedler, 1867], Prints and Photographs, Library of Congress).

The classification of the 1867 fair was considered a vast improvement over any previous exhibition, with the U.S. commissioners calling it "the most comprehensive and exact ever made."[26] The system consisted of ten departments subdivided into ninety-five classes, which might suggest an evenly branching, decimal structure. But it was not really symmetrical; the number of classes in each department varied from five (works of art) to twenty (common arts). Like the order of the 1834 and 1839 fairs, the system was supposed to be based on a hierarchy of human needs: food, clothing, dwelling, raw materials, the elaboration of raw materials in manufactures, the liberal arts, and the fine arts.[27] These translated into the seven departments installed in the main building:

- Food, fresh or preserved, in various states of preservation
- Clothing, including fabrics, and other objects worn on the person
- Furniture and other objects used in dwellings
- Industrial products, raw and manufactured, of mining, forestry, and so on
- Apparatus and processes used in the common arts (machinery)
- Apparatus and applications of the liberal arts—printing, artist's materials, and industrial art; musical, medical, and mathematical instruments; maps and astronomical apparatus
- Works of art

Ironically, these departments were supposed to represent universal needs, but they did not account for the full range of goods on display at a universal exposition, so two more departments were added:

- Livestock and specimens of agricultural buildings
- Live produce and specimens of horticultural works

These were displayed in separate areas, on the island of Billancourt, in the middle of the Seine, and in a part of the Champs-de-Mars known as the Reserve Garden. Finally, a tenth department was added to the system and installed in the innermost ring of the main building:

- Articles exhibited with the special object of improving the physical and moral condition of the people

This was an entirely new category, which would become a defining feature of French fairs. It originated in a special class of affordable goods for the home, which the organizers had added to the 1855 exposition. These provided a balance to the luxury items that the French excelled in producing, which had already become a conspicuous feature of the fairs. The tenth department of the 1867 fair represented an expansion of this practice with a larger category of "social" goods. As the French commissioners reported, "The tenth group touches on everything contained by the other seven classes. It teaches successively the best ways to educate man, to nourish him, to cloth him, to house him, to provide him with work."[28]

Every world's fair is by definition a microcosm, a picture of the world in miniature. At the 1867 fair, this picture took on a particularly graphic and systematic form. The main building was set in a picturesque landscape, with winding paths and smaller pavilions erected in national styles by foreign governments; many reproduced well-known monuments. In a metonymic sense, a person could visit the fair in Paris and see the rest of the world. Furthermore, with all its displays, the main building itself constituted a microcosm. The original intention had been to erect a perfectly round structure, but the rectangular shape of the site favored an elongated footprint—a rectangle bracketed by two semicircular ends. In spite of this alteration, the building was still perceived as a kind of globe. As an official publication reported, "To make the circuit of this palace, circular, like the equator, is literally to go around the world."[29]

The arrangement in the main building was a rounded version of Prince Napoléon's dual system, with national exhibits installed in radial, pie-shaped

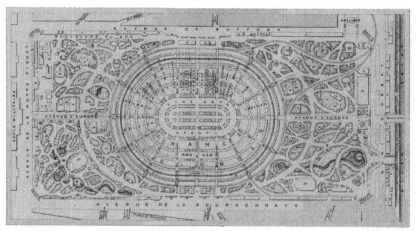

1-5. "Paris Universal Exposition 1867. Plan of the Building and Park" (United States, Commission to the Paris Exposition, 1867, *Reports*, vol. 1, n.p., University of California Library, Berkeley). *Enlarged plate appears on page 230 of the appendix.*

sections and departments in concentric, ringlike galleries; it was as if the prince's table had been turned around on itself to form a giant wheel of knowledge (fig. 1-5).[30] According to the Imperial Commission, the arrangement represented "the complete panorama of universal production"—a telling remark.[31] The round structure of the Panorama National had been a conspicuous part of the 1855 fair. But in a more general sense, the panorama was a staple feature of nineteenth-century visuality, a form of mural painting that provided the spectator with an apparently complete view of a city, a battlefield, or some other significant landscape. It could be unrolled in front of a stationary audience, which enjoyed the illusion of travel, or it could be mounted inside a circular structure. In the latter case, the ideal viewer was a single, centered subject who enjoyed an illusion of power. Etymologically, the word *panorama* is a combination of Greek roots meaning "all" and "sight." Phenomenologically, the panorama promised a totality of vision, a privileged point of view, and an all-encompassing simulation of sensory experience—a nineteenth-century form of virtual reality. The exhibition was similarly comprehensive, visual, and virtual; it provided a vast collection of things, an apparently unlimited vista of consumption, which might or might not be actualized by a purchase. The fact that the 1867 fair was installed in a round building only made the analogy of the panorama that much more concrete and compelling.

Vienna, 1873

"A classification presupposes some arrangement or placing of objects in accordance with it," observed William Phipps Blake, the man most associated with the order of the Centennial.[32] In other words, a system of classification implies a plan of installation. This was the case in Paris, at the 1867 exposition, but not in Vienna. The 1873 Weltausstellung took place on a 280–acre site in the Prater, a large public park located south of the city center, in the floodplain of the Danube (fig. 1-6). In contrast to the Paris fair, where the single main building had expressed the unitary ideal of the Great Exhibition—everything under one roof—the Weltausstellung was divided between five large halls devoted to industry, machinery, agriculture (east and west buildings), and art. As in Paris, the halls were surrounded by a number of smaller structures—more than two hundred in Vienna.[33]

The Weltausstellung celebrated Austria's recovery from defeat in the war with Prussia and Vienna's reconstruction as a modern city. The latter included not only the creation of the Ringstrasse and its monuments in the

1-6. "Birds Eye View of Vienna Exhibitin [*sic*] Buildings," by L.E. Petrovitch (Joe V. Meigs, *General Report upon the Exposition at Vienna* [Washington: Gibson Brothers, 1873], n.p., Library of Congress).

space once occupied by the old walls but also the relocation of the Danube canal and the creation of a new commercial district along its banks.[34] In fact, some of the large halls, or at least parts of them, were supposed to remain after the exhibition closed—the so-called Palace of Agriculture as a railroad depot; the large, domed rotunda of the main building, the Palace of Industry, as a new corn exchange.

Significantly, the plan of the industrial palace mandated a purely geographic arrangement of displays (fig. 1-7). The building consisted of a single, long nave, centered on the rotunda, with a number of small courts branching off on either side. Each court was supposed to be occupied by a single country, or a group of countries collectively responsible for the installation of that area. The result was to be a legible map of the world, with Austria and Germany located at the center, and the other nations distributed on either side according to their geographic relationship to central Europe; the United States, for example, was situated at the extreme western end of this map. (There were comparable arrangements in the buildings devoted to machinery and agriculture.) But the critics complained that the Weltausstellung read as a series of isolated, national fairs, rather than an international exhibition; the sections were integrated only in the sense that they were gathered together in large buildings devoted to broad typological areas.[35] "There was consequently no system comparable with that at Paris," wrote Blake. "The classification did not become a guide to the exhibition, and one great result attained at Paris was lost or not realized."[36]

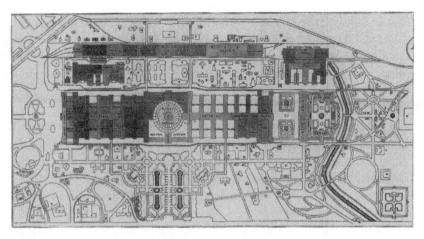

1-7. "Vienna International Exhibition, 1873. Plan of Exhibition Buildings" (United States, Commission to the Vienna Exhibition, 1873, *Reports*, vol. 1, pl. 3, University of California Library, Berkeley). *Enlarged plate appears on page 231 of the appendix.*

As we have seen, the order of the 1867 exposition was based on a hierarchy of human needs. In contrast, the Austrian system represented a developmental series from simple to complex, from raw materials to the most "cooked" products of human community. The system consisted of twenty-six major categories subdivided into a varying number of minor groups. The first fifteen categories were conventional, but the last eleven were unusual and reflected an Austrian expansion of the French idea of social goods. These included, in order, two devoted to the military ("The art of war" and "The navy"), one to architecture and engineering, three to the house and its contents ("The private dwelling-house," "The farm-house," and "National domestic industry"), one to museums of industrial art (the one in Vienna rivaled London's Victoria and Albert in age and influence), three to the arts themselves ("Art applied to religion," "Objects of fine arts of the past," and "Fine arts of the present time"), and one to education.[37] Thus, what were subdivisions of a single group in Paris were elevated to the status of separate categories in Vienna. The exhibition was becoming ever more heterogeneous.

THE CENTENNIAL EXHIBITION

On March 3, 1871, the U.S. Congress approved an act calling for "an Exhibition of American and Foreign Arts, Products, and Manufactures" to celebrate the coming centennial of American independence. The act provided for a representative body consisting of one delegate and alternate from each state and territory, which was to be responsible for the design of the exhibition in the largest sense. This body, which became known as the United States Centennial Commission, was to choose a site in Philadelphia and provide Congress with building plans, as well as a plan for receiving and classifying the goods on display.[38]

The Centennial Commission met in Philadelphia for nine sessions, the first one taking place in March 1872. At that time, William Blake, the alternate commissioner from Connecticut, spoke on the subject of "Previous International Exhibitions," focusing on the 1853–54 Exhibition of the Industry of All Nations in New York and the 1867 Exposition universelle in Paris. Blake had been involved with both, and he spoke at length about the French exposition, but his remarks about the failed fair in New York were relatively brief. Noting that "the great and immediate functions of exhibitions are to stimulate and educate," he criticized the organizers for being motivated by "the hope of pecuniary profit." He blamed their lack of planning for the fact that the palace was not ready on time, the displays were not installed until a late date, and the fair as a whole did not provide a complete picture of even American industry.[39] He said little else about the iron-and-glass building in Bryant Park, except to note that it had burned down. This object lesson was not lost on the organizers of the Centennial.

As we have seen, the French exposition was characterized by a dual system of classification, which located each object by class and country. The corresponding installation consisted of typological departments in concentric galleries and national sections between radial avenues. Blake explained the advantages of this arrangement: "By following one of these galleries the observer passed in succession among the productions similar in kind of different countries. By following the avenues he passed successively through the different productions of the same country. The student, therefore, could investigate the condition of any particular art or industry as manifested by different nations, or he could pursue his studies geographically and note the characteristic productions of each country, and compare them as a whole with those of other countries." Blake also noted that a portion of the central gallery had been reserved for an exhibition of antiquities, to provide "a history of human labor," and he recommended that a comparable space be set aside at the Centennial.[40]

A few days later, Blake argued that the commission should adopt a dual system for the Centennial. He noted the exhibition's ambitious program, which was to display "the objects and products of the whole range of human industry in every country," and he asked the delegates to consider their motives in arranging this collection:

> One of the first questions arising is, under what general plan shall this great diversity of objects be arranged? Are we to place them within the walls of a building so as to best please the eye and promote the general effect regardless of the source or the nature of the articles, or shall we adopt a plan by which the products and objects from each country being kept together, they shall at the same time be grouped according to a common system, and such a system as will best facilitate the comparison and study of similar classes of objects, and promote the higher purposes of such exhibitions?[41]

Blake was posing a rhetorical question: Should the exhibition appeal to the eye, or should it signify to the mind? This was a dilemma that cut to the heart of the Centennial as a project and would prove critical in its design. For the moment, the commission opted for significance, resolving, "That the arrangement and classification of objects shall be both geographical and systematic, and that a committee of three be appointed by the President to prepare and report a system of classification and arrangement combining these two elements."[42]

The commission's decision to adopt a dual system of classification *and* installation denotes an ideal of transparency, of clear and unambiguous representation, that played a major role in Enlightenment thought. In the case of language, this ideal was expressed through a binary theory of semiotics in which signifier and signified communicated with each other directly. This was in contrast to the three-part form of the Renaissance in which the intermediate term of resemblance provided a necessary but frequently hidden link between form and content.[43] During the Renaissance, language was conceived as an opaque system of representation, and knowledge was the interpretation of relationships that were once apparent in the natural, well-constructed language that men spoke before Babel. In contrast, during the Enlightenment, language was conceived as a transparent system, and knowledge was the analysis of the arbitrary relations between things. By extension, the exhibition could be seen as a kind of text, as a clear and unambiguous representation of knowledge.[44] The arrangement of displays could speak of the order of the exhibition, which was supposed to be the order of the world; the objects could speak for themselves. They did not require interpretation, and so they were displayed with an enigmatic directness that we would find puzzling today.

The commission's decision to adopt a dual system also signifies a passion for the systematic, which was itself an Enlightenment preoccupation pervading the entire exhibition. To discipline their project, the organizers of the Centennial erected an intensely bureaucratic structure of rules and records; they attempted to make every aspect systematic—the order of the exhibition, the arrangement of displays, the evaluation of goods. We should note, however, that the word, systematic, has more than one meaning. It has the general sense of "arranged or conducted according to a system, plan, or organized method," which is consistent with a bureaucratic structure. But it also has the more specific sense of "pertaining to, following, or arranged according to a system of classification." Furthermore, the plural, systematics, has long been a synonym for taxonomy itself.[45]

To be systematic, then, is to be scientific, but in a manner peculiar to the Enlightenment—what Michel Foucault called the "Classical age." This was the heyday of natural history, which is defined as the systematic study of objects in nature, whether animal, vegetable or mineral; biology per se did not yet exist.[46] Now, natural history is obviously not history as we know it today; nor is it history as it was understood in the Renaissance. Foucault explained the difference in *The Order of Things:* "Until the mid-seventeenth century the historian's task was to establish the great compilation of documents and signs—of everything, throughout the world, that might form a mark, as it were. . . . The Classical age gives history a quite different meaning: that of undertaking a meticulous examination of things themselves for the first time, and then of transcribing what it has gathered in smooth, neutralized, and faithful words."[47] The idea of a transparent relationship between words and things was central to Foucault's thesis about knowledge, but his observations have more intriguing implications for our study of the exhibition. As epitomized by the Linnaean system, natural history was preoccupied with nomenclature and taxonomy, with naming and ordering things in nature. By the time of the Centennial, these were no longer very compelling scientific problems, but they had come to dominate the study of other kinds of things—"words, languages, roots, documents, records."[48] We might as well add goods, for the classification of the exhibition clearly represents the extension of a scientific method to the material world; the creation of "cultural history," as it were, out of natural history. This may seem strange, but it should not be surprising; with the rapid expansion of production and consumption in the nineteenth century, an expansion paralleled by the steadily increasing size of each industrial fair, culture must have loomed as large and complex as nature had for an earlier period. Furthermore, the installation as realized at the 1867 exposition, and as planned for the Centennial, was precisely the kind of tabular space that Foucault proposed as the archeology, the underlying structure, of Enlightenment knowledge.[49] This makes the exhibition a surprisingly conservative project, anachronistic in its inception.

The Space of Knowledge

The first three members of the Committee on Classification were Joshua Nye of Maine, John L. Campbell of Indiana, and William Blake of Connecticut.[50] Nye's resume is lengthy with accomplishments, but his role on the committee is unclear. He had served in the legislature, had been elected treasurer of a railroad, and had even been appointed to state office. But his real passion was liquor, and his biography described him as a temperance advocate and a champion of Prohibition.[51] Campbell's interest is more apparent; a professor of mathematics and natural philosophy (physics) at Wabash College, he was by some accounts the first person to propose a Centennial exhibition in an 1864 speech at the Smithsonian Institution.[52]

It was Blake who had the most to offer the committee, and who played the most public role in the development of the Centennial system. A geologist and mining engineer, he traveled all over the country in the course of his work, even venturing as far as Japan and Santo Domingo. He is especially associated with the American West, having worked for the Pacific Railroad Survey and explored the California gold country before being appointed a state mineralogist and a professor of geology and mining. His interest in classification reflected these professional activities, which would have included the identification of both mineral specimens and fossil remains. But it also reflected an involvement with exhibitions going back to the 1853–54 exhibition, for which he had started to organize the mineralogy department before leaving to work on the railroad survey. He represented California at the 1867 exposition, edited the six-volume report of the U.S. commissioners, and then served as an American commissioner to the 1873 Weltausstellung.[53] He was eventually elected executive commissioner of the Centennial Exhibition, where he organized the mineral collection in the U.S. Government Building.

It was Blake who submitted the committee's first progress report at the second session of the Centennial Commission. The report stated that the committee had studied the order of previous exhibitions and that it proposed to adopt a classification for the Centennial combining features of the systems used at the 1851 London and 1867 Paris fairs. Like the British system, the Centennial classification would be based on a division of the world into four general categories:

1. The natural products useful to man, the basis of manufactures (raw materials)
2. The manufactures and results of the combinations of these products
3. The means and appliances by which such results have been accomplished (machinery)
4. The resultant effects of such productive activity

These formed a rough hierarchy of the material world, recalling Prince Albert's four broad sections. The difference was in the last category, which the committee had expanded from Albert's "sculpture and plastic art" into a broader grouping that could encompass the "the higher achievements of intellect and imagination."[54]

Like the French system, the Centennial classification was further divided into ten departments, which represented an expansion of the four categories:

I. Raw materials—mineral, vegetable, and animal—and their immediate derivatives
II. Materials—the result of manufacturing processes, chemical compounds, manufactures, and products
III. Textile and felted fabrics, including ready-made clothing and costumes
IV. Furniture and manufactures of general use
V. Tools, implements, motors, machines, and processes
VI. Apparatus and methods of transportation
VII. Apparatus and methods for the increase and diffusion of knowledge
VIII. Civil, mining, and military engineering, public works, and architecture
IX. Fine arts
X. Objects illustrating the methods and the results of efforts for the improvement of the physical, intellectual, and moral condition of man

These departments corresponded to some degree with those in the French system, allowing for small changes in name and order; the biggest differences came at the opposite ends of the range. At the bottom of the Centennial classification, we see the compression of quite diverse groups of things—products of the forest and mine, food, live animals, and plants—

into a single broad category of raw materials. These had been situated near the middle of the French system. Toward the top of the classification, we see the emergence of new categories out of old ones: tools and transportation out of what the French had called the common arts; engineering and architecture out of the fine arts. Significantly, photography migrated from the liberal to the fine arts, suggesting that it enjoyed a different status in the United States than in France. What did not change in the creation of the Centennial classification was the situation of department ten, either in its definition or hierarchical position. The department included a variety of projects that the French had introduced into their expositions, such as public health, nutrition, housing, and education; religious, scientific, and industrial organizations; social services for the young, needy, old, and sick; as well as government and justice. Not surprisingly, occupying the most prominent position at the top of the classificatory pyramid, the crowning achievements of human culture, were the fairs themselves, in all their variety—county, state, national, and international; agricultural, industrial, and artistic.[55]

In a lecture on the Great Exhibition, the British scientist William Whewell had observed, "Suitable gradation is the *felicity* of the classifying art."[56] In keeping with this philosophy, the Committee on Classification did not intend the ten departments to comprise the full extent of the classification. According to the report, each department was to be divided into ten groups, and each group into ten classes. In theory, this would have produced a symmetrically branching, treelike structure, but the committee did not plan on filling every space in the system. The report stated that each department and group could be as large or as small as it needed to be: "If we can properly put all that belongs in each Department into five, six, or eight groups, we propose to do so, leaving the other numbers blank; so, also, of the Classes."[57] Apparently, the system did not need to be symmetrical, but it did need to be complete, capable of accounting for the full diversity of things on display.

The proposed classification of the Centennial, then, was designed to be ample, flexible, and transparent. The neat arrangement of departments, groups, and classes suggested a decimal system of notation, with departments numbered from I to X, groups from 1 to 100, and classes from 1 to 1,000. In theory, the number of any class would indicate its precise position in the entire system, relative to a department and group. For example, the notation of Class 207, Carpets, would show it to be a subdivision of Group 21, Woolen Yarns and Fabrics, in Department III, Textile and Felted Fabrics.[58] Still the committee did not find the relations between classes, groups and departments to be sufficiently clear, so Campbell later reported a change in the system of notation, with group numbers beginning at 10, not 1, and class numbers at 100, not 10. The aim was to make "the figures for any class determine to the eye at once its *place* [my emphasis] in the system."[59] Class 207, for example, became Compound Portable Food, Meat and Vegetable Extracts, a subdivision of Group 20, Extracts and Compounds of Animal and Vegetable Origin, in Department II, Materials and Manufactures Used for Food, or in the Arts.[60] This change was consistent with the Enlightenment ideal of transparency, but it also implied a spatial conception of knowledge that was typical of the Centennial as a project.[61]

Those who know Foucault are familiar with his use of spatial analogies to explain the structures of knowledge in three epistemes—the circle of the Renaissance, the table of the Classical, the linear series of the modern—which he excavated in *The Order of Things*. In fact, space and its structuring was a central theoretical device for Foucault, at least at this early stage, and his work stands as a primary source of all postmodern spatializations of nonspatial phenomena. Significantly, Foucault defines the episteme as a *field* "in which knowledge . . . grounds its positivity," and he describes the aim of his own archaeological project with the prediction that "what should appear are those configurations within the *space* of knowledge which have given rise to the diverse forms of empirical knowledge."[62]

In the case of the Centennial, what is striking is the degree to which the organizers also conceived of knowledge in spatial terms. This was implicit in the dual system of classification and installation, which mapped the order of the exhibition in the arrangement of displays. But the Committee on Classification went further by invoking the startling analogy of the city to explain the notational system, comparing it to the plan of Philadelphia, "where the number of the house at once indicates its location with respect to the streets."[63] This refers to a series of improvements carried out in the 1850s, when the space of the city was rationalized in the same spirit that had led to the political consolidation of Philadelphia and its suburbs. Previously, this space was not as regular as Penn's gridded plan; house numbers were unsystematic, and street names changed from neighborhood to neighborhood. Beginning in 1853, the names were made continuous in the center of town; the city councils (Philadelphia had two) extended this plan to the rest of the community in 1858. The councils further standardized addresses in 1856, assigning each block of land a series of 100 numbers. These counted up from the Delaware River on streets running east and west, with even numbers on the south; they counted up from Market on streets running north and south, with even numbers on the west. At the time of the Centennial, this kind of urban order was still enough of a novelty that guidebook authors felt called upon to explain the system to their readers.[64]

Significantly, the analogy of Philadelphia applied to more than just the system of notation. The dual system implied a gridded arrangement of displays, which made the exhibition a mirror of the city itself. In both the city and the exhibition, the grid was a figure of Enlightenment rationality; a graph for plotting systematic relationships between different points in a field; a device for leveling the differences between commodities—plots of land or types of goods. Furthermore, the grid represented that great table of identities and differences, which Foucault offered as the deep, unconscious structure of Enlightenment knowledge. In this context, his description of the historical documents proper to this period is startlingly evocative of the space of the exhibition, especially as the organizers of the Centennial hoped to construct it: "The documents of this new history are not other words, texts or records, but unencumbered spaces in which things are juxtaposed: herbariums, collections, gardens; the locus of this history is a non-temporal rectangle in which, stripped of all commentary, of all enveloping language, creatures present themselves one beside another, their surfaces visible, grouped according to their common features, and thus already virtually analyzed, and bearers of nothing but their own individual names."[65] As the mother of all collections, the exhibition was clearly one of these "unencumbered spaces" in which things were identified and arranged according to their identities and differences. Ideally, the continuity of this space would not be interrupted. The Committee on Classification did not oppose the mounting of special exhibits in separate buildings, especially for goods like flowers, trees and livestock, which were impractical to display indoors, so long as their removal did not interrupt the full range of things on display. If these things needed to be removed, the committee suggested that "their appropriate position in the classification may be indicated by stuffed or preserved specimens, thus preventing any break in the visible realization of the system"—an appropriation of museum practice.[66]

As Foucault argued it, the space of Classical knowledge did not tolerate disruptions.[67] The space of the exhibition was similar in this and one other way: it was "a non-temporal rectangle," which did not accommodate the display of historic artifacts. These were objects illustrating the history of art and industry in the United States and elsewhere; they could include prehistoric tools, unspecified objects from the colonial and revolutionary periods of American history, as well as the furniture, clothing, "tools, arms, machines, and vehicles" of the early Republic.[68] Blake recommended making room for such a display, but the Committee on Classification seemed to be of two minds. In one place, the committee argued for the inclusion of historic artifacts within existing departments.[69] In another, it proposed the creation of a separate exhibit, comparable to a national section and encompassing all ten departments of the exhibition, in which these artifacts could take their proper position in the typological stream of goods. This would make the past truly the equivalent of another country: "We may also, in following out the geographical element of our plan, give a section of the entire range of products and industry to objects of historical interest, especially those showing the progress of industry and invention in the United States during the century. By so doing, each object will find its appropriate place under the classification—the printing press of Franklin, for example[,] in the same range with those of Hoe, Adams, and Bullock."[70] Time was a problem in either case. The grid of the classification provided only two dimensions of comparison: type of object and country of origin. There was literally no space for the past, which may help to explain the insistent presentness of the exhibition. In spite of occasional forays like the Centennial's colonial kitchen, the exhibition was a statement of *now;* history was an insubstantial sideshow in comparison to the great spectacle of the present condition.[71]

THE MYTH OF PROGRESS

Progress was the spirit of the modern age, and it has been the explicit theme of nearly every world's fair until now. "Progress is the law of life," wrote J.S. Ingram, one of the chroniclers of the Centennial, "and Exhibitions, at once the outcome and the forebears of that very progress, have experienced its influence and have in turn reacted on it."[72] The organizers of the 1876 fair considered the demonstration of this law to be part of their official program; after all, Congress had described the Centennial as "an Exhibition of the natural resources of the country and their development, and of its progress in those arts which benefit mankind in comparison to those of older nations."[73] But it would be difficult to do this without a convincing display of historical artifacts.

Progress was an Enlightenment idea, an offshoot of the cult of reason, which was receiving its scientific rationale from the theory of evolution. Darwin's *Origin of the Species* had been published in 1859, just seventeen years before the Centennial, so it is not surprising that the organizers were under its influence. In May 1874, at the fifth session of the Centennial Commission, the Committee on Classification described the order of the exhibition as "a system based on the idea of evolution or derivation of manufactured products from the crude materials of the earth."[74] In reality, this was a bit of a fiction; the system was supposed to be progressive, but it was really just a hierarchy of things. Furthermore, it is evident that there was some tension between the static order of the classification and the world of evolutionary change. Like the Classical systems of nature, language, and economic exchange, the table of the exhibition with its fixed relationships did not accommodate development. It could only be shifted whole, in jumps and starts, from one place in history to another.[75] At best, the classification represented what Barthes described as "the glorious term of a great trajectory, that of substance, transformed, sublimated by man, through a series of episodes and stations."[76] Thus we have the four great divisions of the exhibition: raw materials mechanically transformed into manufactures, which supported the production of social and cultural goods.

The report submitted at the fifth session also indicates the scope of the committee's investigations. These included the classification of fairs held in London (1851, 1862, and 1871–1874), Paris (1867), Moscow (1872), and Vienna (1873), as well as the alphabetical system used by the U.S. Patent Office. Furthermore, the report confirms that the proposed classification of the Centennial was based on systems used at the 1851 Great Exhibition and the 1867 Exposition universelle, while evaluating their strengths and weaknesses, including their capacity to represent progress.[77] The British system "was one of the best that has been proposed," but it was not "universal" in the sense that it did not provide a place for "all materials and industries"; it is not clear whether this remark was meant to include the conspicuous omission of painting as a fine art. Furthermore, the system did not express "the evolution principle and idea," which was part of the Centennial's congressionally mandated brief. In contrast, the French system was "more universal and comprehensive in its scope than any which had been proposed before," but it was not a convincing demonstration of progress. According to the report, "the evolution idea was broken up, and there was no natural sequence or connection of the groups."[78] The system was supposed to be based on the wants of man, with the ten departments arranged to form a hierarchy of human needs, but the actual classification contained some odd juxtapositions: "There is a certain gradation based on this idea of the supply of man's wants, but it is an interrupted, disjointed sequence, an arbitrary system, which presents the incongruity of the group of raw materials, and the extractive industries in the midst of the series, and according to the arrangement and notation, the Fine Arts in the first group, while Live Stock, Agriculture, and Horticulture were at the other end of the series, next to Group X, devoted to education and the intellectual wants of man." Nevertheless, the report noted, "the great charm of the system of 1867 was its *duality*," with goods ordered and displays arranged in two ways, by country and by class.[79]

In spite of its evident "charm," the dual system was not without its detractors, who would have preferred a more explicit demonstration of each nation's individual progress: "There have been some hypercritical persons demanding perfection, where only an approximation of it is possible, who have thought that the zonal [i.e., systematic] distribution of objects prevented that vivid view of the products and art of each country which is deemed essential. In other words, that at Paris it was not easy to see the contributions of each country by themselves as segregated from those of other countries."[80] While admitting that the boundaries between national sections could have been better indicated at the 1867 fair, the report insisted that the dual system was a vast improvement over any used before and recommended it for future use. This did not happen at the 1873 Weltausstellung, where the branching plan of the industrial palace dictated a geographic arrangement of displays. The virtual disintegration of the fair into a series of national courts, not to mention the construction of separate pavilions for machinery, agriculture, and the fine arts, made it difficult to perceive the fair as a comprehensive unity—a *universal* exposition. Worse still, the geographic arrangement made it difficult to compare like objects from different countries, which, after all, was supposed to be the purpose of a world's fair.[81]

While allowing that the order of the exhibition and the arrangement of displays are not always the same thing, the report recommended that the two approximate each other as much as possible. The footprint of the exhibition hall could be circular, elliptical, or rectangular, but the committee recommended the construction of a functional shed, in contrast to the elaborate industrial palace erected in Vienna: "Our preference is for a compact building, of the simplest and cheapest construction consistent with due protection of the objects, a parallelogram in form, with broad avenues separating the departments, and narrow passageways between the groups."[82] This expression of utilitarian modesty remained a consistent theme in the architecture of the Centennial.

By the time of the fifth session, the commission had already made a number of important decisions about the physical design of the exhibition. It had fixed the site in Fairmount Park, already the largest in the United States, with an area of 2,740 acres on both sides of the Schuylkill River and its tributary, the Wissahickon. It had also appointed a seven-member Committee on Plans and Architecture, with instructions to obtain preliminary designs for a single 50-acre hall. Nearly twice the size of the 1851 Crystal Palace, this enormous structure was supposed to contain the entire exhibition.[83]

Astonishingly, there does not seem to have been any consultation between the Committee on Classification and the Committee on Plans and Architecture. The former predicated the design of its system on the construction of a single large hall. Meanwhile, the latter committee had decided to erect not one but a number of buildings in the park; it had also announced an architectural competition.[84] In a report submitted at the fourth session, the committee had explained its decision by raising the issue of the site in Fairmount Park: "To secure the best architectural effect, and for a proper classification of the articles on exhibition, the topography of the ground selected naturally suggests the erection of more than one building, viz[.]: A main building, including the memorial-building, an art-gallery, a machinery hall, and conservatory, covering together about fifty acres of floor-space; the first to be erected on Lansdowne Plateau, the second on the east, and the third on the west of the main building."[85] Not surprisingly, this development had a significant effect on the classification. The arrangement of the ten departments was theoretically neat but structurally unrelated to the architecture. At the sixth session in May 1875, the director-general of the exhibition, Alfred T. Goshorn of Ohio, explained the need to revise the classification—the first in a series of accommodations that the organizers would be forced to make in the design of their project.[86]

The responsibility for revising the classification fell to John Campbell, who was by then the secretary of the Centennial Commission, and to his assistant Dorsey Gardner. The two supervised the downsizing of the system from ten to seven departments, roughly corresponding to the architecture of the exhibition. Three of the new departments—Mining and Metallurgy, Manufactures, and Education and Science—would be installed in the Main Building. The other four—Art, Machinery, Agriculture, and Horticulture—would be installed in Memorial, Machinery, Agricultural, and Horticultural Halls, respectively. It was this version of the classification, first published in July 1875, which eventually determined the arrangement of the official catalogue.[87]

THE CATALOGUE OF THE EXHIBITION

If there is a counterpart to the confusion of a library, it is the order
of its catalogue.[88]

—Walter Benjamin, "Unpacking My Library"

The literature of the exhibition was vast, consisting of official reports, descriptive histories, illustrated surveys, and frequently lengthy articles in
newspapers and magazines. The reports, histories, surveys, and articles were
all important because they continued to disseminate the lessons of the exhibition to the audience beyond the fairground, as Blake explained in his reading of the 1867 exposition: "These printed results make the exposition a
permanent one. The teachings survive the demolition of the buildings. The
press is the right arm of such displays, carrying the useful and best results
into the remote corners of the earth, interesting and instructing artisans and
others who could not leave their homes to see with their own eyes."[89] In this
context, the catalogue was a peculiar document, since it was supposed to be
used at the fair itself. Like the guide, although in much more detail, the
catalogue was a finding aid that helped visitors locate displays.

At the Centennial, the catalogue identified American exhibits in the
larger halls by letter and number, which indicated the location of the nearest column. The structural notation of the Main Building was explained in
this way: "The letters—A, B, C, to U—designate the width of the building;
the figures, the numbers of the column in each range, counting eastwardly
from the western wall, the entire length of the building, from 1 to 79."[90]
This is a very rational way to describe the structure of a building, which is
still used today and which has its origins in the analytical geometry of the
seventeenth century. At that time, René Descartes and Pierre de Fermat
developed the now familiar system of locating points in space by means of
perpendicular axes and numbered coordinates. It is not clear when this abstract conception was first applied to architecture, but it had to be related to
the rationalization of building space and structure that took place in the
nineteenth century and that was apparently still noteworthy at the time of
the Centennial.[91] The commission explained that the British had used the
same form of notation for the Crystal Palace, while once again invoking the
analogy of Philadelphia to explain the location of displays.[92] This reinforces
the idea of a deep but not entirely unconscious relationship between the
gridded structure of the building, the city, and the exhibition.

In addition to its practical function as a finding aid, the catalogue served an ideological function by reinforcing the idea of order in the exhibition. The catalogue encouraged visitors to view the world through a screen of classification, as they moved about the fairground with their books in hand (fig. 1-8). The Centennial catalogue was published in four volumes, which indicated the correspondence of buildings and departments. Volume 1 pertained to the Main Building and its annexes, as well as Departments I to III; volume 2 to Memorial Hall, its annexes, outdoor works of art, and Department IV; volume 3 to Machinery Hall, its annexes, special buildings, and Department V; volume 4 to Agricultural and Horticultural Halls, their annexes, and Departments VI to VII. Furthermore, each volume re-presented the entire system of classification in synopsis and an appropriate section in detail. Like the system, the catalogue was both "geographical and systematic" in its organization; the entries were listed first by department, then by country, group, and class. This made comparison possible, bringing together like things in the space of knowledge that may not have been adjacent in the exhibition. A three-digit number, based on the system of notation, indicated the precise position of each object in this space.

Surprisingly, given this apparent concern for order, the catalogue was not alphabetized. The entries were listed in an apparently random sequence, which may reflect nothing more than the difficulty of compiling such a

1-8. "The Centennial—wall paper printing press, Machinery Hall" (*Harper's Weekly* 20, no. 1043 [23 Dec. 1876]: 1041, Prints and Photographs, Library of Congress).

work. In fact, based on the experience of previous fairs, there had been doubts as to whether an accurate and complete catalogue could be prepared before the opening on May 10, 1876.[93] But a number of American publishers lobbied for a concession, and the Centennial Board of Finance, which Congress had established in 1872 to manage the money of the exhibition, responded with a request for proposals to produce a four-volume catalogue. The board received twelve bids by the noon deadline of September 15, 1875, and awarded the concession to J.R. Nagle and Company of Philadelphia.[94]

As it turned out, Nagle and Company lacked the experience to produce something so complicated as the catalogue, and the Centennial Commission was forced to assume much of the responsibility itself. Dorsey Gardner, by then chief of the Bureau of Publications, described the jobbing out of this immense project: "The securing of advertisements was given to an agency in New York, the typesetting for the first edition to four different offices in Philadelphia, and for the revised editions to a single large office in the same city, while the printing was done in Boston, and the book-binding partly in that city, partly in New York, and partly in Philadelphia." Foreign commissioners were supposed to provide information about their displays by December 1, 1875—more than six months before the opening; domestic exhibitors were to do the same before receiving an allotment of space in the buildings. But submissions continued to arrive until September 1876, and the bureau was unable to prepare the catalogue on time. Gardner reeled off a list of other difficulties:

> American applicants who had undertaken to exhibit, but changed their minds, failed to give notification of their withdrawal, and allowed their Catalogue entries to stand; and others, who had secured space, and really exhibited, made either no Catalogue entries or inaccurate ones; while not a few forwarded the text of entries without giving either their names or addresses. Foreign commissions, again, furnished matter for the Catalogue in forms wholly unavailable. Many gave no indication of the groups of the Classification to which they referred exhibits, or of the Exhibition building in which they purposed installing them; several, after examining the buildings, shifted their exhibits from one to the another, without notifying the editor of the Catalogue; while other Commissions submitted lists of exhibits for which application had been made in their own countries, but which were never shipped; and still others made no entries at all until long after the opening of the Exhibition.

A four-volume publication was in fact ready to sell on opening day, but it was a sorry affair, riddled with mistakes. A team of thirty people immediately set to work on a second edition, a revised manuscript was ready for printing by June 15, and the first volume was available in late July. The fourth and final volume did not appear until mid-August, three months after the opening. Not one of the twelve hundred pages of this edition matched the originals.[95]

Gardner's experience did not make him optimistic about the future of the catalogue. "In general," he wrote, "it may be said that the experience of the Centennial Exhibition confirms that of all its predecessors,—that it is hopeless to attempt publishing an Official Catalogue by the opening day, and doubtful whether one really trustworthy can be made in such season as to render its publication desirable." In fact, he recommended that the book be abandoned in favor of "a system of descriptive labels affixed to each object"—as in a museum. Gardner went on to suggest that the evaluation of goods, so central to the exhibition's function, should not depend on the production of a catalogue; the judges should prepare their own lists after the opening, when it would be apparent who or what was part of the show. "A catalogue made from exhibitors' entries is worthless," he concluded, "while one collected from exhibits actually in place cannot be got ready for sale until several weeks after the completion of the Exhibition; and an Exhibition of such proportions is not really completed for a long time after its opening."[96]

In the end, the catalogue stands as an emblem for the exhibition as a whole. They were both immensely complex structures that defied rational planning. They were indeterminate in the sense that they could not be known in all their parts, so they could not be reduced to a closed system, no matter how carefully contrived. The organizers had imagined the exhibition as a transparent representation of knowledge, a scientific collection of things, a tabular space that reconciled the empirical desire to arrange everything by class with the chauvinistic impulse to organize everything by country. The reality was something different, less ideal; the exhibition was in fact a perennially incomplete project, as was the catalogue.[97] This experience was not unique to the Centennial, as a writer in the *Nation* observed: "Each international exhibition has been the child of circumstances, not to say of adversity. The Paris exposition of 1867 made the nearest approach to symmetry and completeness of arrangement. Yet it was only an approach, although it was the supreme effort of the most enlightened and proficient despotic bureaucracy that the world has probably ever seen. The other exhibitions all outgrew the ideas and capacity of those who projected them. To speak paradoxically, they succeeded too well, inasmuch as they succeeded in exhausting the resources of their managers."[98]

This ideal of a universal exposition, of "symmetry and completeness" in the arrangement of all things, must seem strange to us now. It is in the nature of our postmodern condition that we value the tolerant fragment and distrust the absolute whole. The complexity of our experience demands many centers and multiple points of view, but the organizers of the Centennial were still thinking with the optimistic and well-ordered mind of the Enlightenment—at home with progress if not entirely sure what to do about evolution. They were confident in their ability to know and order the world; the problem was that it had become a much larger and more complicated place since the time of the Enlightenment. Because of this disjunction, between what was and what was only imagined, the organizers would have to revise their project on many occasions, bringing it into line with conditions that could not be known at the start. That explains why their accounts are tainted, if not by failure, for no one would say that the exhibition was not a success, then by a sense of diminished capacity and reduced expectations, as they came to recognize the limits of their control.

THE ARCHITECTURE
OF THE EXHIBITION

But the end of the Classical age, which Friedrich Nietzsche
announced as an end without return, was in reality the exhaustion of
something that still inspires—at least to some degree—what we have
come to refer to as the modern project. This end is an "illusion," but I
wish to bring into play here the ambiguity of that term in Castilian, for
it can also express a sense of wishful belief, *ilusión* as simultaneously
hope and delusion. Illusion implies a process, and that this process is
oriented toward a certain end. In this sense, the project of the
Enlightenment, the basis of modernity, still participates in a secular
theism, in the idea that it is possible to discover an absolute reality,
within which art, science, and social and political praxis can be
constructed on the basis of universal rationality. When this system
enters into crisis (and it does enter into crisis, precisely as a result of
the impossibility of establishing a universal system), we find ourselves
faced with the *real* crisis of the modern project and the perplexing—
we might say critical—situation of our contemporaneity.
                              —Ignasi de Solà-Morales Rubió, "Weak Architecture"

The distinction between architecture and engineering as separate fields of
expertise is a well-established one that originates in the Renaissance division between civil and military practice. In modern terms, the distinction
has its roots in the seventeenth and eighteenth centuries in the establishment in France of state-sponsored schools and academies. In Great Britain,
the development of such boundaries did not occur until the eighteenth century; in the United States, it happened later, in the critical period immediately following the Civil War.[1] Even then the distinction between architecture
and engineering as different kinds of building was already well established
and is evident in the conventional form of the nineteenth-century railroad

station. In the dichotomy between the head house and the train shed, we see, in front, a monumental public building, conceived in more traditional materials and methods of construction, with the intention of creating an artful, symbolic, representational form, that is, one that signifies and communicates. In back, we see a functional, utilitarian building, conceived in more modern materials and methods, with the intention of creating a rational space and structure. This dichotomy demonstrates that the distinction between architecture and engineering is rooted in social and technological developments, specifically in the emergence of complex building types and in the advent of iron and steel as primary materials of construction. (Since ancient times, iron had been used to reinforce masonry, but that is a different story.) Architecture presumed more of a familiarity with the art of building and the functional arrangement of space; engineering with the design of long-span structures based on a more precise knowledge of building science. Thus, the distinction between the two fields implies not only different kinds of building but also two fundamentally different ways of solving building problems.[2]

Since science is the dominant form of knowledge in Modernity, a truly modern profession must be scientific; it must involve the rigorous application of scientific theory to the solution of well-formulated, repeatable problems. By this standard, engineering is the epitome of the modern profession; it is "strong" in the sense that it is based on an autonomous, well-defined body of "hard" knowledge—rational, objective, quantifiable, demonstrable. This strength is a source of professional authority, along with the fact that engineering is institutionally well defined in the university, that has helped engineers to create and maintain an effective monopoly for their services.[3] Architecture is comparatively weak—this in spite of the best efforts of certain twentieth-century modernists, whose functionalist program can be defined as an attempt to remake their field along the lines of engineering, that is, to render it more rational and scientific.[4] But architectural knowledge has remained very soft—contingent, ambiguously defined, intuitive, subjective, qualitative, difficult to substantiate in utilitarian terms. As a result, in spite of the fact that their profession is equally well defined in the university, architects have never been as successful in securing their own professional monopoly, and they continue to compete with engineers, builders, and unlicensed designers in the market for their services.

This is not to say that architects cannot be rational, or that engineers never think in representational terms. Nor is it to say that a person trained in one way might not practice in another. During the nineteenth century, in the

United States, the line between these two fields was not as well defined as it is now. But by the time of the Centennial, there was already considerable divergence between architecture and engineering as professional cultures, a divergence created and reinforced by the schools, magazines, and societies that had already begun to define each set of practitioners. This helps to explain the mentality of the men, largely, who managed the Centennial, and the character of the exhibition they designed.[5] Among the major figures in this story, one was a geologist (William Blake), one was an economist (Gen. Francis A. Walker), and three were engineers (Henry Pettit, Herman J. Schwarzmann, and Joseph M. Wilson).[6] Thus, representatives of the rational, scientific point of view had an outsize voice in the fair's design.

LONDON, 1851

In keeping with the scientific mentality of their age, the organizers of the Centennial were systematic in all things. This approach included the history of their project, which they studied in a search for precedents that might guide their design of the fair.[7] As we have seen, at the Centennial Commission's first session, William Blake was asked to speak about the 1853–54 Exhibition of the Industry of All Nations in New York and the 1867 Exposition universelle in Paris. The commission later received a set of plans and specifications for the 1873 Weltausstellung that would take place in Vienna. These had been secured from the Austrian government by John Jay, the U.S. ambassador to the Court of Vienna.[8] At the second session in May 1872, Blake, who had by then been elected executive commissioner, was asked to obtain reports and proceedings from previous world's fairs, especially the 1851 Great Exhibition in London and the 1867 exposition.[9] At the third session in December 1872, the commission decided to send an official delegation to study the Weltausstellung in person.[10] As of February 1873, Gen. Joseph R. Hawley, the president of the Centennial Commission, had appointed eleven members to the delegation.[11] Blake also went to Vienna, as did Herman Schwarzmann, at that time the engineer of Fairmount Park, and Henry Pettit, a civil engineer for the Pennsylvania Railroad.[12] Both Blake and Pettit submitted reports on the fair at the commission's fifth session in May 1874.[13] Blake's was the more detailed, but Pettit buttressed his own more compact account with a large selection of documents—books, articles, lithographs, maps, plans, photographs, official reports and forms, catalogs, even flag samples—all relating to exhibitions held since the first "great" one in London.[14]

The British had been slow to follow the example of the French fairs, but, once Prince Albert had made the proposal of an international exhibition, the idea quickly gained support. Within six months, at the beginning of January 1850, the Queen appointed a Royal Commission to manage the exhibition. The Building Committee announced an international competition in March; received 233 designs in April; displayed and rejected them in June. During that same month, the commission published its own proposal, and Joseph Paxton submitted his sketch of an idea for a greenhouse-like building to the engineer, Robert Stephenson. Paxton was, at that time, a landscape gardener; Stephenson was a member of the Building Committee. Paxton's design was developed (the team included Paxton, builder Charles Fox, and members of the Royal Commission), published, and accepted, all by the middle of July, and construction began by the end of September, on a twenty-six-acre site in London's Hyde Park.[15]

The 1,848-foot-long building that emerged from this process was both the symbol and centerpiece of the Great Exhibition. Visitors were amazed by what *Punch* dubbed the "Crystal Palace." Queen Victoria described it as "astonishing, a fairy scene"; the *London Times* observed, "It hardly seemed to be put together by design or to be the work of human artificers." Historians have remembered the building more prosaically, as an early and significant example of architecture transformed by the Industrial Revolution. Everything about it was rationalized; the design was based on a three-dimensional module of 24 feet, which made it possible to conceive of the structure as an open system of standardized, prefabricated parts. The cast-iron girders and columns, the 10-by-49-inch sheets of plate glass that formed the largely transparent skin of the building, the wooden mullions and sash bars that held the glass in place, and Paxton's own patented wood gutters, designed to carry away condensation from the inside of the roof, were all manufactured in large quantities at remote locations, often using machines especially designed for the purpose. Even the assembly of these parts was carefully worked out to maximize efficiency. For example, when it became clear that the process of glazing the roof would make it difficult to complete the building on time, Fox devised a cart, running on the tracks of Paxton's gutters, which permitted a pair of men, their materials, and a boy helper to fly over the open frame of the building. This kind of thinking made it possible for the eighteen-acre building to go up for only £79,800 ($965,840 in 1876; over $14 million today) and over an amazingly short period of seventeen months. It also made it possible for the entire structure to be taken down and rebuilt in somewhat altered form at Sydenham in South London, over a two-year interval beginning in 1852.[16]

Blake's and Pettit's reports both make it clear that the Crystal Palace was still vividly remembered in the 1870s, although by that time impressions of the original building were likely to be confused with its reincarnation at Sydenham. The technological lessons had already been assimilated, and both men—one, a geologist; the other, an engineer—described the palace in surprisingly experiential terms. According to Pettit, "The characteristic features of this building, which excited universal admiration and wonder at the time, were the 'airy lightness of the whole structure,' and the superb vistas afforded by a nave 1800 feet long, 72 feet wide, and 64 feet high"[17] (fig. 2-1). Blake echoed this sentiment, arguing that broad avenues and extended views were desirable in exhibition halls for their aesthetic effects. "No one," he insisted, "can ever forget the charm of the long vista of the crystal palace at Sydenham."[18]

This compelling idea of the vista, of the view that penetrates a mass of displays, became a central issue in the design of the Centennial. The vista was a way of seeing and knowing; it presumed that the extended space of the building should be experienced as a one-point perspective, which al-

2-1. "The Nave of the Great Exhibition" (Tallis, *Tallis's History and Description,* vol. 1, n.p., Library of Congress).

lowed the viewer to command the space with his/her gaze. It posed a visual argument for the idea of the classification, which asserted that the myriad and distracting details of the exhibition could be assembled into a meaningful whole. In this sense, the vista created an illusion of power, which suggested that the fair and the world it represented could both be visually controlled by a single, centered subject.[19] This was consistent with the basic premise of the exhibition, which was meant to be an encyclopedic collection of things—what the French so appropriately called a *universal* exposition. In this totalizing ambition, the exhibition was an effect of Enlightenment knowledge, which had the aspect of a catalog, and especially of early modern science, which was preoccupied with problems of taxonomy. With its glass skin, the Crystal Palace was the architectural embodiment of an Enlightenment ideal of transparency, of an unmediated correspondence between subject and object, sign and referent; between the exhibition inside and the world outside the building. Light, of course, was a preoccupation of the period, and the brightly lit, rationally organized interior of the Crystal Palace was a representation of the Enlightenment mind: a space of inspection illuminated by the lamp of reason.

PARIS, 1867

The British mounted a second world's fair in 1862, but it appears to have had no impact on the design of the Centennial. As far as the organizers were concerned, the next great event after the Great Exhibition was the 1867 Exposition universelle in Paris. The design of this fair was inspired by the dual system of classification and installation, which Prince Napoléon had proposed in his report on the 1855 exposition. The prince had apparently been thinking of a rectangular structure, so it was necessary to adapt his tabular concept to the "elliptical" plan of the main building at the 1867 fair. As a result, the exhibits were located by class of object in concentric galleries, and by country of origin in radial sections. This arrangement was supposed to promote serious study and rational comparison. By pursuing a radial path, a person could study all the goods of a single country; by making a circuit around the building, a person could compare every thing of a single class.[20]

The construction of a transparent relationship between the order of the exhibition and the arrangement of displays was tremendously appealing to observers, as we have seen, but the iron-and-glass architecture of the main building, as designed by engineer Jean-Baptiste-Sébastien Kranz, inspired contradictory reactions. The verdict of the French critic, Théophile Gautier, was succinct and surprisingly positive: "En cherchant l'utile, on a, sans le vouloir, rencontré le beau."[21] In contrast, the director-general of the 1873 Weltausstellung, Baron Wilhelm von Schwarz-Senborn, recalled the same building as an awful, monotonous structure. Speaking to a group of Viennese architects and engineers, he said, "It resembled a gigantic gasometer, and made but very poor impression on the mind, certainly no such impression as was created by the Exhibition building of 1851, in London."[22] A gas tank was certainly no match for the Crystal Palace, but why? Eugene Rimmel, an exhibitor at the 1867 fair, provided a compelling explanation that recalls Blake and Pettit's reaction to the Crystal Palace. "The external appearance of the structure is far from attractive," Rimmel remarked. "The interior of the palace is not more striking than the exterior; its continual curves[,] so fatiguing to the eye, do not offer at any point those long vistas which usually form the beauty of this species of building."[23] Pettit expressed a similar concern, observing that many visitors became disoriented in the long, looping spaces of the French structure (fig. 2-2): "The interior effect from a curved gallery or corridor, prolonged to a great length[,] is so confusing that the public often becomes uncertain as to which part of the curve they may be in at the time."[24] Blake seemed to accept Schwarz-Senborn's basic criticism. "Externally the effect was heavy," Blake remarked, "and by no means imposing," but he concluded that the design "was admirably adapted

2-2. "Salle des Machines." 1867 Exposition universelle in Paris (*L'Exposition universelle de 1867 illustrée* [Paris: Ch. Lahure, 1867], vol. 1, n.p., Smithsonian Institution Libraries).

to the purposes for which it was intended." He elaborated on this theme, striking a utilitarian note that would characterize future discussions of the Centennial's architecture: "The buildings erected for previous great exhibitions are generally known as palaces, but the structure on the Champ-de-Mars had nothing in its appearance suggestive of the name. In its plan and construction architectural effects were subordinated to the great end in view—the exhibition of objects of all nations in such a manner as to invite and facilitate comparison and study."[25]

The actual arrangement of displays in the main building proved to be less ideal than Blake's statement would suggest. The system of classification was based on a hierarchy of human needs—food, clothing, dwelling, raw materials, machines, liberal arts, and fine arts. But the installation of the fair, from outside to inside, indicated a different order of needs—food, machines, raw materials, clothing, dwelling, liberal arts, and fine arts. This reflected the logistical problem of matching departments of differing sizes to the varying areas of concentric galleries and passages. Furthermore, the installation of national sections was based on the assumption that each country could muster a complete and proportionately similar range of displays, encompassing the entire system of classification, no matter how large its exhibit was in the aggregate. This could never be the case; human needs may be universal, but the means to satisfy them are not. As a result, some countries could not fill the areas allotted to them, while others overflowed into the space of their neighbors. According to Pettit, the resulting exhibition, far from being an orderly representation of the world's goods, was "confused and 'unphilosophical'"—that is, unscientific.[26] Nevertheless, the idea if not the reality of the Paris building, of a structure that could symbolize the global dimension of a world's fair, while expressing national identity and giving concrete form to a universal system of classification, continued to inspire the organizers of the Centennial.

Vienna, 1873

The organizers of the Centennial were naturally most interested in the Weltausstellung that was taking place in Vienna while they were planning their own exhibition. In addition to Blake, Pettit, and members of the Centennial Commission's official delegation, eight representatives of the city of Philadelphia visited the 1873 fair. Architecturally, it consisted of five main halls, along with a number of smaller buildings, all located on a large site in the Prater. The fair's central feature was the immense industrial palace, which had been built for the display of manufactured goods. Designed by Karl von Hasenauer, the architect with Gottfried Semper of several monuments of Vienna's new Ringstrasse, the industrial palace was a 3,000-foot-long structure, crossed by a number of relatively short transepts and centered on a 352-foot-diameter rotunda (fig. 2-3). This was enclosed by a conical iron dome, designed by British engineer Scott Russell. In a manner typical of local construction, the walls were made of brick covered in plaster, which was colored like stone and worked into elaborate sculptural decoration (fig. 2-4).[27]

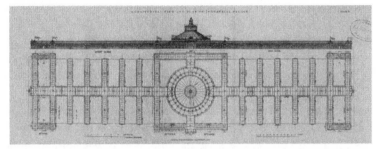

2-3. "Longitudinal View and Plan of Industrial Palace." 1873 Weltausstellung in Vienna (United States, Commission to the Vienna Exhibition, 1873, *Reports*, vol. 1, pl. 2, University of California Library, Berkeley). *Enlarged plate appears on page 232 of the appendix.*

2-4. "Rotunde mit Hauptportal" *(Weltausstellung in Wien 1873.* [(Vienna): Wiener Photographen-Association, 1873], no. 191, Prints and Photographs, Library of Congress).

On first impression, the relatively lavish architecture of the industrial palace inspired the admiration of our American visitors. The Philadelphia representatives, for example, seemed to be at a loss for words: "No description can give an idea of the size and beauty of the Industrial Palace, with its magnificent dome—the largest ever constructed—and its elaborately ornamented facades and portals."[28] On second thought, however, the representatives came to the Quakerish conclusion that this kind of extravagance would not be appropriate for an American fair: "The cost and extent of the Vienna buildings are given with a view rather to avoid them either in magnificence or outlay; and while we should endeavor to celebrate our nation's Centennial in a manner worthy of our nation's dignity, it is not necessary in order to do so that we should attempt to imitate the grandeur and dazzling beauty of the expositions of the old world, but rather desire to appear for what we really are—a plain, practical and common sense people."[29]

Pettit's reaction to the Weltausstellung was similarly equivocal. He rejected the purely functional approach to exhibition architecture, voicing a desire for a more impressive style of building that was not uncommon at this time in the United States, but he criticized the means taken to create the monuments of the Vienna fair:

> The stucco finish admits of the most elaborate ornamentation, being introduced at a small cost, and produces an effect which is wonderfully beautiful and apparently monumental, so long as one forgets that it is all a sham, and that the columns, cornices, window-architraves, balustrades, vases, and statuary are made of a substance but a little better than common plaster. . . . With our varied-colored bricks, tiles, and slate, and proper introduction of terra-cotta, and cast and wrought iron work, we ought, however, to produce an equal monumental effect, and be much more true to the construction, and consequently improve upon the immense stucco shams which are so characteristic of this exhibition.[30]

Pettit's antipathy for "sham" is striking, especially when compared to the response of the Philadelphia representatives. More important, his prescription for a more truthful style of building makes him a party to nineteenth-century arguments about structural and material honesty, arguments like the one made by John Ruskin in *The Seven Lamps of Architecture* (1849). These came to inform twentieth-century Modernism.

Blake's reaction to the industrial palace was the most consistently critical, in keeping with his utilitarian evaluation of the main building at the

1867 exposition. He described the great dome of the palace as "expensive and unimpressive," classifying it among the building's major problems. In considering the "expensive and elaborate" plaster decorations that so impressed the Philadelphia representatives, he asked a significant question: "Shall our building in 1876 be subordinated to the exhibition of the products of the country and of industry generally, or shall the buildings form a part of the exhibition?" To what degree the architecture itself should be on display, competing for attention with the objects in the collection—this is still a critical issue in the design of buildings like museums. In the case of the centennial's temporary structures, Blake advocated an economical, "subordinated" architecture. In the case of the permanent building, however, he favored a more traditional monument. The city of Philadelphia and the state of Pennsylvania had together appropriated a total of $1.5 million for the construction of a museum that was to remain in Fairmount Park as a memorial to the U.S. centennial. "In such a structure," he wrote, "we may and should show fully our skill and taste in construction."[31]

As we have seen, the plan of the industrial palace, with its long nave and many short transepts, ensured that the dual system of classification that had been introduced in Paris was not employed in Vienna. The "systematic" was abandoned in favor of the "geographic"; national groups predominated, and the arrangement of displays by type was accomplished only insofar as there were specialized buildings devoted to broad areas of material culture.[32] This combined with the sheer size of the palace made it physically difficult to study the exhibition, as explained by the *Nation:* "One who wished to compare English and Japanese porcelain, for instance, was compelled to walk the entire length of a building over 3000 feet long, because the English department was at one end and the Japanese at the other."[33] Nevertheless, the plan of the palace made it possible to install the exhibition as a kind of world map centered on Austria and Germany. As described by Pettit, this arrangement was easy to understand: "North and south America occupy the extreme western end of the building; England and Western Europe come next, and so on until we reach the extreme eastern transepts, which are appropriated to China and Japan."[34] The plan was also friendly to crowds, with the nave and rotunda serving as natural gathering places, according to Blake: "The tendency is to keep with the crowd, and the crowd always gravitates to the main halls and passage-ways. . . . This generalization should be kept in mind in designing our building. People gravitate to exhibitions, not only to see the objects displayed, but to see each other—to see the crowd and to be in it. This being the case, broad avenues or promenades

2-5. "Industriepalast: Innen, Ansicht der östlichen Hauptgalerie" *(Weltausstellung in Wien 1873.* [(Vienna): Wiener Photographen-Association, 1873], no. 99, Prints and Photographs, Library of Congress).

should constitute a feature of exhibition-buildings." This observation, that people came to a fair not only to view things but also to look at and be with other people, is an important one that we will encounter again in this work. Intriguingly, Blake insinuated that visitors may actually have avoided the exhibit areas for the "avenues or promenades." Unfortunately, these areas, which constituted the space of the vista, were blocked in Vienna by a crowd of showcases, "most of them of unusual height and size" (fig. 2-5).[35] Arriving before the opening of the exhibition, Pettit observed that these displays were not only obscuring the view but also making it difficult for people to orient themselves in the enormous building: "Some of these show-cases are so large that they almost touch the roof, and are so wide as to completely close up the vista both down the nave and transepts."[36]

In addition to preventing the implementation of the dual system, the overly articulated plan of the industrial palace had other disadvantages. In addition to making construction unusually expensive, the plan created an excess of wall. This would be desirable in an art museum, where hanging space is at a premium, but not at a fair, where exhibitors preferred freestanding displays.[37]

The plan did have one inadvertent virtue: as the exhibition outgrew the building, the courtyards between the transepts could be enclosed to provide more room. This was an expensive solution, but Hasenauer's fancy facades made it difficult to expand the building in any other direction.[38] As a result, Pettit was emphatic about the need for flexibility in the architecture of the Centennial, "owing to this primary fact: that it is impossible to know positively, at this early state of the work, the exact kind of exhibits that will be sent, or the area in square feet each State or country may need."[39]

THE CENTENNIAL EXHIBITION

In the end, the story of the Austrian industrial palace teaches the same lesson as the Centennial catalogue: the exhibition was an indeterminate structure, the parts of which could not all be defined in advance and the behavior of which could not be entirely predicted. This made it difficult to describe in words, let alone contain in a building—an obstacle to modern, rational planning. Hasenauer had employed the traditional forms of monumentality—the domed rotunda, symmetrical plan, articulated spaces, and Classical language—but his fancy facades belied the fact that there could be no such thing as a finished building where the exhibition was concerned. The Crystal Palace had shown how architecture could frame the fair as a persuasive picture; the elliptical hall of the 1867 exposition had illustrated the synchronous power of a dual system of classification and installation. The industrial palace reinforced both these lessons while demonstrating that the fair was a charged social environment. Synthesizing these precedents would not be easy, as the exhibition hall was a relatively new building type, the form of which was still in flux. The Centennial Commission could not be blamed if it did not know what to build, and it would have to consider many alternatives before making up its collective mind. In such circumstances, a competition was clearly in order.

In the nineteenth century, when American architects were establishing their authority as a profession, there was an already accepted tradition of architectural competitions in the United States. This dated to 1789, when a competition was held for the design of a new building for the Library Company of Philadelphia. A gentleman architect, William Thornton, earned the modest first prize of one share in the library, and he went on to produce the winning design in the U.S. Capitol competition of 1792–93. Over the next one hundred years, competitions would be held for a variety of important public buildings. These included the White House (1792), the Second Bank of the United States (1818), the Ohio State Capitol (1838–39), the Smithsonian Institution (1846), the New York State Capitol (three separate contests held in 1863 and 1866), and the city hall in Philadelphia (1871).[40] More to the point, the managers of this country's first world's fair, the 1853–54 exhibition in New York, sponsored an international competition for the design of the building in Bryant Park.[41] Given this history, it is not surprising that the organizers of the Centennial eventually decided to hold their own competition. It was the appropriate thing to do in the case of an important public commission, particularly one of national significance that included the design of a permanent museum building in Fairmount Park.

At the Centennial Commission's first session in March 1872, Hawley appointed the Committee on Plans and Architecture.[42] The seven members were instructed to return to the second session with a preliminary design and construction estimates for a single, fifty-acre exhibition building—nearly three times as large as the original Crystal Palace.[43] How the members were expected to proceed is not clear, but at some point they evidently began to consider a competition. During the recess, they met with groups of architects in three major cities—Philadelphia, New York, and Boston—and published their views in three short reports submitted at the second session.[44] The architects were all wary of competitions, and they raised issues that would make the program more or less fair to competitors—prize money; the amount of time provided to develop schemes; the importance of returning unpremiated designs; and, most important, the need to guarantee the commission to the winner. They also voiced a concern for the client's interest that was not incompatible with a desire to limit the program to qualified professionals. The architects of Philadelphia and New York, for instance, both proposed that the competitors submit cost estimates—a condition tending to rule out amateurs. In the same vein, the New York architects suggested that references be required.[45]

The report of the Boston architects is the most significant because it most clearly articulated the idea of a two-stage competition. The architects preferred a limited, paid competition, but if the Committee on Plans and Architecture did not want to assume the responsibility of choosing a select group of ten practitioners, they reluctantly suggested an unpaid, open competition as a preliminary stage, warning that this could lead to a dilemma. On one hand, the Centennial Commission could find itself in the awkward position of having to hire "an incompetent or otherwise undesirable person"—someone, we can imagine, who was not a professional. On the other hand, if the commission did not intend to fulfill its commitment to award the commission to the winner, "competent and responsible architects" would boycott the program. "These evils are inseparable from public competitions," stated the report, "and account for the failure which has generally attended them."[46]

The report of the Boston architects appears to have had the most influence on the Committee on Plans and Architecture. In its own report to the commission, the committee considered the merits of limited and unlimited competitions. A limited competition, open to all comers, would provide an opportunity for unknown architects to be recognized. This seemed more egalitarian, more in the spirit of a national event like the Centennial. But a limited competition, closed to all except invited architects, would ensure that the commission obtained the advice of leading professionals. Ultimately, in an effort to promote both equity and quality, the committee proposed a two-stage competition. The first stage would consist of two parts, with ten architects chosen from the open part, and ten invited to compete in the closed. Each would receive a premium of $1,000 and would have the opportunity to compete in the second stage of the competition for six prizes ranging in value from $2,000 to $15,000.[47]

This program did not meet with the immediate approval of the Centennial Commission, which sent the entire report back to the committee. In an apparently contradictory move, the commission did appropriate the generous sum of $50,000, "for the purpose of procuring plans and estimates for the erections of the buildings and appurtenances contemplated by this Commission."[48] This sum was never actually provided, as the country was in the grip of a financial panic that had begun with the collapse of Jay Cooke's Philadelphia bank.[49] As a result, the Board of Finance—the entity charged with raising and spending money for the Centennial—was having trouble selling stock in the exhibition.[50] At the third session, the committee reported that, for lack of funds, it had not been able "to procure plans and estimates," as instructed.[51] The commission responded by providing the members with the smaller sum of $20,000 ($270,000 today), "to be used as they deem best, to procure plans and specifications of the buildings."[52] This appropriation was confirmed on February 25, when the committee was officially informed that the funds were available.[53] The competition could finally proceed.

THE FIRST STAGE

On April 1, 1873, the Committee on Plans and Architecture published an advertisement inviting "Architects, Engineers, and others" to submit pre-

liminary plans for the buildings of the Centennial Exhibition.[54] This word-
ing is significant, since it suggests that the commission did not want to
restrict the competition to either architects or professional designers—a sign
of the architect's weakness and of the amateur's continuing credibility.[55]
The advertisement appears to have generated a strong response; the committee answered the 173 inquiries with a package that included a brief set
of specifications, a topographical map of Fairmount Park, indicating the
proposed location of the exhibition buildings, and a short pamphlet explaining
the dual system of classification.[56]

The specifications described a simpler competition than the committee
had originally proposed. The first stage was completely open, but the July
15 deadline gave competitors a little more than three months to prepare a
basic set of drawings: a "block" or site plan, building plans of the ground
floor and galleries, north and south elevations, and cross sections if necessary. If the entries were satisfactory, the committee promised to select ten
finalists, each receiving a $1,000 prize (approximately $13,500 today) and
advancing to the second stage of the competition. In addition to these ground
rules, the specifications affirmed the idea of a fifty-acre fair but not in its
original form. Because of the nature of the site, the plan was no longer to
erect a single large hall, but at least four separate structures—the Main
Exhibition Building, an art gallery, a machinery building, and a plant conservatory. The competition was only concerned with the design of the first
two—the Main Building, with at least twenty-five acres of floor space, and
a "fire proof" art gallery with no more than two acres of space. To make
matters more complicated, the Main Building was to be a hybrid design
incorporating both a temporary exhibition structure and a five-acre building
known as Memorial Hall. The latter was to be "of such a character, and
constructed of such substantial materials, as that it shall remain after the close
of the Exhibition for a *permanent* Art Museum."[57] Significantly, the specifications did not specify a budget for the construction of these buildings.

The Centennial Commission received forty-three entries, all but eight
of which were the work of easterners, and held a public exhibition on the
University of Pennsylvania campus. In addition, for the convenience of competitors, all of the drawings were photographed, and the written descriptions reproduced in pamphlet form.[58] In general, solutions to the problem of
the Main Building took four forms. The most common was a conventional
palace block elaborated by courtyards and pavilions, with Memorial Hall
embedded somewhere in the middle or front of the temporary structure.
Many entries showed the influence of previous exhibition buildings, spe-

cifically the nave-and-transept design of the industrial palace at the 1873 Weltausstellung and the elliptical plan of the main building at the 1867 Exposition universelle. Finally, there were a few idiosyncratic proposals for star-shaped buildings, ostensibly as a patriotic reference to the American flag.

On August 8, 1873, the Committee on Plans and Architecture selected ten finalists to compete in the second stage of the competition. A slight majority were from Philadelphia: Samuel Sloan; John McArthur Jr. and Joseph M. Wilson; James C. Sidney; Edward Collins and Charles M. Autenrieth; Francis R. Gatchel and Stephen P. Rush Jr.; and Henry A. Sims and James P. Sims. The rest were from various locations in the East and Midwest: Joseph S. Fairfax of Wheeling, West Virginia; Calvert Vaux and George K. Radford of New York; Thomas M. Plowman and Bartholomew Oertly of Washington, D.C.; and Josse A. Vrydagh of Terre Haute, Indiana.[59]

The name of Calvert Vaux (1824–1895) stands out among the finalists. Born in England, Vaux was an architect and landscape designer who came to the United States to work with Andrew Jackson Downing, best known for writing books such as *The Architecture of Country Houses* (1850). During the course of their short-lived partnership, Vaux and Downing established a reputation for designing English-style country houses and their surroundings. Vaux contributed to Downing's scheme for a picturesque rearrangement of the Mall in Washington, D.C., before Downing died in a steamboat accident. Vaux subsequently made a partner of Frederick Law Olmsted, with whom he produced designs for Central Park in New York (1857 competition), Prospect Park in Brooklyn (1865–68), and the picturesque suburban community of Riverside, near Chicago (1868 plan). Vaux was an early member of the American Institute of Architects (AIA), established in 1857. His association with English-born engineer George K. Radford dated from the time of the Centennial competition and lasted until 1892.[60]

Vaux also was the author of an extremely popular pattern book, *Villas and Cottages,* which was published five times between 1857 and 1874.[61] Another of the finalists, Samuel Sloan (1815–1884), was a prominent Philadelphia architect as well as a prolific author of pattern books: *The Model Architect* (1852 and 1860), *City and Suburban Architecture* (1859), *Sloan's Constructive Architecture* (1859), *Sloan's Homestead Architecture* (1861), and *American Houses* (1861). He was also the publisher of *The Architectural Review and American Builder's Journal* (1868–1870), the first architectural magazine in the United States. His designs were familiar to readers of the popular woman's journal, *Godey's Lady's Book*, where they began to appear in 1852. At the same time, Sloan directed an expanding practice known mostly for the production of schools and mental hospitals.[62]

John McArthur (1823–1890) was the architect of Philadelphia's new city hall, begun in 1872 and the largest and tallest building in the United States when finished in 1901. McArthur was also the architect of the Continental Hotel (1858–60), a six-story, six-hundred-room block where the Centennial Commission met in Philadelphia.[63] McArthur's partner in the competition, Joseph Wilson (1838–1902), had a degree in civil engineering from Rensselaer Polytechnic Institute, and he worked as an engineer for the Pennsylvania Railroad from 1860 to 1886. The Centennial was clearly a turning point in his career; in 1876, he established Wilson Brothers and Company with his brother John A. Wilson, another civil engineer, and Frederick G. Thorn, an architect. Working as an architect and an engineer, Joseph shared with his partners a large and diverse practice that included private houses, public buildings, and functional structures, with railroad stations as a particular speciality. The most important were all in Philadelphia: the Philadelphia and Reading Terminal (1891–93, with Francis H. Kimball as consulting architect), the original Broad Street Station (1880–82), and its enlargement by Wilson Brothers (shed, 1892–93) and Furness, Evans and Company (head house, 1892–94). Wilson is credited with introducing the three-hinge arch into the United States, with Reading and the enlarged Broad Street stations serving as high points in the design of single-span, hinged-arch train sheds in this country. Broad Street was the largest of its type, with a span of just over three hundred feet that was exceeded only by the Galerie des Machines and the Manufacturers and Liberal Arts Building at the 1889 Paris and 1893 Chicago fairs, respectively. Wilson's interests extended to scientific research, and he published a number of technical papers in engineering. He belonged to several learned societies and for ten years served as president of the Franklin Institute in Philadelphia.[64]

The other finalists are less well known today. Henry Sims (1832–1875) was born in Philadelphia, according to one source; in Canada, according to another. Sims practiced as a civil engineer and an architect in Ottawa and in Philadelphia, where he helped to found the local AIA. His brother, James Sims (1849–82), was a graduate in architecture of the University of Pennsylvania. The two of them established a Philadelphia-based firm; their works included the Girard Avenue Bridge (1872–74), a one-hundred-foot-wide, one-thousand-foot-long structure that served as an important link between the city and the Centennial.[65] The Prussian-born Edward Collins (1821–

1902) is believed to have immigrated to the United States in 1849 and was an assistant to John McArthur in the 1850s. During this time, he joined with another German immigrant, Charles Autenrieth (1828–1906), in forming one of Philadelphia's most important and enduring architectural partnerships, which lasted nearly fifty years.[66] Bartholomew Oertly was a Swiss-born architect who worked in the federal government's Bureau of Construction, beginning in 1855 as a draftsman. He rose to the position of assistant architect of the Treasury Department before leaving in 1868 or 1869.[67] Belgian-born architect Josse Vrydagh lived in Dallas and Cincinnati before establishing a practice in Terre Haute in the 1860s. He was an AIA fellow and designed a number of important public buildings in Indiana.[68] Thomas Plowman (d. 1879) began practicing as an architect in 1870, after a career as a carpenter and builder. His only known buildings date from a short-lived partnership in Washington, D.C.[69] James Sidney (c. 1819–1881) was the author of a master plan for Fairmount Park (1859) and of a partially published pattern book, *American Cottage and Villa Architecture* (1850).[70] Joseph Fairfax, who was listed as one of two architects in the 1867–68 Wheeling directory, was responsible for the design of the West Virginia State Capitol in Wheeling, completed in 1876.[71] Stephen Rush (d. 1877) worked with his father in a local company of architects/builders; the identity of his partner, Francis Gatchel, has not yet been determined.[72]

THE SECOND STAGE

On August 11, shortly after announcing the winners in the first stage, the Committee on Plans and Architecture published the "conditions, requirements, and awards" for the second stage of the competition. These affirmed the initial specifications with two important changes. The first required the finalists to provide estimates of the time and money required for construction of their proposed buildings. The second mandated an express relationship between the architecture and order of the exhibition: "The temporary buildings, being connected with the Memorial Building, whether they be rectangular, elliptical, semi-elliptical, circular, or semi-circular, must admit of the dual application of the systematic and geographical classification."[73] In this way, what had only been suggested in the first stage became an explicit part of the competition program.

The September 30 deadline gave the finalists less than two months to revise their original schemes. During this time, they could study the photographs and written descriptions of their competitors' first-stage designs. On

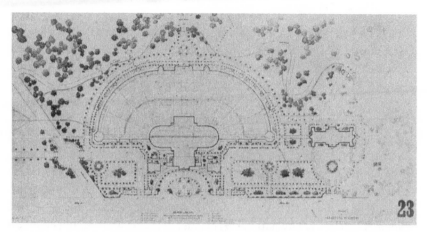

2-6. "Block Plan" (site plan), by Edward Collins and Charles M. Autenrieth (United States Centennial Commission [USCC], *Photographs of Plans for Centennial Exhibition Buildings* [albums, 1873], 3:73, Business Science and Industry Department, Free Library of Philadelphia). *Enlarged plate appears on page 233 of the appendix.*

October 15, the Committee on Plans and Architecture began to consider the second-stage entries; on November 1, the committee issued a report announcing the results. In spite of the fact that the Centennial was supposed to be a national celebration, the winners were all from Philadelphia. Edward Collins and Charles Autenrieth received the first prize of $4,000 (about $54,000 today); Samuel Sloan, the second prize of $3,000; John McArthur and Joseph Wilson, the third prize of $2,000; Henry and James Sims, the fourth prize of $1,000. The plan had been to award a single premium of $10,000, but the committee decided to split this amount four ways after consulting the finalists.[74] This was not a good sign, as it was common practice for a dissatisfied jury to divide the prize among the competitors.[75]

Collins and Autenrieth submitted a design that was clearly based on the main building at the 1867 Exposition universelle. They cut the ellipse in half the long way and positioned Memorial Hall at the center of the resulting hemicycle, where a courtyard had been in the French structure (fig. 2-6). They located the art gallery east of the Centennial's Main Building, on an extension of its long axis, and oriented the whole complex toward Elm Avenue, which would be the southern boundary and main entrance of the exhibition. In this scheme, the temporary structure provided a relatively subdued backdrop to Memorial Hall, which was a grandiose building with a cruciform plan, domed rotunda, and triumphal-arch entry (fig. 2-7). The plan of the exhibition space seemed to accommodate the dual system; Me-

2-7. "South Elevation," Main Building, by Edward Collins and Charles M. Autenrieth (USCC, *Photographs of Plans,* 3:84, Centennial Collection, Historical Society of Pennsylvania).

morial Hall served as the focus of thirteen radiating avenues, which were named after the thirteen original states and which intersected five concentric galleries (fig. 2-8). The high, arched space of the central Massachusetts Avenue continued the north transept of Memorial Hall and provided the orienting device that Pettit and others had found lacking in the French structure.[76] The outermost gallery was bordered by a ring of restaurants, which served as a kind of continuous food court. Noting that the 1873

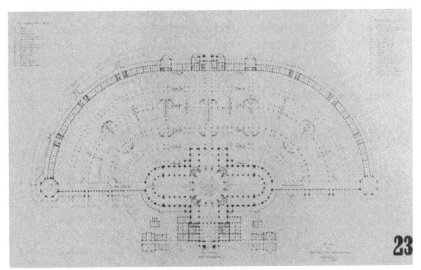

2-8. "Ground Plan," Main Building, by Edward Collins and Charles M. Autenrieth (USCC, *Photographs of Plans,* 3:75, Business Science and Industry Department, Free Library of Philadelphia).

2-9. "Block Plan," by Samuel Sloan (USCC, *Photographs of Plans,* 3:34, Business Science and Industry Department, Free Library of Philadelphia). *Enlarged plate appears on page 234 of the appendix.*

Weltausstellung, like all previous exhibitions, had required more space than originally planned, the architects proposed to use this ring, and the twenty-five-foot-deep verandah surrounding it, for display if necessary.[77]

Samuel Sloan adopted a similar approach to the Main Building, cutting the ellipse across the short axis and positioning it behind Memorial Hall (fig. 2-9). He expressed the difference between the two parts of the Main Building in stylistic terms, with Memorial Hall designed in "the modernized classic of Palladio" (fig. 2-10) and the amphitheater of the temporary structure in what he called a "Venetian" mode (fig. 2-11); the future museum faced the art gallery across a large terrace. Going beyond the require-

2-10. "A Geometrical Elevation of the East Front of the Permanent and Temporary Buildings Connected . . . ," by Samuel Sloan (Prints and Photographs, Library of Congress).

2-11. "Perspective View of the Permanent and Temporary Buildings as They Will Appear Together from the North and South West," by Samuel Sloan (USCC, *Photographs of Plans*, 3:44, Business Science and Industry Department, Free Library of Philadelphia).

ments of the competition, Sloan also submitted a design for Machinery Hall, which he situated on axis behind the Main Building. Like Collins and Autenrieth, Sloan situated his buildings on a line parallel to Elm, but he rotated the complex of the Main Building so that it faced roughly east, toward the center of Philadelphia. He believed that east was the traditional orientation of a monumental structure, but he also thought that, after the art gallery was demolished, it would be more appropriate for Memorial Hall to look toward the city and not toward Elm, which he feared would develop as a commercial and industrial corridor.[78]

In contrast to these two schemes, John McArthur and Joseph Wilson submitted a design that rejected the elliptical prototype. McArthur and Wilson conceived Memorial Hall as a brick structure with a cruciform plan and a gigantic square tower at the crossing (fig. 2-12 and 2-13). Sheathed in galvanized iron, the tower would be built on a wrought-iron frame, 120 feet wide at the base and comparable in size to the iron dome of the U.S. Capitol. The written description is replete with such comparisons; for instance, the 500-foot-high tower would be the world's loftiest building, 50 feet taller than the stone skyscraper that McArthur had designed for Philadelphia's new city hall. The projected roof span was 216 feet, which would make the building larger than the 200-foot-wide shed of New York's first Grand Cen-

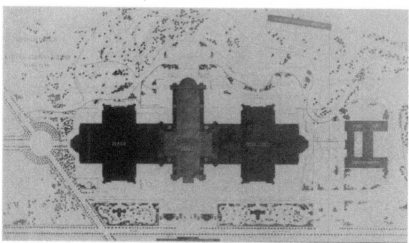

2-12. "Block Plan," by John McArthur Jr. and Joseph M. Wilson (USCC, *Photographs of Plans,* 3:55, Business Science and Industry Department, Free Library of Philadelphia).

tral Station (Isaac C. Buckhout and J.B. Snook, 1869–71).[79] The height of the nave was 148 feet, which would put the building in a league with religious monuments like Cologne cathedral and St. Peter's in Rome.[80] These comparisons all added up to something of a mixed metaphor, which was inherent in the design. McArthur and Wilson were the only ones to use the Gothic style; this and the cruciform plan made the building look like a church. Yet, as depicted in the rendering (fig. 2-14), the cavernous space with its arched, wrought-iron roof trusses recalls nothing so much as a railroad station, particularly the shed of St. Pancras in London (William H. Barlow

2-13. "Proposed Centennial Exhibition Building South Front," by John McArthur Jr. and Joseph M. Wilson (USCC, *Photographs of Plans,* 3:64, Business Science and Industry Department, Free Library of Philadelphia).

2-14. Main Building, interior perspective, by John McArthur Jr. and Joseph M. Wilson (Prints and Photographs, Library of Congress).

with R.M. Ordish, 1865–67; head house and hotel by Sir George Gilbert Scott, 1868–77). This should not be surprising; Wilson was an engineer for the Pennsylvania Railroad, after all.

In the McArthur and Wilson design, Memorial Hall joined two sizable temporary structures, which also had cruciform plans. Built in brick on a timber frame, these structures would be attached on either side of the transept. Placed end to end, the three buildings would form a 2,224-foot-long complex covering more than twenty-five acres and providing nearly seventeen acres of "classified" exhibition space. Lacking any precise information, McArthur and Wilson did not describe a fixed installation, insisting only on the preservation of open space for the sake of the vista. "A central aisle is absolutely necessary for a proper display of the building and its exhibits," they explained, "and there is no reason why we should not produce even *grander* effects than those which have been attained at Sydenham." In arranging the displays, McArthur and Wilson explicitly rejected the complicated, elliptical installation of the 1867 fair. Instead, they proposed to use a rectangular plan, which would accommodate a dual system while providing for "an uninterrupted interior view of 2224 feet." Thus, they in-

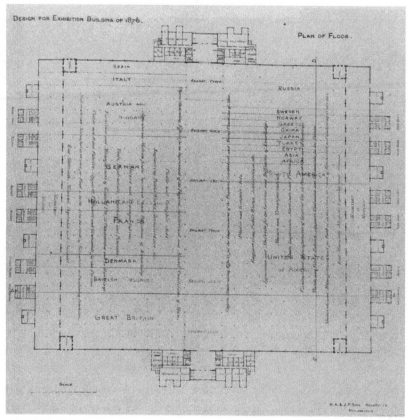

2-15. "Plan of Floor," Main Building, by Henry A. Sims and James P. Sims (USCC, *Photographs of Plans,* 3:26, Business Science and Industry Department, Free Library of Philadelphia).

tended to combine the look of the British fair with the logic of the French one.[81]

While the preceding schemes were all professional, Henry and James Sims took fourth prize with a straightforward, even amateurish design that nonetheless managed to attract the jury's attention. Like McArthur and Wilson, the Sims brothers adopted a rectangular plan for the Main Building, proposing to install the exhibition in an orthogonal version of the dual system (fig. 2-15). A long, barrel-vaulted nave, recalling Francis Fowke's design for the 1862 London fair, provided both a focus and a promenade, while bisecting the building into two large, equally sized exhibition spaces. The Sims had originally intended to construct the nave in permanent materials, thinking that it would remain as Memorial Hall after the temporary

2-16. Memorial Hall, exterior perspective, by Henry A. Sims and James P. Sims (USCC, *Photographs of Plans,* 3:31, Business Science and Industry Department, Free Library of Philadelphia).

structure had been taken down. In revising their design, they determined that Memorial Hall should be a freestanding structure. (The Committee on Plans and Architecture eventually came to the same conclusion.) Noting that the specifications had imposed a maximum size of five acres, they argued that it would be impossible to erect "a thoroughly permanent and substantial building" of that size for the $1.5 million that had been appropriated. Instead, they proposed to make the hall a one-acre, neo-Romanesque monument in stone and brick (fig. 2-16), with the Main Building as an entirely separate, temporary structure in brick and iron. In this part of the design, they made a surprisingly modern distinction between "served" and "servant" spaces, between display and ancillary functions. The nave of the Main Building terminated at both ends in 120-foot-square, domed pavilions (fig. 2-17). These were fronted by smaller structures containing restaurants, dining rooms, and kitchens; "retiring rooms" for men and women; telegraph

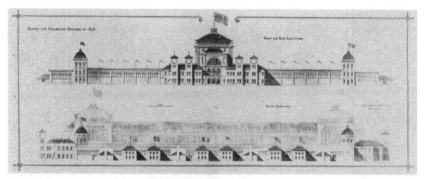

2-17. "Front and Rear Elevations" and "Flank Elevations," Main Building, by Henry A. Sims and James P. Sims (USCC, *Photographs of Plans,* 3:30, Business Science and Industry Department, Free Library of Philadelphia).

and newspaper offices; committee and jury rooms. Similarly, the east and west sides of the building were lined with boiler houses and smaller service structures. The big box of the exhibition hall was otherwise undifferentiated, except for the long axis of the nave and the square bays of the column grid. The result was an open, uninflected interior, very much like the rationalized space of twentieth-century factories and warehouses. The resemblance was heightened by the use of a sawtooth or "spinning shed" roof, with long skylights supported on a system of iron trusses. This makes the design, for all its naïveté, remarkably prescient.[82]

THE PAVILION PLAN

These prize-winning schemes illustrate the two main sets of questions that faced participants in the 1873 competition. First, how should the architecture of the Centennial accommodate the dual system of classification? Should the temporary structure have a rectangular plan, like the Crystal Palace? This would be cheaper to build and easier to salvage, but it would also create the vista that everyone seemed to think was a desirable feature. Or should the structure have an elliptical plan, like the main building at the 1867 exposition? This would be more expensive to build, but it would suggest the panoramic, comprehensive character of a world's fair. Second, how should the two parts of the Centennial's Main Building relate to each other? Should Memorial Hall and the temporary structure be connected, as originally specified and as assumed by most of the competitors? Or should the parts be separated, as Henry and James Sims had determined? One would

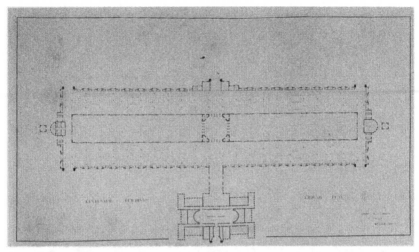

2-18. "Ground Plan," Main Building, by Thomas M. Plowman and Bartholomew Oertly (USCC, *Photographs of Plans,* 3:11, Business Science and Industry Department, Free Library of Philadelphia).

be permanent; the other, temporary. One was expected to be a representational form that signified an important event and a public institution; the other, a rationalized space providing the most benefit for the least cost. One was architecture, as this was understood in the nineteenth century; the other was engineering—and yet both would be monumental buildings of some kind. The rub was that such buildings were still largely defined in traditional terms, which included the choice of an appropriate style of architecture. This was a contentious issue in the nineteenth century, and yet, putting aside Sloan's argument about Venetian vs. Palladian, there was surprisingly little talk of style among the competition's finalists.

The designers of unpremiated schemes responded to these questions in much the same way as the winners. Plowman and Oertly, for example, proposed another orthogonal plan, in which the temporary structure took the form of a rectangle centered on a domed rotunda (fig. 2-18). Memorial Hall was a semidetached Second Empire palace, situated on axis with the rotunda; the art gallery was a small, doughnut-like building to the southeast. Plowman and Oertly wanted to house Department IX, Fine Arts, in the art gallery, and Department VIII, Engineering, Public Works, and Architecture, in Memorial Hall. The rest of the exhibition would be installed in the temporary structure along the lines of the dual system, with typological departments in long strips, and national courts in short sections.[83] In con-

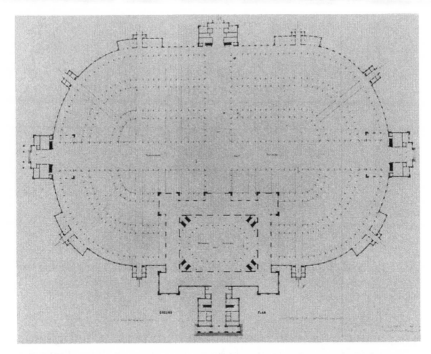

2-19. "Ground Plan," Main Building, by James Sidney (USCC, *Photographs of Plans,* 3:3, Business Science and Industry Department, Free Library of Philadelphia).

trast, James Sidney and Josse Vrydagh both followed the elliptical proto-type. In fact, Sidney was the only finalist to explicitly cite the French build-ing as his inspiration. In his design, Memorial Hall was almost completely submerged in the temporary structure, which took the form of a nearly com-plete ellipse accommodating the dual system in rings and sections (fig. 2-19).[84] Like Sloan, Collins, and Autenrieth, Vrydagh proposed that the temporary structure take the form of a half ellipse behind Memorial Hall (fig. 2-20). However, like the Sims brothers, he detached the permanent building from the temporary structure, citing their contrasting characters: "Each is to fulfill a different object and usage: the one is to be good for one year, and the other for a century of more. . . . Hence the difficulty to incor-porate two buildings so widely different in nature in one structure, and har-monize them in construction and according to taste and art. Either the Memorial would look temporary or the Exhibition Building would look permanent, if blended into one."[85] The most distinctive aspect of Vrydagh's design, however, was the plan of installation. Not satisfied with a dual sys-

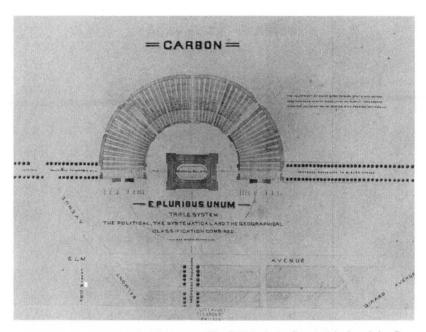

2-20. "E Pluribus Unum / Triple System / The Political, the Systematical and the Geographical Classification Combined," installation in temporary structure, by Josse A. Vrydagh (USCC, *Photographs of Plans,* 3:98, Business Science and Industry Department, Free Library of Philadelphia).

tem, he envisioned three divisions promoting "the departmental, geographical, and political comparison of arts and manufactures." The addition of the last division would permit each of the American states to mount their own individual exhibits, alternating with those of foreign nations in radial courts. This arrangement of equality between states and nations was meant to accommodate the overwhelming number of exhibits that could be expected from the host country, at the same time acknowledging the country's delicate situation after the Civil War. "While we do not believe in States rights to divide the country and alienate the right of any of her citizens," explained Vrydagh, "we wish to encourage the doctrine that more progress towards good will be arrived at by the strict observance of their individuality than by centralization or agglomeration into one mass."[86] (The design of Centennial finally recognized such individuality in the form of separate state pavilions.)

Gatchel and Rush proposed the single star-shaped structure to make it into the second stage of the competition. This was, in their words, "the only

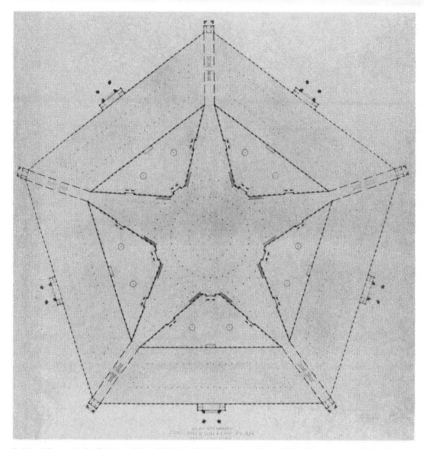

2-21. "Ground & Gallery Plan," Main Building, by Francis R. Gatchel and Stephen P. Rush Jr. (USCC, *Photographs of Plans,* 3:18, Business Science and Industry Department, Free Library of Philadelphia).

design for an Exhibition Building that . . . is at all significant of our nationality." The five-pointed star of Memorial Hall was centered on a domed rotunda and surrounded by the pentagon of the temporary structure (fig. 2-21). Gatchel and Rush claimed that the ringlike space of the structure would accommodate an arrangement of displays that was similar to the one used at the 1867 fair, or at least a polygonal variation of it. After the fair, the pentagon would be dismantled, leaving only the domed star of Memorial Hall.[87] Joseph Fairfax submitted another radial design, which was reminiscent of Philadelphia's Eastern State Penitentiary (John Haviland, 1823–25). In Fairfax's design, each of the eight arms of the Main Building terminated

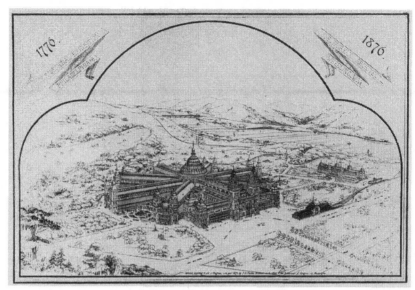

2-22. Bird's-eye view of the exhibition buildings, by J.S. Fairfax (USCC, *Photographs of Plans,* 3:95 reverse, Business Science and Industry Department, Free Library of Philadelphia).

in a two-towered pavilion; the largest facing Elm Street was Memorial Hall (fig. 2-22). Fairfax proposed to install one or two whole departments in each arm, so that visitors could examine every department in turn by making a clockwise circuit of the building.[88]

None of these schemes would have changed the course of architectural history, but there was one unpremiated design that, if it had been built, would certainly have become a part of the canon. This was Vaux and Radford's "Pavilion Plan"—without doubt, the most original and imaginative entry to the 1873 competition. As we have seen, Vaux was an architect; Radford was an engineer. Their association, like that of McArthur and Wilson, was a sign that larger and more complex projects were already demanding interdisciplinary cooperation, a bridging of the distinction between architecture and engineering. Their design was distinctive in being a real synthesis of these two kinds of building, these two ways of solving building problems. Unfortunately, they quarreled with the terms of the program, like the Sims but less successfully. Arguing that Memorial Hall could not be designed until the form of the Main Building had been determined, Vaux and Radford declined to propose a scheme for either the hall or the art gallery, and the jury disqualified their submission.[89]

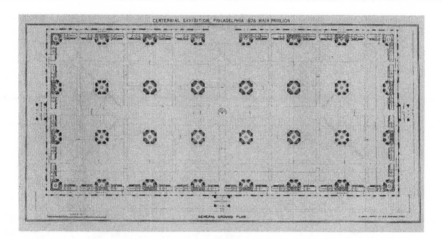

2-23. "General Ground Plan," Main Building, by Calvert Vaux and George K. Radford (U.S. Congress, Senate, *The National Centennial*, [Washington: GPO, 1874], n.p., University of California Library, Berkeley).

Vaux and Radford seem to have learned the lesson of the Crystal Palace, which was to determine the details of the building before its overall form. They began with a spatial and structural idea—a square bay or "pavilion"—which they refined and multiplied in two directions to form a single large exhibition hall (fig. 2-23). Each bay had a vaulted roof with wide, flattened groins; these converged in small, diamond-shaped courtyards, which drained the roof while supplying light and air to the vast interior. Unlike the other finalists, Vaux and Radford conceived the hall entirely in wood; the vaults were supported by arched timber trusses springing directly from the ground, making the wall and roof one continuous surface. An impressive perspective drawing (fig. 2-24) illustrates what this space would have looked like from the inside, with the cloth-covered ceiling divided into painted panels. A structural model (fig. 2-25), the only one to be presented in the competition, shows the outside wrapped by a repeating, screenlike facade. The style of this wall, which contained a narrow band of rooms, was High Victorian Gothic, and a square-domed pavilion in the form of a triumphal arch provided a central focus to each long side. Putting aside these historical allusions, there was something very modern about this design, which Vaux and Radford conceived not only as a rationalized kit of parts and spaces but also as a systematic method of construction. The problem, as they saw it, was to provide lateral support for the pavilions while

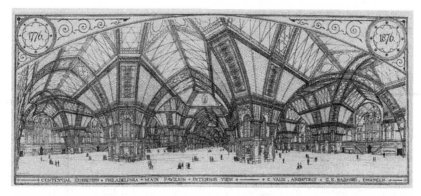

2-24. "Main Pavilion. Interior View," by Calvert Vaux and George K. Radford (United States Congress, Senate, *National Centennial,* n.p., University of California Library, Berkeley). *Enlarged plate appears on page 235 of the appendix.*

they were being erected; the solution was to make each bay stable in itself, by setting one pair of trusses at right angles to another. The trusses could then be raised at the same time, using the same type of scaffolding, which could ostensibly be taken down and reused in the construction of the next bay.[90]

2-25. Main Building model, by Calvert Vaux and George K. Radford (USCC, *Photographs of Plans,* 3:67, Centennial Collection, Historical Society of Pennsylvania).

Vaux and Radford proposed to accommodate the dual system of classification with an orthogonal version of the elliptical French plan. This was not a grid of knowledge, as proposed by McArthur and Wilson, but an arrangement of concentric zones for Departments I to VI, which would be installed in the Main Building; Departments VII to X, "being of a special nature," would be in Memorial Hall. In this arrangement, the United States occupied a favored position along the south side of the Main Building, facing the main entrance on Elm Avenue, with Germany and Great Britain in the flanking corners, "supporting the United States and typifying the sources from whence her population is mainly derived." (Vaux and Radford were clearly considering only Europeans.) France filled a third corner, Russia and Belgium a fourth, with the other countries taking strips of whatever was leftover.[91] The entire exhibition would be installed on one floor, although Vaux and Radford did allow for a fringe of raised galleries to be used for serving refreshments and for viewing the displays from above. Standing on the floor or in the galleries, the effect would have been spectacular: "The various parts of the building are thus included in one grand whole; and the result becomes a spacious hall, adequate to the emergencies of the occasion, with long vistas, central and intermediate points of emphasis, direct lines of transit throughout its length and breadth, diagonal lines of communication where really needed, and an entire relief from any appearance of contraction anywhere; for the visitor is always in an apartment over 200 feet wide, that opens without any intermediate corridor, into other apartments, also over 200 feet wide."[92] In spite of this reference to the vista, the exhibition as projected by Vaux and Radford was not a one-point perspective, as their drawing shows. The Pavilion Plan embodied a fundamentally different way of seeing, with galleries and "diagonal lines of communication" implying oblique views, and the repetition of nearly identical bays suggesting multiple and equivalent vantage points. The proposed space was isotropic, that is, the same in any direction; Vaux and Radford did mark the axes of the building with "central and intermediate points of emphasis"—raised roofs, cupolas, and pavilions—but these were really superficial effects. The axes are invisible in plan, and the drawing shows that there were no favored spaces in the design—one "apartment" was as good another. The result was a remarkably "modern," multipurpose space, which was not axial, not hierarchical, not permanent—the antithesis of a traditional monument.

Ultimately, the Vaux and Radford design was a true synthesis of the rational and the representational. It was rational in the systematic method of construction and the modular, uniform space, but also in the distinction it made between this space, which was functionally undefined, and the fringe of more functionally specific rooms that surrounded it. In this there is more than a hint of ideas that we associate with twentieth-century architecture: Louis Kahn's distinction between rooms that are servants and rooms that are served; Ludwig Mies van der Rohe's related notion of a universal space that is minimally encumbered by columns or fixed partitions and that can theoretically accommodate all things. The building as designed was representational in the painted decoration of the vaults, of course, but also in the use of the vaults themselves. These referred to Gothic architecture and all it represented, particularly the structural rationalism of the French architect Eugène-Emmanuel Viollet-le-Duc, who argued that medieval architecture could be a rational source of contemporary structure. Thus the Vaux and Radford design was not only rational but also a conscious representation of rationality.

A Change of Plan

If the 1873 competition had one fatal flaw, it was the omission of a construction budget for the specified buildings. The estimates submitted in the second stage varied widely, from a low of $2,871,500 for Vaux and Radford's disqualified Pavilion Plan, a figure that only accounted for the temporary structure, to a high of $10,050,000 for Collins and Autenrieth's first-prize-winning complex. By comparison, the cost of the industrial palace in Vienna had been $3,144,509, not counting the enclosure of the courts.[93]

This omission helps to explain the position taken by the Committee on Plans and Architecture in its November 1 report to the Centennial Commission. The committee praised the quality of the ten schemes, all of which displayed "great care, skill and labor," and professed to be embarrassed by the difficulty of choosing among them, but it described the selection process in a mysterious, strangely qualified manner: "In order to make the awards for this second competition, the relative merits of the different designs have been discussed and decided upon solely with respect to their meeting the requirements stated in the specification. The Committee has not been influenced by any additional points now deemed of equal importance, but which have presented themselves since the issue of the specifications. Such action was of course the only just one to the competing parties, but results in giving the awards to some designs which are radically different from that which it now deems advisable to erect." After announcing the four winners, the committee added this surprising disclaimer: "At the same time, however, that it recommends the above awards . . . it would distinctly state that in its judgment no one of the above designs can be considered as representing entirely satisfactorily what is required for the Centennial Buildings."[94]

What were those "additional points" that the committee had chosen to ignore? And what prevented it from endorsing any of the winning entries? The committee did not say outright, but Alfred T. Goshorn, in his own final report as director-general, described a number of problems that had not been addressed in the competition, the most important of which was money:

> The Committee, however, had to consider the great difference in the estimated cost of the buildings proposed; and it was also influenced by considerations which had arisen since the publication of its proposals,—(1) that it was essential, from considerations of economy and time, to combine the Art Gallery and Memorial Hall in a single building; (2) that the Art Gallery should be distinct from the Main Exhibition Building; (3) that buildings not previously contemplated would be required; (4) that certain principles of economy should be regarded in the construction of the Main Building, and also its capacity for extension in case of need.[95]

As an arm of the Centennial Commission, the Committee on Plans and Architecture was not responsible for the cost of construction—that was technically the job of the Board of Finance—but it could not completely ignore economic reality. The state of Pennsylvania and the city of Philadelphia had together appropriated a sum of only $1.5 million for the construction of Memorial Hall.[96] Furthermore, the financial panic of 1873 had developed into a major depression that would last another five years and that was already making it difficult for the board to sell stock in the exhibition.

In these circumstances, the Committee on Plans and Architecture had no choice but to alter its original plans. These had included a five-acre Memorial Hall as part of the Main Building and a separate, two-acre art gallery. In the November 1 report, the committee announced its decision to downsize these two structures into a single and significantly smaller one-and-a-half-acre pavilion, which would be located on a prominent site just north of the Main Building. This change was based not just on "considerations of economy and time," as Goshorn had stated, but also on a fundamental reevaluation of responsibilities. A close reading of the appropriations for Memorial Hall had convinced the committee that the Centennial Commission probably did not have jurisdiction over the building, and that the designs properly belonged to the State Board of Centennial Supervisors, which had been established to oversee construction.[97] The committee had also come to the surprisingly late conclusion that the function of the art gallery was incorporated in the legally mandated program for Memorial Hall, which was to remain in Fairmount Park as a museum.[98] Furthermore, in its report, the committee enumerated the size and type of the Centennial's other structures. In addition to Memorial Hall, there was to be an enlarged Main Exhibition Building of thirty-six acres, a ten-acre Machinery Hall, a five-acre Agricultural Hall, and a greenhouse of unspecified size. The total enclosed area of the fair was now well over the fifty acres that had originally been proposed. It would grow to more than seventy-one acres by opening day.[99]

Having announced and then renounced the results of the competition, the Committee on Plans and Architecture set about creating a hybrid scheme, using parts of both the Sims brothers' fourth-prize-winning design and Vaux and Radford's disqualified Pavilion Plan. The result was a large, rectangular building, 2,040 feet long and 680 feet wide. Based on a 136-foot-square bay, the building would be a combination of iron and brick, or iron and wood if brick proved too expensive. The nave, transept, and projecting corner pavilions would be covered by Vaux and Radford's groin vaults; the rest of the building, by the Sims' sawtooth roof.[100] The Committee on Plans and Architecture presented this hybrid to the Centennial Commission's Executive Committee on November 6, 1873, just five days after announcing the results of the second stage.[101] In a surprising move, the Executive Committee approved the scheme and referred it to Vaux and Radford for further development. They in turn convinced the committee that their original Pavilion Plan was a better design that would be just as economical as the hybrid. The committee accepted this argument, and two versions of the plan were sent out to bid, one in wood and the other in iron. The estimates showed that iron construction would be too costly, so Vaux and Radford reproduced the building in wood, with some iron protection. The committee approved this version, the price of which was estimated to be a mere $103,000 per acre, but the Building Committee of the Board of Finance refused to accept a wood structure on the grounds that it would not be fire safe.[102]

What followed was a kind of limbo dance in which Vaux and Radford bent ever more backward to satisfy the increasingly stringent demands of their clients. The Executive Committee asked them to redesign the building in iron, using smaller, more economical roof spans; they produced a structure estimated to cost $182,000 per acre. The committee approved it, but the Board of Finance demanded deeper cuts. Vaux and Radford were able to reduce the price to $124,000 per acre, which only provoked a drop in the maximum to $100,000 per acre. At this point, Henry Pettit entered the picture. Pettit, who had become a consulting engineer to the Centennial Commission, suggested an entirely new scheme with central pavilions and shedlike wings. He believed that this would be easier to expand, in contrast to the industrial palace at the 1873 Weltausstellung. Vaux and Radford were either unable or unwilling to make much of this idea, and Pettit was asked to prepare his own design. He refused, correctly reminding the Board of Finance that it already had a contract with Vaux and Radford.[103]

Eventually, there were three schemes on the table, all prepared by Vaux and Radford. The first was the Pavilion Plan with the addition of arched iron ribs; the second consisted of three vaulted galleries set between smaller aisles; the third, which corresponded to Pettit's proposal, was similar to the second but incorporated triangular roof trusses. The Building Committee replied by once again asking Pettit to prepare his own design. This time, he relented and created a fourth scheme incorporating his original suggestions. All four went out to bid; number two and number four came back at roughly the same price, although number four was considered superior; number one came in at over half a million dollars above the other two. (Number three seems to have disappeared as an alternative.) As a result, on June 30, 1874, the Board of Finance adopted number four, Pettit's scheme, and Goshorn approved it on July 4 at the direction of the Executive Committee.[104]

Joseph Wilson was generous in his description of the adopted design as "the final result of the successive efforts of many talented in their profession, developing step by step from the grand idea of the original requirements to a practical basis which could be met by the resources at hand. All those who contributed towards the attainment of this end—be it more less—are entitled to due credit for it." This kind of collective recognition was apparently not enough to satisfy Vaux and Radford. Having redesigned the Main Building several times, only to lose control of the concept to Pettit, they seem to have lost their enthusiasm for the project. "A professional issue arising," as Wilson discretely put it, "Messrs. Vaux and Radford declined to execute their work." As a result, Wilson and Pettit were appointed both architects and engineers of the Main Building and Machinery Hall.[105]

A NEW PROGRAM

The preceding account may suggest that the 1873 competition was a failure, and for good reason. The program had lasted six months and consumed twenty thousand dollars in prize money. In the end, the specifications were judged to be inadequate, the results were set aside, and the commission for the Main Building went first to the designers of a disqualified entry, and then to a pair of in-house engineers. However, if a competition can be considered an investigation of a building type, then this one can be judged at least a partial success. The Committee on Plans and Architecture had started out with only a very dim idea of what should be built. After studying all the entries, the committee was able to reach a number of very important, quite specific conclusions about the architecture of the Centennial, the Main Building in particular. These conclusions, which were stated in the November 1 report, in effect constituted a new program for the exhibition.

In the report, the Committee on Plans and Architecture rejected the prototype of the main building at the 1867 Paris fair, with its elliptical plan and its system of concentric galleries and radial sections. Instead, the committee called for a rectangular structure covering at least thirty acres and allowing for expansion as required. It recommended against the use of mezzanines as display areas but allowed for the incorporation of observation platforms from which visitors could obtain an overview of the displays. This was a new way of seeing the Centennial that had not previously been considered. The committee placed a high value on the construction of the exhibition as both a visual experience and a social environment, stating that "the interior arrangement should allow of vistas and attractive promenades, and afford opportunities for the convenient assembling of a large number of people." These were features associated with the reconstructed Crystal Palace at Sydenham and "the most successful English exhibition buildings." The committee decided that the Centennial's Main Building should be constructed of fire-resistant brick and iron, using standardized parts that could be salvaged after the exhibition was over. Regarding the massing of the building, the committee acknowledged the importance of "domes, towers and central massive features" in creating a beautiful and dignified structure, but it recommended against such "ambitious and expensive constructions." Instead, the committee envisioned a structure whose architectural impact was based on the abstract qualities of mass, composition, and space. "The Grand Pavilion," as it was called, "being a temporary building, must trust for its impressiveness to its great size, the proper treatment of its elevations, and to its interior vistas and arrangement, and not to any central feature erected at a great expense only to remain a few months."[106]

When combined with the selection of Wilson and Pettit as designers of the Main Building, this prescription is significant, because it anticipates the rationalist, modernist architecture of the twentieth century, just as it rejects the representational monumental architecture of the nineteenth. In fact, the Centennial was an engineer's landscape; the site plan and most of the major buildings were designed by men who, up until that time at least, were engineers by virtue of education, training, or professional experience. Many of the buildings, both large and small, were remarkably simple and straightforward—even utilitarian—when compared to the architectural pretensions of Memorial and Horticultural Halls. (This helps to explain why the buildings of the Centennial, some of which were quite significant in their own right, have been so neglected by architectural historians.) This was all in striking contrast to the 1893 World's Columbian Exposition in Chicago, where a committee of architects under the direction of architect Daniel Burnham was very much in control of the design, while the engineers were administratively reduced to one professional consultant. The neoclassical buildings of the fair were self-consciously monumental, employing precisely those "ambitious and expensive constructions" that had been eschewed by the Committee on Plans and Architecture. Their formal arrangement around the Court of Honor was a promise of the visual order that architects would deploy in the City Beautiful movement.

The comparative absence of architects at the Centennial can be read as a sign of weakness, as the complete apparatus of professional institutions had not yet appeared in the United States. The American Institute of Architects dates to 1857; it foundered in 1861 but was reestablished after the Civil War. The first professional program in architecture was organized in 1868, at the Massachusetts Institute of Technology; the first professor was Henry Ware, one of the Boston architects who had advised the Committee on Plans and Architecture on the 1873 competition. The first successful professional journal, *The American Architect and Building News,* began publication in the Centennial year and continued to appear under some variation of that name until 1938, when it was absorbed by the present *Architectural Record.* Legal recognition would come at the end of the century, when the Illinois legislature passed the first architectural licensing and registration law in 1897. This was clearly a critical time in the formation of architecture as a modern profession, and engineering was undergoing a parallel development. The process would continue into the twentieth century, but it was well enough advanced by the 1890s—architects had been successful enough in defining their role and selling their image to the public—that engineers were displaced as plausible designers of public buildings at the Chicago fair.[107]

THE INSTALLATION IN THE MAIN BUILDING

> The Centennial Commission . . . had well-nigh committed a serious
> error in adopting plans for the buildings, when the element of cost
> intervened and compelled their abandonment and the substitution of
> designs for structures of less expense and pretensions, but of greater
> utility. After expending a large sum in payment of awards for
> competitive plans, and the virtual adoption of a design for the Main
> Building, the services of the architects were dispensed with,—the
> original scheme was abandoned as impracticable, and the subject
> was referred to the engineers in the employ of the Commission. An
> experience, no doubt, not unlike that of other Exhibitions.
> —Alfred T. Goshorn, "Report of the Director General"

Surprisingly, the first real site plan of the Centennial Exhibition was not
prepared until October 1873, some time after the finalists had submitted
their revised designs in the second stage of the competition. Henry Pettit
was the author of this plan, which he presented to the Executive Committee
on November 6, in the form of a still-extant, six-foot-long drawing (fig. 3-
1). At that time, the Committee on Plans and Architecture was still proposing a hybrid scheme for the Main Building, combining Vaux and Radford's
vaulted pavilions with the Sims' simple sheds. Pettit placed a version of this
scheme parallel to Elm Street, along with Machinery Hall, a long, narrow
building reminiscent of the Galerie du Quai at the 1855 Paris fair. The two
structures straddled the existing diagonal of Belmont Avenue, which continued across the site after being interrupted by the southwest corner of the
Main Building. Memorial Hall was a relatively tiny pavilion situated on
axis behind the Main Building; Agricultural Hall, another linear structure
connected to Machinery Hall.

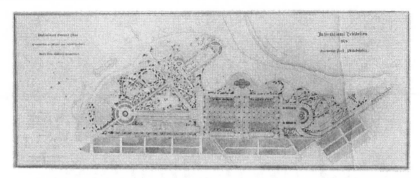

3-1. "Preliminary Ground Plan Submitted by the Committee on Plans and Architecture of the United States Centennial Commission" (Pettit, "Centennial Exhibition," 1:46, Historical Society of Pennsylvania [Philadelphia] architectural drawings collection on loan to the Athenaeum of Philadelphia, with the support of the Pew Charitable Trusts through its Museum Loan Program). *Enlarged plate appears on page 236 of the appendix.*

The long axis of the Main Building terminated to the east in a semicircular terrace; it continued to the west as Centennial Avenue, a broad, tree-lined boulevard intersecting a new diagonal street at a large rond-point. Running roughly east-west and forming a cross axis with the north-south line of Belmont Avenue, the diagonal connected the southwest corner of the fairground with Horticultural Hall, which was dramatically situated at the end of the street, on a plateau between Lansdowne and Belmont Valleys. This extremely formal arrangement indicates that Americans were already acquiring a taste for Grand Manner planning, well in advance of the 1893 Chicago fair. In the United States, such planning usually signifies the influence of French urbanism, particularly the interventions made by Baron Georges-Eugène Haussmann in the city of Paris. But more than that, the basic structure of Pettit's plan recalls the armature of the 1873 Vienna fair, where a long axis also met a diagonal in a rond-point, and the axial, symmetrical arrangement of major buildings contrasted with the picturesque arrangement of smaller structures. This combination of the formal and the picturesque had been a feature of the 1867 Paris fair, and it would also come to characterize the layout of the Centennial.

With this scheme, Pettit succeeded in establishing the fairground's essential features, which Herman Schwarzmann, as head of the Centennial Commission's Department of Engineering, developed in a series of "situation" plans. The last one showed the Main Building and Machinery Hall both positioned parallel to Elm Street, as in Pettit's scheme (fig. 3-2). The

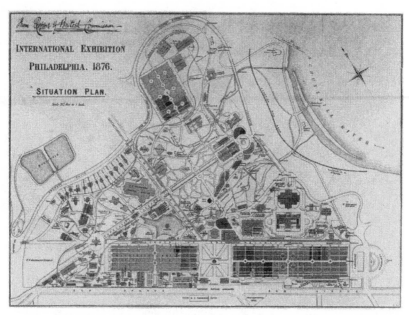

3-2. "Situation Plan." Autograph: "From Report of British Commission" (Pettit, "Centennial Exhibition," 1:53, Historical Society of Pennsylvania architectural drawings collection on loan to the Athenaeum). *Enlarged plate appears on page 237 of the appendix.*

3-3. "Main Building" (Centennial Photographic Company [CPC] 1289, Print and Picture Collection, Free Library of Philadelphia).

3-4. "Machinery Hall" (CPC 871, Print and Picture Collection, Free Library of Philadelphia).

Main Building (fig. 3-3), a twenty-acre, iron-and-wood structure designed by Wilson and Pettit, was shifted westward, allowing Belmont Avenue to continue unimpeded through the site and creating space for a rectangular entry plaza. Machinery Hall (fig. 3-4), a fourteen-acre, timber-framed building that was also designed by Wilson and Pettit, was moved northward, in line with the Main Building, so that the two halls appeared to form a single, three-quarter-of-a-mile-long front along the Avenue of the Republic. This much enlarged version of Pettit's Centennial Avenue, on axis with George's Hill, stretched the entire length of the fairground, intersecting the diagonal street at a more modest version of his original rond-point.[1] The diagonal was named Fountain Avenue after the two elaborate drinking fountains that marked its middle and western end. Erected by the Pennsylvania Sons of Temperance and the Catholic Total Abstinence Union, these were among the many fountains being erected in cities across the country in an effort to dissuade Americans from slaking their thirst with alcohol.

Memorial Hall (fig. 3-5), designed by Schwarzmann in what the Centennial Commission reports called a "modern Renaissance" style, was still in its original position behind the Main Building. Erected by the city of Philadelphia and the state of Pennsylvania as a permanent addition to the park, the 1.5-acre hall was the only major structure of the Centennial to be designed as a traditional monument in permanent materials—brick, granite, glass, and iron. Horticultural Hall (fig. 3-6), designed by Schwarzmann

3-5. "Memorial Hall" (CPC 1578, Print and Picture Collection, Free Library of Philadelphia).

3-6. "Horticultural Hall" (CPC 702, Print and Picture Collection, Free Library of Philadelphia).

in what the reports termed the "Mauresque style of architecture," also retained its location between Lansdowne and Belmont Valleys. Like Memorial Hall, this 1.25-acre, glass-and-iron conservatory was intended to be a "permanent decoration of Fairmount Park," as were the arboretum and botanical gardens on either side of Fountain Avenue. Lansdowne Drive was realigned to create a new site for Agricultural Hall on the other side of Belmont Valley (fig. 3-7). As designed by the architect, James H. Windrim, this hall took the form of a long nave crossed by a welter of transepts to form a complicated cross. The reports described it as a "cathedral ten acres in extent, though its materials were of the simplest." It was made of wood, covered an area of 8.72 acres, and looked, not inappropriately, like a big barn.[2]

The most striking development in the evolution of the Centennial's plan was the addition of a large number of entirely new buildings (fig. 3-8). These included ethnic and national eateries, such as the American Restaurant across Belmont Valley from Agricultural Hall; the 16 small, house-like structures erected on a winding drive by the American states; looming over the state houses, the U.S. Government Building, designed by Windrim for a site at the intersection of Fountain and Belmont Avenues; across Belmont from the U.S. Government Building, Schwarzmann's Women's Pavilion,

3-7. "Agricultural Hall" (CPC 829, Print and Picture Collection, Free Library of Philadelphia).

3-8. "From the Reservoir" (CPC 2064, Print and Picture Collection, Free Library of Philadelphia). *Enlarged plate appears on page 238 of the appendix.*

the first to be erected at a world's fair; also by Schwarzmann, Judges' Hall, situated in a prominent position at the head of the entry plaza; and free-standing additions to the major pavilions, such as the Art Gallery Annex and Photographic Hall, both situated near Memorial Hall. These were just a few of the 249 structures that were erected on the fairground by opening day—15 by foreign governments, 24 by American states and territories, 56 by private exhibitors, and 41 by assorted concessionaires.[3]

To orient visitors in this vast and crowded landscape, the organizers developed an elaborate system of signs. According to Schwarzmann, each building was supposed to be identified by a national flag and a banner (in practice, a shield) with a letter and number indicating the building's nationality and location. "By this means," reported Schwarzmann, "persons traversing the grounds had an unmistakable direction to every building they encountered."[4] The official guide explained that the space of the exhibition was divided into four quarters, with those structures situated south of the Avenue of the Republic numbered from 1 to 50; those north of the Avenue of the Republic and west of Belmont Avenue, from 50 to 100; those east of Belmont and south of Fountain, from 100 to 150; those east of Belmont and north of Fountain, from 150 to 200. The buildings were further divided into five groups, with those erected by the Centennial Commission flying a blue flag; those erected by the federal government and the American states, a red flag; those erected by foreign nations, a white flag; restaurants and places of entertainment, a yellow flag; and miscellaneous structures, a category that included the Women's Pavilion (!), a green flag. To make matters even more complicated, the banner was supposed to be similarly coded, with the border colored to match the flag, and the number colored to indicate the quarter in the fairground.[5]

The proliferation of such structures, and especially the presence of national buildings like the one erected by the U.S. government, has inspired some historians to cite the Centennial as the source of the pavilion idea.[6] Rather than attempting to display as much as possible under one roof, as was done at the 1851 London and 1867 Paris fairs and as was originally intended for the Philadelphia fair, the pavilion idea implied the disintegration of the international exhibition into specialized groups of exhibits in architecturally distinct halls. The exhibits could be organized around broad typological themes—machines, manufactures, art, and agriculture—as was common in the nineteenth century, or they could embody political or economic forms of organization—the country or corporation—as became prevalent in the twentieth.

In reality, in spite of the unitary ideal represented by the 1851 and 1867 fairs, the exhibition was fragmented from the very beginning. As early as the 1855 Exposition universelle, the exhibits had been divided among seven buildings—the Palais de l'Industrie, the Galerie du Quai, the Rotunde du Panorama, the Palais de Beaux-Arts, and three other buildings devoted to the display of agriculture, carriages, and bargain goods. Twelve years later, the elliptical hall of the 1867 exposition, which appeared to contain the whole world, was actually surrounded by a host of smaller structures. These were national in the sense that they represented characteristic types and styles of architecture, but they were not pavilions, as one source claims, in the sense that they did not contain collective exhibits.[7] The first true national pavilion was probably the structure erected by the U.S. government at the Centennial Exhibition. This is in the sense that it was not merely an office building, like the Queen Anne–style home of the British commissioners, but a real exhibition hall, with extensive displays of native peoples and natural resources.

Whatever the source, the emergence of the pavilion idea was a significant development, since the construction of specialized buildings reified the system of classification in the landscape of the Centennial. This was consistent with the original ambition of the organizers, which was to effect a transparent correspondence between the order of the exhibition and the arrangement of displays. At the same time, the construction of these buildings illustrated the deficiencies of a supposedly comprehensive system of classification, with "miscellaneous" buildings like the Women's Pavilion suggesting categories of material culture that the Centennial's mostly male organizers had not originally considered in the order of the exhibition.

THE MAIN EXHIBITION BUILDING

As designed by Wilson and Pettit, the Main Building was an elaboration of the scheme that Pettit had submitted to the Board of Finance as an alternative to Vaux and Radford's "Pavilion Plan." The building was a series of parallel sheds, the central one being a nave 120 feet wide, 70 feet high, and 1,832 feet long. Reputedly "the longest avenue of that width ever introduced into an Exhibition Building," the nave was flanked on either side by 100-foot-wide avenues and 24- and 48-foot-wide aisles (fig. 3-9). Three transepts, identical in section to the nave and avenues, crossed the building from north to south, creating nine large, column-free spaces in the heart of the hall.[8]

In the massing of the building, Wilson and Pettit deviated from the recommendation of the Committee on Plans and Architecture, to avoid "ambitious and expensive constructions," but only slightly. The roof over the crossing was raised to create the spatial focus that Pettit had considered so important in his report on the 1873 Vienna fair. Four 120-foot-high towers broke through the roof at the crossing; four 75-foot-high towers rose from the corners of the building; four 90-foot-high arcaded pavilions projected

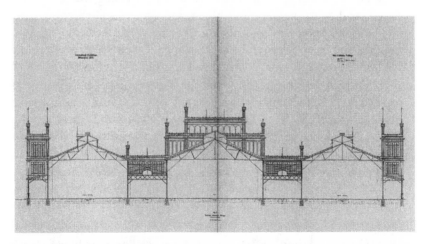

3-9. "Main Exhibition Building. No. 7. Section through Wings," by Henry Pettit and Joseph M Wilson (Pettit, "Centennial Exhibition," 2:20–21, Historical Society of Pennsylvania architectural drawings collection on loan to the Athenaeum).

3-10. "Main Building." North central entry (CPC 926, Print and Picture Collection, Free Library of Philadelphia).

from the middle of the four sides (fig. 3-10).[9] Bristling with trophies and turrets, and containing entries, offices, restaurants, and rest rooms, these pavilions interrupted the long horizontal march of the elevations, giving the design a vertical emphasis, albeit not enough to satisfy critics whose tastes had been formed on more compact and conventional structures.

Although the effect is lost in the engravings and black-and-white photographs, the Main Building was actually quite colorful. The seven-foot-high walls at the base of the building were constructed of red and black brick laid in a diaper pattern, but this gesture toward constructional polychromy was an anomaly: the circular hoppers topping the windows were treated to imitate stained or painted glass, and much of the decoration was painted. The outside was tinted in what Wilson described as "an agreeable tint of buff, relieved by darker shades, with bright colors in the chamfers, the rustic and foliated work at the entrances, the caps of columns, etc., being of a green bronze picked out with gold." Inside, the ceiling was whitewashed and stenciled; the ironwork of the roof was colored buff with crimson details; the columns and woodwork were painted several shades of light olive green, with decorations in crimson, blue, and gold. "On entering," Wilson thought, "the effect of the coloring is quite pleasing, harmonizing well with the rich display of exhibits, and fully justifying the reasons which led to its adoption."[10]

All of this color was applied to what was essentially a rationalized, industrial artifact. This was an engineer's building, after all, and it was conceived in a systematic fashion, like the Crystal Palace, as a kit of parts.[11] The plan was based on a twenty-four-foot-square module, and the structural members were built up from standardized elements that were prefabricated at remote locations and bolted together on site. Because of the committee's concerns about fire safety, the columns, girders, and trusses of the frame consisted almost entirely of wrought iron.[12] The Centennial Commission reports described the triangular roof trusses as being "similar in form to those in general use for depots and warehouses"—a sure sign of kinship with these utilitarian buildings.[13]

To our eyes, the Main Building looks like a factory, particularly the horizontally organized, nave-and-aisle type of factory that became common after 1900. In fact, it was an iron-trussed railroad shed. In Europe, this type of structure had become a familiar sight by the 1840s, but it did not appear in the United States until 1865. In fact, it was Wilson who built the first major example at the Washington terminal of the Baltimore and Potomac Railroad (1873–77). This had a length of 510 feet and a span of 130—much shorter than the 800-foot-long sections of the nave that stood on either side of the crossing of the Main Building, and only 10 feet wider. In fact, the Main Building can be seen as one of the first and largest of these sheds, which were built in this country between 1870 and 1900.[14]

The use of standardized, prefabricated parts made it possible to erect this immense structure in just eighteen months, and at a cost of only $1,763,600.17 (roughly $26 million today).[15] The site was graded during September and October 1874.[16] The foundations, consisting of rubble brick piers with granite caps, were laid in the fall of that year; winter brought an end to construction, and no other site work was performed until the following spring.[17] In the meantime, the mills, shops, and glassworks were busy fabricating the various parts of the building. The Board of Finance described the extent of this enterprise: "Some idea of the large amount of material which enters into the requirements of a structure covering 20 acres may be formed from the statement that to complete it 3,928 tons of iron must be rolled and fitted, 237,646 square feet of glass made and set, 1,075,000 square feet of tin roof-sheeting (equal to 24-5/8 acres) welded and spread."[18] The first column was erected on May 8, 1875, the ironwork was completed by December 2, and the building was accepted from the contractor, Richard J. Dobbins, on February 14. "For all practical purposes," stated the reports, "it was completed by January 1, 1876, four months before the opening of the Exhibition, the date announced officially by the Centennial Commission, during the spring of 1874, as the time when the building would be ready for the reception of goods."[19] Writing in *Lippincott's,* Edward Bruce described the process that had brought the building to such a swift conclusion: "All had been done with the precision of machinery, no pillar varying half an inch from its line. Machinery, indeed, rolled the quadrant-shaped sections of each column and riveted their flanges together with hydraulic hammers; great steam-derricks dropped each on its appointed seat; and the main tasks of manual labor in either building were painting, glazing, floor-laying and erecting the ground-wall of masonry, from five to seven feet high, that fills in the outer columns."[20] Bruce painted an enthusiastic picture of industrial production—standardized, mechanized, and unfailingly accurate. Photographs of the site being prepared by men and horses tell a different story; still, the Main Building was not so much built as assembled out of identical, factory-made components, with traditional craftsmanship limited to a few areas.[21] In this sense, the Main Building was as modern as anything being constructed today—perhaps more so, given the degree to which its design was rationalized. More important, the Main Building, like the Crystal Palace, represented a fundamentally modern conception of "uniform, infinite, isotropic space," which had been prefigured in the perspective constructions of the Renaissance and given a mathematical and philosophical formulation by René Descartes and his followers.[22]

Consistent with this conception, the Main Building represented a particularly modern type: the loft. We know this type under a variety of institutional guises—the factory, the warehouse, the department store, the office tower, the exhibition hall, and even the museum. (The most notorious example is the Centre Pompidou by Rogers and Piano, 1972–76, Paris.) As a type, the loft relies on the rational idea of space as open, undifferentiated, and minimally ordered by a column grid. The functional interpretation of this space is defined not so much by architecture as by an extra-architectural structure or set of structures—the physical arrangement of workers, machines, goods, or furniture, as opposed to the organization of rooms. Partitions are possible but not essential—they might even be said to be contrary to type—and architecture is devalued in relationship to space planning.

As an exhibition hall, the space of the Main Building was defined by the installation of displays. This was described by Pettit as "the practical work required to carry out in the buildings and grounds a previously adopted system of classification and arrangement." The Centennial Commission had presumed a close relationship between the two at its first session, when it adopted a dual system of classification *and* arrangement. However, the precise nature of this relationship was always up to debate. Writing after the exhibition, Pettit argued for transparency, with the audience able to read the order of the exhibition in the installation: "Generally the visiting public have no need for a system of classification, except as it is embodied in the arrangement, and this fact should establish the rule that a system of 'classification' for exhibits and 'arrangement' for exhibits should be considered as practically one and the same thing."[23] But William Blake had originally suggested only a loose relationship: "A classification presupposes some arrangement or placing of objects in accordance with it; but, though connected[,] classification and arrangement are not necessarily one, objects may or may not be placed in the order or relations established by classification."[24] For its part, the Committee on Classification, of which Blake was a member, advised the commission not to be too stringent in pursuing its 1872 mandate: "We must not lose sight of the fact that the classification and the arrangement of objects, though connected, are not the same. . . . The objects may or may not be arranged in accordance with the classification, as we elect or as necessity dictates. The arrangement may conform generally, and there may be exceptions without destroying the symmetry and system." Ultimately, the committee adopted a compromise position, stating that "a general conformity is presupposed, and should be secured."[25] It was this position that inspired the earliest ideas about the installation of the Main Building.

THE INSTALLATION AS PLANNED

This desire for transparency, for legibility, was not peculiar to the Centennial; it was in fact a common characteristic of the three major fairs preceding the one in Philadelphia. At the Great Exhibition, the British had originally intended to arrange the displays in the Crystal Palace according to the four broad divisions of the classification. For practical reasons, they were only able to effect this plan in the British section. At the Weltausstellung, the Austrians had organized the exhibition in the main building like a map of the world centered on Vienna, with foreign countries arranged on either side to approximate their geographic relationship to the metropolis.[26] Finally, at the 1867 Exposition universelle, the French had adopted the most famous and influential of these plans—a dual system with typological departments in concentric rings and national areas in radial sections. Blake explained how this arrangement worked: "By following one of these galleries, the observer passed in succession among the productions similar in kind of different countries. By following the avenues he passed successively through the different productions of the same country. The student, therefore, could investigate the condition of any particular art or industry as manifested by different nations, or he could pursue his studies geographically and note the characteristic productions of each country, and compare them as a whole with those of other countries. The arrangement facilitated exhibition, prompted study and comparison, and in these respects fully realized the intentions of its authors."[27] The organizers of the Centennial were especially impressed with this way of mapping knowledge, since it was "both geographical and systematic," in the words of the resolution.[28]

Now, the systematic ordering of the world was an Enlightenment preoccupation, as was the ideal of transparent representation. But the immediate appeal of the dual system was the way it responded to the competing demands of chauvinism and empiricism, which were inherent in the design of any international exhibition. The solution was to render the world in tabular form, with nation on one axis and type on the other, so that an artifact could be located in a Cartesian space of knowledge that embraced both the classification and the installation of the exhibition.

As first proposed, the arrangement of displays in the Centennial's Main Building was supposed to be a rectangular version of the French installation, with countries in cross sections and departments in longitudinal divisions (fig. 3-11). This relationship was suggested by Dorsey Gardner, Pettit's assistant in the Bureau of Installation, whose description of the arrangement is remarkably similar to Pettit's explanation of the French plan: "The exhibits in a given group were to occupy a band of floor-space running lengthwise of the building; while every exhibiting country was to be allotted a band intersecting at right angles,—so that the visitor might follow, at his option, either a single line of products as shown by all contributing nations in succession, or else might examine the products in every department of each nation separately."[29] The choice of an orthogonal plan for the Centennial cannot be explained by the economy of rectangular structures alone, although that was certainly a consideration. Americans had a long-established preference for the grid as a way to organize space; the street system of Philadelphia was only the most immediate example of a pattern

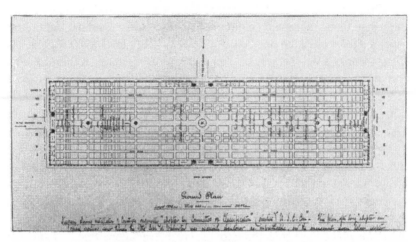

3-11. "Ground Plan." Main Exhibition Building. Autograph: "Diagram showing installation of Countries originally 'adopted by Committee on Classification' (scientists) 'U.S.C. Com.' This plan, after being 'adopted' and official drawings issued through the State Dept[.] at Washington was necessarily abandoned as impracticable, and the arrangement shown below adopted in its place" (Pettit, "Centennial Exhibition," 1:61, Historical Society of Pennsylvania architectural drawings collection on loan to the Athenaeum). *Enlarged plate appears on page 239 of the appendix.*

that included the Commissioners' Plan of New York (1811) and the continental grid anticipated by the Congressional Land Ordinance (1785). So it is not surprising that the planned installation of the Main Building took the form of a giant grid of knowledge, which the visitor penetrated in search of artifacts. The exhibition was thus a metaphor for the larger American landscape.

The proposed arrangement of displays also reflected the influence of the geocentric Austrian installation; it produced not just a grid of knowledge but a map of the world as drawn from an American perspective. The United States claimed a large section in the middle of the floor, with the other nations arranged in geographic order on either side. To the west was a reserved space of fifty thousand square feet, set aside for those countries that had not yet accepted their invitations to participate in the exhibition or appointed their commissioners.[30] Twelve Latin American nations came next, arranged in order of their proximity to the United States; then a group of countries in which this country had an interest—Haiti, the Sandwich Islands, and Liberia; finally, China and Japan, at one extreme of this American-centered world. Great Britain, Canada, India, Australia, and the rest of the British Empire occupied an area just east of the central transept. This

British section fronted a long line of European countries, which were arranged so that geographic neighbors had contiguous exhibits. Behind Europe, a group of Asian and African powers—Russia, Turkey, Egypt, and
Siam—implied the theoretical continuation of this map around the other
end of the building.

Problematically, the proposed arrangement was based on the expecta-
tion that each nation would be able to fill every part of its allotted space.
The Committee on Classification confidently asserted "a tolerably uniform
relation between the bulk of the products of the industries in every country"—a statement indicating a sympathy for the ideal of universal human
needs that had been built into the design of the 1867 Paris fair. Essentially,
the committee was assuming that every country develops in the same way,
that each nation had to supply its citizens with the same basic goods and
therefore would have something to display in every department of the exhibition. The committee proposed to deal with exceptions by allowing the
exhibit of a particular country to expand beyond its boundaries, but it did
not provide for the case of a nation without displays in a particular department, as it should have.[31] The Paris fair had shown that some countries
specialized in the provision of raw materials; others, in the production of
finished goods.

The limitations of this plan ultimately prevented its implementation,
but not before it had been adopted by the Committee on Classification and
communicated to all the invited nations.[32] "Of course its absurdity as a system became evident to the foreigners themselves who had exhibited at other
exhibitions—and it was abandoned," observed Pettit. He blamed "a Committee composed largely of scientists" for attempting to enforce an impracticable plan on the exhibition.[33] This statement is remarkable, both
for his use of the term *scientist,* which was still relatively new, and for the
disparaging tone.[34] In Pettit's words, we read the disdain of an engineer
for the impractical schemes of theorists. We also read an indication that
the organizers of the Centennial understood the classification and installation of the exhibition as an expansion of an already established scientific project—the taxonomic ordering of plants and animals—to include
the world of goods.

THE INSTALLATION AS REALIZED

Dorsey Gardner did not seem to share Pettit's professional prejudices, but
he did cast doubt on the possibility of ever achieving the desired correspon-

dence between the order of the exhibition and the arrangement of displays. The organizers simply did not have the power to make the world as represented by the exhibition conform to their expectations: "This logical and theoretically perfect arrangement might perhaps in time be accomplished in a permanent museum, where one management controlled the collection and installation of exhibits. It is clearly impossible in the case of an International Exhibition of short duration, where each foreign Commission arranges its goods to its own taste, and a large proportion of the participating countries are unrepresented in many of the presupposed groups."[35]

Implicit in Gardner's statement was an apt comparison between the exhibition and the museum. The Centennial was supposed to be a museum of everything in one place—in French terms, a *universal* exposition. This connotes the kind of totalizing program that we have to come to associate with the "unfinished" project of modernity, as Jürgen Habermas has called it. In this sense, the exhibition was a cousin to other modern projects, like the Linnaean classification of plants and animals, like the encyclopedia. In fact, as a vast collection of physical object lessons, the exhibition was a fulfillment of the encyclopedia as it was conceived by Denis Diderot: he proclaimed that "a glance at the object or its representation says more than a page of discourse."[36] All these projects suggest a nostalgia for the wholeness of pre-Enlightenment knowledge, a longing for a prelapsarian state of epistemological innocence, when the world seemed small enough to be apprehended by a single, well-educated person—that or a ferocious naïveté in the face of the world's full complexity.

In the case of the Centennial, this nostalgia/naïveté manifested itself in the first plan of installation. This called for a single building containing all the displays, organized by a comprehensive system of classification. As the size and site of the exhibition became known, the organizers abandoned this plan, and the unitary, universal ideal survived only in fragmentary form, in the installation of the Main Building. As originally conceived, this was supposed to be the most comprehensive part of the exhibition, comprising nine of the original ten departments. (Art was to be housed in a separate gallery.) After the expansion of the Centennial and the revision of the classification, this number was reduced to three of seven departments—Mining and Metallurgy, Manufactures, Education and Science.[37]

In the second plan of installation (fig. 3-12), the four great powers of industry—France, Britain, Germany, and the United States—were allotted the most prominent positions at the center of the Main Building, underneath the raised ceiling of the crossing or Central Pavilion, as it was called.

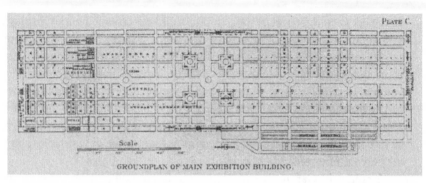

3-12. "Ground Plan of Main Exhibition Building" (USCC, *International Exhibition, 1876*, vol. 9, pl. C, University of California Library, Berkeley). *Enlarged plate appears on page 240 of the appendix.*

The intention, as described in the Centennial Commission reports, was to create an "installation by races": "France and Colonies, representing the Latin races, were given space adjacent to the northeast central tower. England and Colonies, representing the 'Anglo-Saxon' races, were given space adjacent to the northwest central tower. The German Empire, and Austria and Hungary, representing the Teutonic races, were granted space adjacent to the southwest tower. The United States was placed in the southeast section." The other countries were supposed to be located according to a specious scheme of racial proximity: "It was very much desired, in order to make the installation by races complete, to place all the exhibiting nations of Latin extraction in the northeast quarter, adjacent to France, and of Teutonic extraction in the southwest quarter, with German, etc., etc." However, like the grid of knowledge, the installation by races was never achieved, at least not in its original form. The problem was the indeterminate structure of the exhibition—the perennial difficulty of obtaining reliable information from foreign commissions; the increasing, and increasingly desperate, requests for space by American exhibitors—which was itself a representation of the provisional state of knowledge that was available to the organizers. As a result, the four industrial powers were located around the Central Pavilion, as planned, but the rest of the installation was an awkward compromise. Brazil and Mexico, for example, were placed opposite the United States, in French territory. No specific provision had been made for the Asian countries, so China and Japan, "being geographically west of America," were allocated space in the west wing, behind Germany and Austro-Hungary. Spain, Egypt, Turkey, and the Netherlands were all given what the reports described as "positions of honor," but none found a geographically meaningful place in the installation.[38]

In spite of these evident difficulties, Robert Rydell has cited the second plan of installation as proof of a racist program in the design of the Centennial.[39] If this were the case, how would we account for the fact that race, with the conspicuous exception of the so-called installation by races, was simply not an explicit issue for the organizers, at least as demonstrated by the official literature? How would we explain the exclusion of race as a category in the classification? This by "scientists," who devised the order of the exhibition with such care, at a time when the emerging field of anthropology had already begun to give the concept a "scientific" formulation?[40] To answer these questions fairly, we would have to admit that the organizers were as much preoccupied with the cultural order of things as the social order of people. The dual system is evidence of this fact, since it represents their attempt to balance the scientific, "objective" arrangement of things by type with the chauvinistic organization by national groups. We would also have to admit that the installation by races had little to do with what we might think of as racism, and more to do with the linked issues of nationalism and imperialism. To be very specific, the second plan was manifestly not about race in the biological sense, that is, "a division of mankind possessing traits that are transmissible by descent." It was about race in the ethnic or political sense, that is, "a family, tribe, people, or nation belonging to the same stock," or, more ambiguously, in the case of the United States, "a class or kind of people unified by community of interests, habits, or characteristics."[41] This explains why, in the second plan, the world was literally drawn and symbolically quartered between the four great industrial economies. This created a map of balanced power in which the categories of nation and empire subsumed all others.

Admittedly, Rydell's larger argument concerns not just the Centennial but a whole series of world's fairs that took place in the United States between 1876 and 1916. Americans of this period were engaged in "a search for order," states Rydell, after Wiebe; this search was a response to the economic and spiritual crises brought on by the scientific and industrial revolutions. "To alleviate the intense and widespread anxiety that pervaded the United States," Rydell writes, "the directors of the expositions offered millions of fairgoers an opportunity to reaffirm their collective national identity in an updated synthesis of progress and white supremacy that suffused the blueprints of future perfection offered by the fairs."[42]

As issued by the Board of Finance, the design of the Centennial's stock

3-13. Certificate of capital stock no. 7551, United States, Bureau of Engraving and Printing ([Philadelphia: Centennial Bureau of Finance, (1876?)], Broadside Collection, Rare Book and Special Collections, Library of Congress).

certificate represents just such a program. Congress had authorized the exhibition but had also refused to provide any public funds to support it. The fair was supposed to be financed by the sale of ten-dollar shares, and subscribers received a certificate engraved with an elaborate allegory of progress (fig. 3-13). At the apex of this triangular composition, the female figure of Liberty receives the tribute of the nations, with the Arts and Sciences at her feet. In the background, on either side, stand Independence Hall and the U.S. Capitol, as well as the figures of four American inventors. These are the individual agents of progress, holding their discoveries like attributes. Beneath them huddle the archetypes of labor—on one side, a miner, a planter, a farmer, and a trapper, all above an indignant-looking Indian who, in a significant gesture, is turning away from this picture; on the other side, a tailor, a sailor, a black man reading, a mechanic, and soldiers of different eras comparing weapons. In the bottom left vignette, the old is replaced by the new—clipper ship by steamboat, covered wagon by railroad train, the hand-held scythe by the horse-drawn reaping machine. In the bottom right, a despairing native sits in front of a dilapidated windmill, while mill-town chimneys belch smoke in the rear. This picture, "of the stupefied savage confronting the signs of civilization on the march," was one of the favorite tropes of nineteenth-century American landscape painting.[43] At the bottom center, the circle of progress is completed by an image of John Trumbull's famous painting, *The Declaration of Independence, 4 July 1776* (1787-1820).

The design of the stock certificate, which combines a progressive theme with racist imagery, seems to verify Rydell's thesis, but it also suggests that the situation was more complicated than he has allowed. The Indian is associated with the old, the antique, and the outdated, while the black man is depicted as educable and enculturated. One is written out of the American story, as indicated by his departing position at the bottom of the triangle; the other is given a future in it and a role to play, as indicated by his rising position in the composition. This difference in treatment can be explained by the historical context; with the end of the Civil War and the beginning of Reconstruction, progress meant freeing the African slave and teaching him to read so that he could become a good, self-supporting citizen. But progress also meant removing the human obstacle of indigenous people, who inhibited the westward expansion of American civilization. The certificate's depiction of the native was surely informed by the Indian War that was then being waged by the U.S. government and that would reach a symbolic peak during the summer of 1876 with the defeat of General Custer and his troops at Little Bighorn.

In keeping with this context, the Centennial was the site for a pioneering ethnographic exhibit, of the type that would become such a disturbing feature of later fairs.[44] This was the large collection of Indian artifacts displayed by the Smithsonian Institution in the U.S. Government Building. As Rydell and Robert Trennert have both observed, native people here served as a primitive counterpoint to American progress, in the Government Building as on the stock certificate. Still, it must be admitted, as Trennert has, that the exhibit inspired unexpected and contradictory reactions.[45] William Dean Howells responded with shocking hostility: "The red man, as he appears in effigy and in photograph in this collection, is a hideous demon, whose traits can hardly inspire any emotion softer than abhorrence."[46] But another writer left the exhibit with a stinging sense of regret at the inverse relationship between American progress and native decline: "With the tragic fate of General Custer and his brave troops so fresh in mind, not many of us are inclined to sentimentalize over the Indian just now; yet there is matter for melancholy and remorse in the position of things. The contrast between this enormous exhibition of what we have achieved since our forefathers came from the other hemisphere, our rapid prosperity, and our incalculable future, with the fate of the true children and masters of the soil, cries shame on us."[47]

In the end, it is difficult to ignore the fact that the Centennial occurred at an unusual juncture in American history—after the Civil War, which had been at least partly fought over the issue of slavery, and during Reconstruction, which had as one of its ends the rehabilitation of freed slaves—when the relationship between white and black was in flux and had not yet hardened into its familiar form. The space of the exhibition was liminal by definition; that it may have been so in a specifically American sense is suggested by this same writer's account, as published in the *Atlantic:* "The Exhibition itself and the streets of Philadelphia . . . constantly presented groups which at any less crowded and cosmopolitan season would strike us as strange; from the first there were parties of blacks and whites, in most cases evidently strangers who had come together from a distance, though whence there was no means of ascertaining except by a direct question. I do not mean the familiar group of Southerners with a colored nurse in tow. Generally speaking, they were women only, and the negresses were the most smartly dressed of the company." The writer concluded with the hope that "perhaps this new association of colors may mark another prejudice conquered, in some quarters at least."[48] It was a vain hope, to be sure, but this kind of evidence suggests the need for a more nuanced understanding of the exhibition as a social phenomenon.

PRINCIPLES OF INSTALLATION

To implement the second plan, the Centennial Commission established an executive department under the direction of Henry Pettit. Known as the Bureau of Installation, this department was responsible for processing applications from American exhibitors, for allocating space in the Main Building (this included "the general installation of foreign countries" as well as "the installation in detail of the American Department"), and for managing the building itself. (The commission established specialized departments—Art, Machinery, Agriculture, and Horticulture—to manage the other principal exhibit halls.)

The Bureau of Installation opened for business in April 1875. As applications poured in, the staff grew from eight to twenty-one people, and the office moved from the commission's building on Walnut Street in Philadelphia, first to a structure near the exhibition's main entrance and finally to a space in the north gallery of the Main Building. The increasing size of the bureau can be explained by the size and complexity of its responsibilities. What the reports described as the "tedious task of allotting space in detail" made it necessary to communicate with each of the 9,266 American exhibitors at least nine times, "either by personal interview, letter, or circular," during the planning phase of the installation.[49]

In keeping with its demonstrated passion for the systematic, the commission endeavored to rationalize all its operations. The Bureau of Installation, for example, standardized communication with a large number of printed forms. Each exhibitor received a copy of the general regulations, as well as an official Application for Space (form no. 63) that required a description of each article on display and a statement of the size and kind of space desired. Upon receiving the application, the bureau sent the exhibitor a receipt (form no. 67) with an identification number that was to be used in all future correspondence. Beginning in December 1875, the bureau sent out an official Permit for Space (form no. 177), as well as a blank letter of acceptance, which was to be signed and returned to the bureau. The permit included a scale drawing showing the dimensions of the space allotted to the exhibitor and its position relative to the nearest column (fig. 3-14); this was indicated by letter and number, as in the catalogue. To avoid the possibility of any misunderstanding, the bureau kept a letterpress copy of each permit. (Letterpress was the nineteenth-century equivalent of photocopying, the inked letters of a document being "pressed" into the treated page of a book, thus leaving a faint impression.) All in all, this system of processing applications appears to have been a complete success—an anomaly in the history of the Centennial.[50]

Because of the number of applications, the Bureau of Installation eventually published a special notice (form no. 131) requiring exhibitors to submit drawings of their proposed displays. (Thousands must have been produced, but I have found only a few examples.) Using these drawings, the bureau allocated space on the basis of two principles, which implied different ways of seeing the exhibition, different ways of knowing the world. The first was familiar: "To create as many long vistas as possible." This principle was consistent with the earliest ambitions of the organizers; its purpose was to convey the vastness of the exhibition to a single, comprehending eye. The second was new: "To accent the corners of intersections of passages, by exhibits of marked interest and attractiveness." This principle was

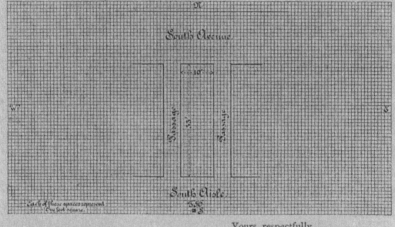

EXHIBIT E.

BUREAU OF INSTALLATION.   [No. 117.]

PERMIT FOR SPACE.—MAIN EXHIBITION BUILDING.

Application No. 1.^   PHILADELPHIA, December 27, 1875.

CAMBRIA IRON CO.,

D. J. MORRELL, GEN. MANAGER,

Johnstown, Penna.

SIR: You have been allotted Floor Space 33 ft. $\times$ 10 ft., with passages on all sides, in the Main Exhibition Building, located with reference to the columns as shown below, and of the following dimensions:

Yours, respectfully,

HENRY PETTIT,

Chief of Bureau.

Permit of entry granted April 24, 1876.

R. M. SMITH,

For Chief of Bureau.

3-14. "Permit for Space" (USCC, *International Exhibition, 1876,* 1:120, University of California Library, Berkeley).

an appeal to the wandering eyes of the audience, which had never been considered before; Pettit justified it as "the only reliable way to sustain the interest of visitors who move about as rapidly and incessantly as Americans generally do."[51] The observation is striking but not particularly unique; it describes the behavior of the nervous and easily distracted urban crowd as later observed by Georg Simmel and Walter Benjamin.[52]

3-15. "Interior of the Main Building Showing the Various Pavilions and Show-Cases Constructed and in Process of Erection" (Norton, *Illustrated Historical Register,* 55, Free Library of Philadelphia).

The first principle represented the organizers' point of view (fig. 3-15). It pictured their intentions in the form of a one-point perspective through the Main Building, the structural grid being equivalent to the net of lines cast out over the space of a perspective drawing. The vista promised the *veduta;* it posited a single, well-positioned subject, visually commanding an array of objects in a totality of understanding. It opened up the kind of rationally ordered, geometrically constructed space that had dominated Western thinking since the Renaissance, when the modern rules of perspective were first formalized and popularized. This kind of space served as the basis for a perceptual dualism between subject and object, which was one of the founding propositions of Classical optics in the sixteenth and seventeenth centuries. This visual regime has been called Cartesian perspectivalism, after the French philosopher, mathematician, and scientist "who adopted the position of a perspectivalist painter using a camera obscura to reproduce the observed world."[53]

For Descartes, seeing was a way of knowing. The ideal eye was the equivalent of the camera obscura, producing passive representations of the world that were actively corrected and interpreted by the rational mind. (An aid to drawing, the camera obscura is a boxlike device with an aperture that projects the image of an exterior scene onto an opposite, interior surface.) The problem with this analogy is the fact that we have two eyes, while the camera obscura has only one aperture. As a result, the Cartesian model, and the perspective theory on which it was based, implied a dramatic reduction of deep, binocular vision to the relatively flat, monocular view of the box and the drawing. Thus, Cartesian perspectivalism, and the Enlightenment philosophy that it inspired, implied a disembodied gaze. It posited not just a single subject and a single point of view, but a single, centered, focused eye that stared at the world without blinking. This ideal eye was removed from time and space, or at least the objects in it; it was the eye of Medusa in its ability to freeze the flux of reality, the eye of God in its objectivity and unchanging distance. This distance, ironically called objectivity, is the source of the eye's superiority over the other sense organs in the Enlightenment and of vision's privilege among the other senses in the larger system of modernity.[54]

In contrast to the first principle and the regime it encapsulated, the second principle of installation represented the reincarnation of vision in the mobile body of the audience (fig. 3-16). It acknowledged the difference between this body and the somewhat scientific mind of the organizers. It implied not the strong, objectifying gaze of the seventeenth and eighteenth

3-16. "The Centennial—West End, Main Building" (*Harper's Weekly* 20, no. 1033 [14 Oct. 1876]: 832, Library of Congress).

centuries but a weaker and more subjective look that began to supplant the gaze in the early nineteenth century—what Norman Bryson has called the glance.[55] Ironically, this reincarnation implied a certain weakening of vision as the privileged sense; as the reembodied eye joined its pair, vision was inescapably united with the other four senses as a real, physiological effect. The weakening of vision in turn implied the replacement of *space* with *place,* of the abstract conception with phenomenally complete experience. The exhibition thus became less a text to be read and more a situation to be encountered by the audience without a priori meaning, as indicated by accounts of its reception.

The Last Days

The Centennial Commission had promised that the Main Building would be ready by January 1, 1876, and, in a substantial sense, it was. Foreign material began to arrive early in January, but the floors and some of the woodwork were not finished until later in the month. As a result, it was not until February that the Bureau of Installation was able to begin marking out the arrangement of displays. This it did quite literally, by drawing the plan on the floor of the building, the boundary of each space in red and the number of each application in black. The result was a full-scale map, which encouraged exhibitors to visit the building well in advance of the opening and to adjust the design of their displays in response to the characteristics of their allotted spaces. It also expedited the movement of material into the building, allowing packages to be delivered to a precise location. The shipment of American goods was further facilitated by the use of special labels that had been issued with the official Permit for Space. In keeping with the system, these bore the number of the application as well as the letter and number of the nearest column.[56]

This was all supposed to make the installation an orderly procedure, but as opening day approached, a flash flood of more than 150,000 packages, a third of which were headed for the Main Building, overwhelmed the system.[57] Many American exhibitors had waited until the last minute to prepare and ship their displays. As a result, on May 1, just ten days before the scheduled opening, chaos reigned in the heart of the exhibition. According to Pettit, an increasingly reckless army of two thousand people—"workmen, porters, janitors, exhibitors and attendants"—was at work in the Main Building: "As the opening day rapidly approached, the anxiety on the part of exhibitors to get their goods in position made them forgetful of every other consideration. Boxes and rubbish were thrown into the main aisles regardless of consequences. In not a few instances articles of considerable value, reported stolen at the time, were afterwards found in boxes which exhibitors had unpacked, and supposing them empty, had thrown into the aisle for removal." Amid the frenzy of unwrapping, trash became an increasingly serious problem: "The accumulation of waste material in the main passages and between the exhibits became enormous. Piles of lumber and loose boards and broken boxes were scattered in every direction, and tons of straw, paper, and other combustible material used for packing were strewn throughout the building." At one point, fifty-eight janitors were removing twenty-five tons of refuse each day. Straw packaging was particularly dangerous; it posed a fire hazard that eventually led to an order to remove all refuse from the fairground and deposit it in an open space east of the Main Building. There it formed an unsightly pile in full view of the carriage entrance.[58]

This fever of preparation reached a climax on the day before the opening of the Centennial. Exhibitors had been instructed to finish unpacking by 4:00 P.M. on May 8, but some worked throughout the night, "both to their own disadvantage and our inconvenience," according to Pettit. Beginning at 4:00 P.M. on May 9, the janitors made one final, heroic sweep of the Main Building. The process took eight hours, but the exhibition opened as scheduled on May 10, 1876—the first fair to do so, according to Alfred T. Goshorn.[59] Boosters insisted that the exhibition was in a high state of readiness, but in reality much remained to be done. Although the five major pavilions were complete, the fairground and many of the smaller buildings were evidently still unfinished. Howells visited a week after the opening and reported that "the first impression was certainly that of disorder and incompleteness. The paths were broken and unfinished, and the tough red mud of the roads was tracked over the soft asphalt into all the buildings."[60] Surveying the Centennial around the same time, the *Atlantic* made an odd virtue of the fact that many countries had not yet installed their exhibits in the Main Building: "This incompleteness, which is not confined to the interior of the buildings, but is to be seen in every direction as the eye wanders over the grounds, imparts to the aspect of the whole place an air of rawness and impermanence which is probably common to all exhibitions on the same plan, but which is also emphatically American. . . . Except the Australians, nobody else has a country where everything is new."[61] Nevertheless, the state of the installation, as described by the *Journal of the Franklin Institute,* testified to the failings of the system: "The Exhibition itself, on the day of opening, displayed much want of completion of arrangement, besides the numerous vacancies, where no attempt to open the packages had been made; in fact, a thousand tons of merchandise and machinery were then upon the cars, without the gates of enclosure; and as much more was known to be yet upon the seas, to arrive in New York or Philadelphia." On May 10, then, the Centennial remained a work in process, but the *Journal* reassured its readers that, as of its June publication, the exhibition was ready to receive visitors.[62]

THE AMERICAN SECTION

Prior to the opening, the Bureau of Installation made one final attempt to effect a correspondence between the order of the exhibition and the arrangement of displays. The location was the 187,700-square-foot American section, which took up the entire southeast quadrant of the Main Building, plus a space in the northeast corner. The passages running the length of the building divided each of these two areas into three belts that suggested the building's three departments. Thus, the bureau proposed to install Department I, Mining and Metallurgy, in the first belt running between the outside wall and the south avenue; Department II, Manufactures, in the second belt running between the avenue and the central aisle; and Department III, Education and Science, in the third belt between the aisle and the nave.[63] Although the categories are not identical, this arrangement recalls "the three great divisions" that Prince Napoléon had suggested for future fairs.

Most of the exhibits in Department I were eventually located in the Mineral Annex, just south of the Main Building, while many of the bulkier items in Department II—"carriages, heating and cooking apparatus, etc."—were exported to the Main Annex, a two-acre addition at the east end of the building. The educational displays were placed above ground, in the east and south galleries, while some special, trophylike structures, such as the elaborate, two-story exhibit of the American Book Trade Association, were located without regard to plan. As a result, the installation of the American section was only a loose expression of the progressive, evolutionary principle of the classification, with raw materials supposedly located near the outer wall, various instruments and social goods close to the nave, and everything else on a rough gradient in between. Pettit explained how this arrangement did or did not work, depending on the path one chose to take:

Thus, walking crosswise, from south to north, through the middle of the section, we pass from ores and minerals in Department I., next the outer wall, to building stone, then marble mantels, then through furniture and musical instruments in Department II. to philosophical instruments and the latest improvements in electric telegraphy in Department III., next the nave, which arrangement shows a strict conformity to the classification.

In another instance the arrangement was different. Commencing at the nave, next to the music-stand, we have, first, diamonds, jewelry, silver plate, electro-plate, and bronzes; then metal, gas-fixtures, glass gas-fixtures, and glass-ware. That sequence, although at variance with the classification, produced the brilliant and strikingly beautiful display which was wanted in that vicinity.

This passage illustrates the failure of the bureau's last, limited attempt to create a meaningful arrangement. The second principle of installation had mandated that the intersections of the Main Building be accented with visually compelling displays—a critical practice at the crossing. Here, at the epicenter of the exhibition, where the four industrial powers faced off across the intersection of the building's two major avenues, the desire to create a "brilliant and strikingly beautiful display" overwhelmed any lingering intention to devise a significant plan. The conflict between significance and appearance was intensified by the fact that, in both the American and foreign sections, the consumer-oriented exhibits in Department II, Manufactures, vastly outnumbered all others. These exhibits were also found to be considerably more beautiful, so that "the middle belt did not afford sufficient space, nor as many prominent locations as were desirable." In practice, then, the second principle was enlarged to cover not only the intersections but also the whole nave, with the most attractive displays in Department II moved forward and the less visually compelling displays, those in Department III, Education and Science, buried in the depths of the exhibition.[64]

In the end, the conflict between the significance of the installation and the appearance of the displays was decisively resolved in favor of the latter, thus overturning whatever remained of the classification's hierarchy. The increased attention given to visual appearance suggests that the organizers had come to realize that they could never achieve the legibility and transparency that they had originally imagined. In spite of their obsession with the vista, for a piercing, penetrating look that could comprehend the whole exhibition, the average person's experience appears to have been a superficial one. The mass of displays remained opaque and impervious to the gaze. That is why the nave and the transept were ultimately surrendered to a glance that could slide more easily across the surface of things.

4

WAYS OF SEEING THE EXHIBITION

> World exhibitions are the sites of pilgrimages to the commodity
> fetish.
> —Walter Benjamin, "Paris: The Capital of the 19th Century"

With the completion of the installation, visitors standing in the nave of the Main Building could perceive the Centennial Exhibition as a great, ordered spectacle, which opened up a vast, interior landscape. The sections lining both sides of the nave formed a street of nations running the eighteen-hundred-foot length of the building (fig. 4-1). The balance between chauvinism and empiricism that had been the aim of the dual system was decisively overturned, and the exhibition was laid open as a site of competitive display between nations—a potlatch of global dimensions, signifying an orgy of mass consumption.[1]

It is hard not to see this street as the equivalent of a shopping center, positioned somewhere between the arcade and the enclosed mall, and comparable to the great gallerias built in cities like Milan. This at least was the view of Samantha, the colloquial heroine of a popular novel by Marietta Holley: "Oh, good land! Oh, dear suz!" writes Samantha. "Why, a hull Dictionary of jest such words couldn't begin to tell my feelins as I stood there a lookin' round on each side of me, down that broad, majestic, glitterin' street full of folks and fountains and glitterin' stands, and statutes, and ornaments, with gorgeous shops on each side containin' the most beautiful beauty, the sublimest sublimity, and the very grandest grandeur the hull world affords."[2] Holley never actually saw the Centennial—her 1878 novel was based on published accounts[3]—but her reading of the exhibition is confirmed by other writers who did visit. Howells complained about "the offensiveness of a mere mart" in certain sections of the Main Building,

4-1. "Main Building." Nave looking east (CPC 814, Print and Picture Collection, Free Library of Philadelphia).

particularly "the extremely shoppy show of the Austrians," while the unnamed writer in the *Atlantic* referred to the American exhibits as "indigenous shops and factories," which of course they represented.[4]

It must have been an amazing experience to walk this street, however "shoppy." Very few visitors had ever seen a real museum or department store, and no one who had never visited an international exhibition could ever have imagined so many things in one place. Confusion was a typical response to this lavish display, according to Joseph Wilson: "Passing down the central aisle, we are lost in bewilderment. The construction of the building permits us to see all over it; the wealth of the world is before us, and our sight is only limited by the exhibits. Where shall we go first? What shall we do? These are the questions one hears on every side."[5] Bewilderment and disorientation in the face of a limitless view of consumption: these are the marks of the phantasmagoria. The term has its origins in the flickering images of magic lantern shows; for Karl Marx, it suggested the complex of illusions associated with the commodity fetish, which mystifies real social relations in the apparent relations of things. For Walter Benjamin, display was the key to understanding the nature of the fetish; in the visual culture of modernity, representation trumped both use and exchange as a source of value. It did not matter whether anything was actually purchased; Benjamin's idea of the phantasmagoria applied to a modern city like Paris, where the center of town had been given over to the possibilities of real consumption, as well as it did to an environment like the exhibition, that ground zero of display, where consumption was largely visual and imaginary.[6]

In addition, bewilderment and disorientation appear to have been the usual response to the exhibition. One reason was the rationalized architecture of the exhibition hall; the sheer size of the enclosed space and the dearth of scale-defining and direction-giving features combined to create an effect of "abstract magnitude" that visitors could find overwhelming.[7] Another reason was the nature of the collection—its mind-numbing size and the peculiar situation of the artifacts on display. Their alienation from any context of origin or intended use and their placement in odd and sometimes violent juxtaposition to each other could combine to make it difficult to apprehend their meaning as artifacts.[8] It was precisely this situation that the system of classification and its optical equivalent, the vista, were meant to address, by creating a new context of stable, predictable, comprehensible order.[9] As we have seen, however, the Centennial was not as well organized as its classification, and the construction of the vista as the space of a penetrating gaze was ultimately compromised by aesthetic, literally superficial considerations. The result was that many visitors perceived the exhibition not as a clear series of precise object lessons but as a blur of faintly received impressions. This was the experience of Frederick A. Tozier of Newberry, Pennsylvania, who visited in early October 1876 and closed an account of his first day by recording, "I have seen a great many things and Icannot [sic] remember the one half."[10]

Good autobiographical evidence of the Centennial is hard to come by, but we get much the same impression from critical and journalistic accounts in books and magazines. These tend to be long and disorganized lists of things seen, which pass distractedly from one subject to another. It took someone with the literary powers of William Dean Howells to penetrate this haze and make some sense of the exhibition. His account is remarkably clear and coherent, but it includes an admission that he and his companions initially found it difficult to form a strong impression of the exhibition: "If we had been the most methodical of sight-seers we could hardly have systematized our observations on a first day. It was enough if we could form a clear idea of the general character of the principal features and their position. Even this we did not at all do. We wandered quite aimlessly about from one building to another, and, if we ever had anything definite in view, gave ourselves the agreeable surprise of arriving at something altogether different." By the third day, Howells was touring Agricultural Hall, which he found to be "absorbingly interesting. . . . There are almost as many attractive show-cases and pavilions as in the Main Building, and they are somehow seen to better advantage." He was impressed by "fanciful and effective arrangements of farm implements; exhibitions of farm products both foreign and domestic; shows of the manufactured and raw material—literally without number," and yet he finally had to admit, "To remember one was to forget a thousand, and yet each was worthy to be seen."[11]

NATIONAL SECTIONS

Individual exhibits were the building blocks of an exhibition, but they did not stand alone. They were gathered together and read by visitors as larger increments of display—the national sections that were the basis for the so-called installation by races. The sections displayed major differences in character, reflecting differences in economic development and social organization.

Reflecting the logic of the installation, the sections of more developed countries—Austria, Belgium, France, Germany, Norway, Russia, Sweden, and the United States—were larger and more central. But they were also fundamentally different in character, with individual companies mounting exhibits that testified to the development of an industrial economy and a consumer society. In the Swedish section, for example, there was a large and well-organized collective display of iron and steel products (fig. 4-2). This was mounted by twenty-eight firms using conventional forms and techniques, as described by J.S. Ingram: "Huge columns and pyramids of iron and steel bars and pipes, great screens towering nearly to the roof of the building, upon which were arranged tires, bars, ingots, etc., collections of iron and pig metal, cases of nails, a reindeer made of spikes, huge railway axles, maps of the mining districts, and drawings of furnaces and machinery, were among the many things seen in this group." In contrast, his description of the French section shows that it was dominated by the displays of luxury goods. These provided ample evidence of French leadership in the production of art manufactures and fashionable apparel, while indicating how consumption was specialized by gender:

The French have a very happy faculty . . . of arranging everything so as to

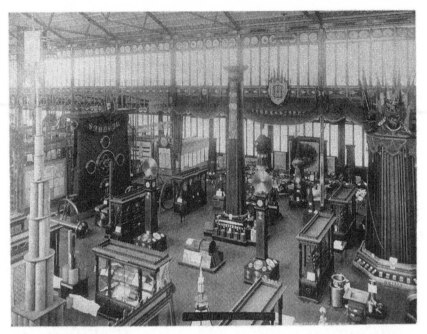

4-2. "Main Building—Sweden" (CPC 1786, Print and Picture Collection, Free Library of Philadelphia).

produce the most attractive effect. Thus the predominance of articles of real beauty, such as bronzes, porcelains, faience, laces, jewelry, and the innumerable host of *articles de fantaisie,* and the systematic and tasteful arrangement of the plainer wares and fabric, combined to make the French section of the Main Building a delight to people of cultivated taste. It was also the domain of the ladies, and its portals might have been appropriately inscribed, *"Place aux Dames,"* for nowhere else were there so many elegant things, such as women most covet—lace shawls of the finest workmanship, silks in a profuse variety of color and pattern, rich brocades and velvets, lovely embroideries, costly Paris dresses, heavy with flowers and real point lace; silk stockings with lace inserted at the instep; the daintiest of shoes and slippers, jewelry, fans, ribbons, artificial flowers, and a thousand quaint and pretty articles for the writing desk, the mantel, and the boudoir-table, all admirable in their way.[12]

One part of the French section, adjacent to the nave, consisted entirely of vitrines, organized in neat rows on either side of an aisle (fig. 4-3). The

4-3. "Main Building—France" (CPC 1317, Print and Picture Collection, Free Library of Philadelphia).

arrangement evoked the well-organized space of the modern city, its center given over to consumption-related display, even the grid of towns like Phila-delphia. In particular, the arrangement recalled the straight corridor streets of Haussman's Paris, with their long vistas, walls of uniform buildings, and traditional monuments. The view down this street was thus appropriately framed by the triumphal arch of a glass exhibit.

The sections of smaller and/or less developed countries and Europoean colonies were situated in more peripheral locations, but many had an unex-pected prominence due to the enclosures that foreign commissioners had built to give shape and character to their sections. The ranks of these coun-tries included European nations like Sweden, Norway, Denmark, and the Netherlands, but most were in other parts of the world—China, Japan, Egypt, Tunisia, Mexico, Brazil, the Sandwich Islands, and the British possessions. With the exception of China and Japan, which mounted exceptional dis-plays of metal and ceramic wares, these areas put predictably less emphasis on manufactured goods and more on exploitable raw materials and natural resources. As a result, their sections took on the character of natural history museums, with maps, diagrams and illustrations, as well as samples of native flora and fauna.[13]

The most memorable of these enclosures was the award-winning Brazilian court, which was designed by Philadelphia architect Frank Furness (fig. 4-4).[14] Like Horticultural Hall, the court was described as being in the "Moresque style," but the design was top-heavy in a manner typical of Furness's work in particular and High Victorian architecture in general. Made of painted wood and decorated with glass tiles, the structure consisted of short, relatively thin columns supporting a heavy arcade of lobed horseshoe arches, all topped by a continuous cresting of conventionalized Victorian ornament. A view of the interior shows how different the Brazilian exhibit was from the French or Swedish (fig. 4-5). The entry was marked by a tall, four-sided pavilion, which enclosed an octagonal showcase containing eye-catching samples of Brazilian birds and bugs. Beyond this case, there were displays of the country's undeveloped mineral wealth, especially Brazilian gold and diamonds, examples of furniture made of local woods, a case of the emperor's jeweled decorations, another with domestically produced splints and surgical instruments, and so on, all displayed in a manner complementing the architecture of the court. The center was taken up by an exhibit of the empire's educational system, with long showcases containing examples of textbooks and student work from various schools. All in all, it was a motley display of things—a cabinet of curiosities illustrating the resources of a nation.[15]

OTHER POINTS OF VIEW

The long perspective of the nave is what greeted visitors who traveled to the Centennial by carriage and accessed the Main Building from the concourse to the east. Those who arrived by train enjoyed a similar prospect, after passing through the main gates at the plaza and entering the building from the west. Those leaving the streetcar on Elm Avenue used gates located just south of the building; their first impression was not the long perspective of the nave but the shorter and more crowded view of the central transept (fig. 4-6).[16] In the foreground, to the right, was the American section and a sign advertising the steam-driven passenger elevator in the southeast tower; to the left was the German section, proclaimed by a sign and a great hanging carpet.[17] (Other carpets hung in the shadows.) Straight ahead, in the middle

4-4. "Main Building—Brazil" (CPC 310, Print and Picture Collection, Free Library of Philadelphia).

4-5. "Main Building—Brazil" (CPC 1502, Print and Picture Collection, Free Library of Philadelphia).

4-6. "Main Building." Central transept from south gallery (CPC 2055, Print and Picture Collection, Free Library of Philadelphia).

of the picture, was the open space of the Central Pavilion, where the art industries of the four major industrial powers faced off across a circular bandstand. At the far end, in the north gallery, one could just make out the ranked pipes of the Roosevelt organ, "one of the prominent features of the exhibition," according to Pettit, with stops suspended over the transept and in the northwest tower.[18]

In the pavilion, above the entrances to the building's four wings, hung trophies designed by Camille Piton, a French painter who had exhibited at the Paris Salon in 1869 and 1870 (fig. 4-7).[19] Measuring forty feet high and forty-eight feet wide, these were large but temporary decorations, made of painted wood and staff or papier-mâché and representing the four quarters of the world—Africa on the north side of the crossing, America on the east, Europe on the west, and Asia on the south. According to the specifications, each trophy was supposed to consist of "representative, characteristic, and symbolical elements."[20] These were drawn from an unusual table that, like the classification and the exhibition itself, collocated a diverse array of things (fig. 4-8). America, for example, was to be represented by the flags of Canada,

4-7. "Main Building." Overview of exhibition from southwest tower (CPC 581, Print and Picture Collection, Free Library of Philadelphia).

Brazil, Mexico, Chile, Argentina, and Ecuador; by George Washington and Benjamin Franklin as representative men; by the female figure of an "Indian Girl (Red)"; by corn and buffalo as characteristic flora and fauna; and by the architectural forms of the "Modern Renaissance"—the described style of Memorial Hall.

The sign advertising the elevator indicated yet another other way to see the exhibition; this was the overview obtained from the observation platforms in the four towers of the crossing (fig. 4-9). These proved to be quite popular with visitors seeking visual refreshment and a broader perspective, as described by Edward C. Bruce, another of the exhibition's chroniclers: "Those [platforms] at the different stages of the central towers proved highly attractive to students who prefer the general to the particular, or who, exhausted for the time, retire to clear their brains from the dust of detail and muster their faculties for another charge on the vast army of art. From this perch one might survey mankind from China to Peru through 'long-drawn aisles' flooded with mellow light."[21] Like the vista, the overview contradicted the confusing details of the exhibition with a look of wholeness and

Trophy.	Flags.	Representative Men.	Female Figure.	Characteristic.		
				Animal.	*Plant.*	*Architect's Motive.*
EUROPE.	France. England. Germany. Russia. Austria. Sweden and Norway.	Charlemagne. Shakspeare.	Caucasian. (White.)	Horse.	Grape Vine.	Composite.
ASIA.	Japan. China. Persia. Turkey. Siam. India.	Confucius. Mahomet.	Bayadere. (Yellow.)	Camel.	Tea.	Indian.
AFRICA.	Egypt. Morocco. Tunis. Liberia. Madagascar. Tripoli.	Sesostris. Rameses.	Slave Girl. (Black.)	Elephant.	Coffee.	Egyptian.
*AMERICA.	Canada. Brazil. Mexico. Chili. Argentine Republic. Ecuador.	Washington. Franklin.	Indian Girl. (Red.)	Buffalo.	Corn (maize.)	Modern Renaissance (eclectic).

*The Colors of United States are shown upon an oriflamme in the centre of each trophy.

4-8. "International Trophies. Main Exhibition Building.—Central Pavilion" (Pettit, *Specifications for International Trophies,* 3, Historical Society of Pennsylvania).

4-9. "The Central Aisle of the Main Exhibition Building" (McCabe, *Illustrated History,* n.p., University of California Library, Berkeley).

4-10. "From S.E. Tower, Main Building" (CPC 1874, Print and Picture Collection, Free Library of Philadelphia).

significance. The overview combined the functions of surveillance and spectacle; it restored the primacy of the gaze and the controlling relationship of the few to the many (both aspects of surveillance) while putting the individual observer on full display to the crowd below (the classic spectacle). Also like the vista, the overview implied a position of power; it was by definition, by virtue of height, a privileged look. It provided a superior kind of comprehension, which was not available to a person on the ground. This ostensibly privileged look was democratically extended to all who could climb the stairs or pay for the elevator.

In addition to the view from the platform, the Centennial provided other opportunities to look out over the world. Above the roof of the Main Building, the four towers were joined by outdoor bridges that provided a 360-degree view of the exhibition. From this position, one could see in the distance, on top of George's Hill, the spindly observation tower that had been erected outside the fairground (fig. 4-10). The tower provided its own panoramic view of the city, the exhibition, and a second tower on Lemon Hill, on the other side of the Schuylkill (fig. 4-11). Thus, the elements of this landscape were knitted together in a chain of reciprocal looks, from floor to platform, from bridge to hill and towers, and back again. A balloon floating overhead took in the whole sight, which was presented to the stay-at-home readers of *Harper's* in the form of a lavish, two-page spread (fig. 4-12). A number of such views were published.

4-11. [Centennial Exhibition from Observatory, George's Hill], by James Cremer ([Philadelphia: James Cremer, 1875], Print and Picture Collection, Free Library of Philadelphia).

4-12. "The Centennial—Balloon view of the Grounds" (*Harper's Weekly* 20, no. 1031 [30 Sept. 1876]: supplement, Library of Congress). *Enlarged plate appears on page 241 of the appendix.*

Looks like these were a staple experience of the exhibition. Visitors took in similar views from the roof and elevated walkways of the main building at the 1867 fair in Paris; from the Eiffel Tower and from the moving platform that carried visitors over displays in the Galerie des Machines, both at the 1889 fair in Paris; from the Ferris Wheel at the 1893 fair in Chicago and the De Forest Wireless Telegraph Tower at the 1904 fair in St. Louis; from the Aeroscope, a revolving tower that hoisted visitors up into the air at the 1915 fair in San Francisco; and from the various sky rides (blimp, balloon, rocket cars) at the 1933 fair in Chicago.[22]

As Roland Barthes has argued in an essay on the Eiffel Tower, the experience provided by such structures constitutes an entirely new way of seeing because it enables us to actively read the landscape as a whole, as opposed to the passive, piecemeal experience of the street. According to Barthes, "In the past, to travel was to be thrust into the midst of sensation, to perceive only a kind of tidal wave of things; the bird's-eye view, on the contrary, permits us to transcend sensation and to see things *in their structure*."[23] Barthes was writing about the city, but his argument is just as applicable to the exhibition, which was similarly "a tidal wave of things," restrained by the space of the vista. Like the streets of Haussmann's Paris, this space was a corridor that parted the blocks of the exhibition without actually penetrating them. The overview obviated the vista by rendering the exhibition more transparent and by encouraging visitors to link the fragments of experience into a more comprehensive and comprehensible whole.

STRATEGIES OF DISPLAY

On returning to the ground, this unified picture of the exhibition once again shattered into its component parts, which were the individual exhibits. Each had its own seeming significance; each constituted a spectacle unto itself. The Bureau of Installation did not control the form of exhibits in detail, but it did publish a set of "Rules and Information for Exhibitors" in the Main Building. (There were similar regulations for exhibitors in other buildings.) These rules established the basic parameters of design; through them, the bureau controlled the use of space, permitting exhibitors to put things right on the floor, or else to construct a display using a variety of elements: platforms, counters, an assortment of vertical forms ("ornamental columns, pyramids, cones, and partitions") and, finally, "show-cases in which the exhibits may be tastefully displayed." The rules specified the maximum height of the elements—fifteen feet above the floor for showcases and partitions; two feet, ten inches for counters along the passageways; one foot for platforms; and two feet, six inches for railings—thus contributing to the visual order of the exhibition. Exhibitors were not allowed "to display products in such a manner as to obstruct the light or vistas through the avenues and aisles," nor could they hang things from the roof of the building without permission. There were to be "no trophies, decorations, portals, fountains, or other special exhibits" in the aisles and avenues unless approved by the bureau, which also kept tight control over signs, regulating their size, location, and material. Exhibitors wanting to identify their merchandise could use official cards, which indicated their "name, address, and place of manufacture, class of objects, catalogue number, and [last but not least] price." Finally, the bureau permitted exhibitors to distribute business cards, circulars, and samples, but not to press them on visitors.[24] Together, these rules suggest a typology of display, from simple to complex, which we can use to understand the forms and techniques that were in use at the time of the Centennial:

Putting things on the floor. Obviously the simplest technique, this was almost entirely reserved for the plants and machines in Horticultural and Machinery Halls.

Platforms. As a change in the datum of display, platforms constituted the minimum degree of distance between observer and observed, but they were rarely used alone. Exhibitors combined them with other forms—railings, counters, walls, or showcases—to construct more complex displays (fig. 4-13).

4-13. "Furniture" (CPC 2571, Print and Picture Collection, Free Library of Philadelphia).

4-14. "Medicinal Preparations" (CPC 2653, Print and Picture Collection, Free Library of Philadelphia).

Individual showcases. These were single, large pieces of wooden furniture. Some were open, with objects displayed on partitions, counters, shelves, or stepped, pyramidal platforms (fig. 4-14). Many took the form of glass-enclosed vitrines, which were associated with museums and the Centennial's French section. In the French fashion, these showcases were often made of ebony or ebony-finished wood, with details picked out in gold; the designs were otherwise varied.[25] The contents were displayed vertically, on a flat, picture-like panel; horizontally, on a covered counter; or in the space of a tall compartment, frequently fitted with a glass top that allowed light to enter the compartment (figs. 4-15 and 4-16).

Compound vitrines. Individual showcases could be assembled into elaborate structures of display. For example, the exhibit of a German maker of ivory products was a Second Empire–style monument in ebony (fig. 4-17). Four two-story showcases marked the corners, while a single three-story showcase formed the center tower. Each was domed and decorated with ivory.[26]

Inhabitable displays. These defined rooms or passages within the space

4-15. "Scientific Instruments" (CPC 1338, Print and Picture Collection, Free Library of Philadelphia).

of the building. Examples include the gazebo-like exhibit of a Philadelphia maker of gas fixtures (fig. 4-18), and the walk-through vitrine of a chemical company, also in Philadelphia (fig. 4-19).

Not all exhibits were equally well contrived; some were even astonishingly casual. But most exhibitors went to some length to construct a display that was attractive or meaningful; the two were not necessarily synony-

4-16. "Toys" (CPC 2017, Print and Picture Collection, Free Library of Philadelphia).

mous. The technique varied with the type of merchandise; large objects like furniture tended to be set out in an open, relatively straightforward manner, but small things seemed to demand an assemblage, some large form of coherent and visually compelling display. At the very least, exhibitors put things in piles and pyramids, as shopkeepers did, or in more or less orderly rows on shelves and counters. In the case of panel-type vitrines, exhibitors

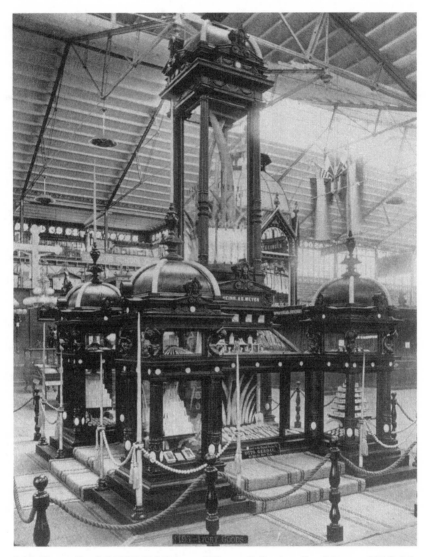

4-17. "Ivory Goods" (CPC 196, Print and Picture Collection, Free Library of Philadelphia).

employed symmetrical, two-dimensional arrangements—geometric patterns (fig. 4-20) and typological arrays (fig. 4-15). The latter bore a striking resemblance to anthropological exhibits, with the objects arranged by type and size to imply an evolutionary series.

4-18. "Gas Fixtures" (CPC 1782, Print and Picture Collection, Free Library of Philadelphia).

The panels had at least two things in common with larger and more three-dimensional displays. First, they represented an attempt to create something eye-catching out of something that was not by itself very attractive. This was an important consideration, given the part that appearance had come to play in the installation. Brass samples and drafting tools, for ex-

4-19. Powers & Weightman exhibit of chemicals (CPC 1479, Print and Picture Collection, Free Library of Philadelphia).

ample, had to compete for attention with "the brilliant and beautiful" exhibits that had been moved forward onto the avenues. Second, the panels represented an attempt to contrive a specious meaning for something that was not by itself extraordinarily significant. This problem was especially critical at the exhibition, where the artifact was detached from a context of use or origin.

4-20. "Buttons" (CPC 2255, Print and Picture Collection, Free Library of Philadelphia).

In more three-dimensional displays, the impulse to make something large and meaningful out of something small and relatively insignificant could lead to the creation of architectural miniatures, like the tiny baldachin of spools in an American display of silk thread (fig. 4-21). Such forms were common enough in retail environments, but, in the large, enclosed space of the Main Building, it was possible to erect full-size structures like the

4-21. "Sewing Silk" (CPC 708, Print and Picture Collection, Free Library of Philadelphia).

baldachin in the exhibit of the English company H. Doulton (fig. 4-22). This took the form of a circular, domed temple, made of terra-cotta tile and enclosing a pyramidal display of the company's faience ware. The result was both eye-catching and informative, and was considered significant enough to be granted a special place in the central avenue of the nave.

4-22. "Doulton Pottery" (CPC 1025, Print and Picture Collection, Free Library of Philadelphia).

The Doulton temple exemplifies a persistent tendency to monumentalize the commodity, which is evident at the Centennial and other exhibitions. This technique is illustrated by an Austrian exhibit that consisted of a large wax obelisk surrounded by samples of wax in chunks and coils (fig. 4-23). This kind of display commands a certain amount of attention, but it does

4-23. "Wax—Austria" (CPC 1680, Print and Picture Collection, Free Library of Philadelphia).

not tell very much about the product itself, except to say, Here is a lot of wax. It exemplifies what I call "the technique of more." Common to both stores and exhibitions, the technique of more represents an attempt to astonish the observer by a display of sheer quantity. On one hand, this piling on of product can be criticized as a distraction from the reality of produc-

4-24. "American Watch Co.—Watches" (CPC 1029, Print and Picture Collection, Free Library of Philadelphia).

tion, a strategy for the creation of a commodity fetish.[27] On the other hand, the technique was an appropriate expression of the power and repetitive character of industrial production, as illustrated by the exhibit of the American Watch Company of Waltham, Massachusetts (fig. 4-24).

Both the town and the company were especially significant in the context of an industrial fair. Waltham was the home of the Boston Manufacturing Company, the prototype of the modern American corporation. In 1814, this entity had established the first large, integrated textile mill in the United States; the investors later went on to build the model industrial community of Lowell, Massachusetts. The American Watch Company was founded at Waltham in 1859, by men from the armory in Springfield, Massachusetts, where the American System of Manufactures had been pioneered. As a result, watchmaking was one of the earliest industries to benefit from the new system of interchangeable parts, and the company went on to great success during the Civil War.[28] Its exhibit at the Centennial took the form of a single vitrine containing twenty-two hundred watches, which represented a day's worth of work at the factory—a small but compelling monument to both the company and the system.

THE STRANGENESS OF THINGS

> Encyclopedic nomenclature, whatever its technological esotericism
> on occasion, actually establishes a familiar possession. This is
> remarkable, for nothing logically obliges the object to be invariably
> friendly to man. The object, quite the contrary, is humanly a very
> ambiguous thing; we have noted that for a longtime our literature
> did not acknowledge it; later (which is to say, on the whole, today),
> the object has been endowed with an unfortunate opacity;
> assimilated to an inhuman state of nature, its proliferation cannot be
> noted without a sentiment of apocalypse or of alienation: the
> modern object is either asphyxiation (Ionesco) or nausea (Sartre).
> —Roland Barthes, "The Plates of the *Encyclopedia*"

To our eyes, there is something raw and unmediated about all these displays. This condition is exemplified by an exhibit in Agricultural Hall, which consisted, as the sign tells us, of three hundred varieties of potatoes, assembled by B.K. Bliss and Sons of New York City (fig. 4-25). The potatoes were arranged without much fuss, on plates identified by small cards, on a long, rough, wooden table that emphasized the crudeness of the display. Exhibitors like Bliss and Sons showed a boundless faith in the power of the object lesson, in the instructiveness of things themselves. Like their contemporaries in other display-oriented environments—like many contemporary scholars of material culture—they relied on the artifact to tell the truth about itself and so provided precious little in the way of explanation. The audience was thrown back onto its own expertise, such as it was, in making

4-25. "Potatoes" (CPC 2407, Print and Picture Collection, Free Library of Philadelphia).

sense of things. As we have seen, however, most of the exhibits at the Centennial provided considerably less access than these potatoes would suggest. Exhibitors used strategies that made the artifact both distant and
strange—distant in the sense of a barrier between observer and observed,
strange in the sense of an abstraction from any meaningful context.

Almost every exhibit had a more or less impermeable boundary that
itself was a source of strangeness. In the case of a collective display of
American carpets, the boundary took the form of a platform, railing, and
partitions around the back and sides of each exhibit (fig. 4-26). These disci-
plined the movement of people in the aisle, separating the spaces of display
and circulation and focusing attention on the goods inside. The boundary,
however, was not absolute; this type of display was meant to be manned, in
contrast to the mute and self-sufficient vitrine, with an attendant making
the goods available to observers. The attendant was *in* the display but not
really *on* display, in the sense that he occupied the space created by the platform, railing, and partitions but was not intended to be the object of a look.

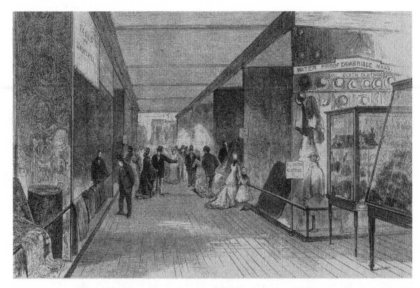

4-26. "The Centennial—display of American carpets, Main Building" (*Harper's Weekly* 20, no. 1039 [25 Nov. 1876]: 957, Library of Congress).

The audience at the Centennial was generally well behaved, but there is one account of transgressive acts, which reminds us that the exhibit boundary was more than a formality. These included a man and a woman in dusty clothes sprawling on expensive Gobelins sofas (this was after breaking down the rope) and people in general mishandling delicate artifacts and pointing at pictures with sharp canes.[29] These cases show that the boundary was obviously a practical necessity, but I would argue that it was also an ideological statement, a model for a particular kind of relationship between subject and object. This relationship was consistent with the visual regime of Cartesian perspectivalism, which was based on the ideal of the camera obscura, with its separation of inside and outside, of observer and observed, and its assertion of an uninvolved, "objective" point of view. The exhibit might seem to have inverted the mechanics of the camera obscura, with the object inside the box and the subject outside, looking in. It nevertheless retained the camera's propensity to isolate one from the other, and to privilege seeing as a way of knowing, since the observer inspected things that were more or less out of reach. This was especially true in the case of the vitrine, which enforced the primacy of the eye with a pane of glass, thus severing anything but a visual relationship between subject

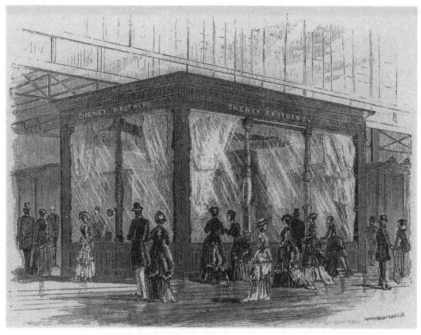

4-27. "Case of Silks, Exhibited by Cheney Brothers" (Bruce, *Century,* 25, University of California Library, Berkeley).

and object (fig. 4-27). Even such a limited connection might be obscured by glare.

This enforced emphasis on the look of things helps to explain how, in Simon Bronner's words, "the sight-oriented, broader world of consumption" came to replace "the touch-oriented, local world of production."[30] The transition from one world to another was evident in all parts of the exhibition. In fact, the pervasiveness of the look suggests the degree to which the material world was already being reorganized along the lines of an emerging culture of mass consumption. It also suggests the boundaries of this culture, as well as possible areas of resistance. Machinery was in; the hall was built like a factory, with the giant Corliss engine silently providing power to all the exhibits, much to the delight of an audience that consumed it all as an experience of the "technological sublime," as David Nye and others have called it (fig. 4-28).[31] Agriculture was in; the display of canned tomatoes behind the Bliss and Sons exhibit signifies the increasing importance of packaged and prepared foods in modern life (fig. 4-25). Horticulture was still out; the plants in the conservatory-like hall were presented in the traditional manner, as so many specimens of a single, natural world (fig.

4-28. "Machinery Hall." North Avenue looking east (CPC 808, Print and Picture Collection, Free Library of Philadelphia).

4-29). Art appeared to be out, but that may have been an illusion born of vestigial strategies of display. The works were presented like originals—mounted and framed or on pedestals—but a great many were in fact mechanical reproductions—engravings, photographs, and serial works of sculpture (fig. 4-30).

The strangeness of things at the exhibition might have reflected the fact that many of them were new, were new versions of old things, or were old things presented in new ways. Even familiar objects that are ostensibly very close to us, parts of our own bodies, might seem strange in a strange context. A display of false teeth is a case in point; it has a surreal quality that is the result of displacement, of seeing a familiar, organic object displayed in an unfamiliar, inorganic setting (fig. 4-31). The flattened teeth encrust a truncated pyramid, which is precariously raised on four small columns; other sets litter the bottom of the showcase. We naturally respond with a sense of shock, of prosthetic anxiety, an uncomfortable identification with all these distorted body parts. The technique of more is at work, producing a strangeness that is the consequence of seeing too many things in one place and in such an unnatural context—out of the body, in an ornate vitrine. Ironically,

4-29. "Horticultural Hall." Interior from west end (CPC 2320, Print and Picture Collection, Free Library of Philadelphia).

the showcase is singular—the design is an odd amalgamation of conventionalized Eastlake-style decoration with very realistically modeled, monopod legs—but the contents are standardized. The form may be specific, but it can in fact contain many different kinds of things—shirts, skates, artist's supplies, corsets, and so on. It thus establishes an equivalency between these things, standardizing our perception of them as goods. To para-

4-30. Memorial Hall, Art Gallery (CPC 1578, Print and Picture Collection, Free Library of Philadelphia).

phrase Benjamin, the display makes the commodity identical to all those which are exhibited in the same way.[32]

We should be reminded here of the Jean Baudrillard's early interpretation of modernity as "an increasing destabilization and mobility of signs and codes." This was a process that began during the Renaissance as a reaction against the social and semiotic hierarchies of earlier periods.[33] It reached a critical stage in the nineteenth century, with the arrival of new and more mobile signs as a result of industrialization and improvements in science and technology. Unlike their predecessors, these signs, which Baudrillard has described as "potentially identical objects produced in indefinite series," do not serve a mimetic function: "The relation between them is no

4-31. "H.D. Justi—Teeth" (CPC 2014, Print and Picture Collection, Free Library of Philadelphia).

longer that of an original to its counterfeit. The relation is neither analogy nor reflection, but equivalence and indifference. In a series, objects become undefined simulacra of each other."[34] By comparison, the artifacts on display at the exhibition were all signs, but they were not entirely removed from their referents. The observer obviously did not forget that potatoes were meant for eating, carpets for covering floors, silks and shirts and teeth for wearing on or in the body. But these things did achieve a certain mobility as signs, a certain self-sufficiency as symbols of exchange. Because of the display strategies employed by exhibitors, the artifacts did acquire a certain equivalence to each other as commodities, inspiring a feeling of indifference on the part of the observer. At the exhibition, if the relationship between sign and referent was not entirely severed, it was considerably loosened.

Mannequins and Model Rooms

In the two principles of installation, we have seen a change in emphasis from the vista to the accent, from the "strong" look of the gaze to the "weak" look of the glance. This paralleled the process by which, in the early nineteenth century, the camera obscura ceased to be the dominant model for seeing and knowing, and vision was reconstituted as a subjective effect of the human body.[35] The accompanying transformation in subject-object relations was similarly reflected at the Centennial in a shift from strategies of display

4-32. "Main Building—England" Howard and Sons exhibit (CPC 712, Print and Picture Collection, Free Library of Philadelphia).

4-33. "Art Furniture at the Centennial—Display of Howard & Sons, London" (*Harper's Weekly* 20, no. 1033 [14 Oct. 1876]: 825, Prints and Photographs, Library of Congress).

that were relatively distant and abstract, implying an objective point of view, to ones that promoted a more subjective identification with the artifact.

The model room was one of these new strategies, and the fact that the Bureau of Installation failed to include it in the general rules is a sign of its novelty. Katherine Grier has stated that the model room made its first appearance at the Centennial, where it is most evident in the exhibits of cer-

4-34. "English Furniture" Howard and Sons exhibit (CPC 1740, Print and Picture Collection, Free Library of Philadelphia).

tain English and American decorators. But I find it hard to believe that it had not already appeared in their own stores and was merely being exported to the exhibition. Similar forms of display had already emerged in other environments; Grier herself suggests that the model room may have originated in colonial-kitchen exhibits built at sanitary fairs during the Civil War.[36] Furthermore, we know that period rooms, which display a collection of objects in a historically accurate setting, were becoming a part of museum practice during the 1870s, although their prominence in American institutions would have to wait until the 1920s.[37]

The inherent drama of the model room permitted the impression of distance and strangeness to be replaced by an illusion of familiarity and intimacy. In contrast to the technique of more, which celebrated industrial output with a display of sheer quantity, the model room represented the artifact in all its singularity. It created an aura of authenticity, which explains its use in the Howard and Sons exhibit, a display of hand-crafted art furniture (fig. 4-32). But the model room was just as applicable to the display of mechanically produced artifacts, since it denied the equivalency of these "potentially identical objects" by placing them in a particular context, in precise relationship to each other. In contrast to the abstraction of other methods, the concrete quality of the model room helped to stabilize the meaning of the objects on display, reducing their mobility as signs within the semantically lubricated environment of the exhibition.

Furthermore, the model room countered the indifference of the observer by lowering the boundary of display. It invited spectators to enter an attractive narrative, a dream world of ease and comfort, a tableau in which they could perform, at least in their imaginations. In contrast to the camera obscura, the model room implied an engaged subject, one that was psychologically enmeshed with its object. This position is represented by a well-known engraving from *Harper's* in which a female figure sits in an overstuffed chair, reading by a fireplace that is set into an enormous Aesthetic overmantle (fig. 4-33). As was common practice, the engraving was based on the photograph of a real woman, posing in the space of the Howard and Sons exhibit (fig. 4-34). Significantly, at some point in the process, a living body was actually on display.

In looking at these pictures, it is not exactly clear who or what is meant to be the focus of our attention. The overmantle is overwhelming, and it very nearly reduces the woman to the status of an ornament, a form of garniture like the ceramic pieces above her. She is clearly intended to be visually consumed along with the other objects on display and thus becomes the object of a complex gaze that vacillates between the figure and the fireplace. Is the figure commodified by the furniture? The fireplace eroticized by its association with the woman? Probably a bit of both—the meaning of one sign literally overlaps/overwhelms the other. Even though we are obviously not looking at the first instance of a body on display, these two images indicate the crossing of some significant cultural boundary. This is not the figure as the object of desire in a work of art, although desire

4-35. "Corsets" (CPC 859, Print and Picture Collection, Free Library of Philadelphia).

plays a part in how these images are received, nor is it the abhorred body of the other in a freak show. This is the body as instrument, a context-giving device that is used to explain the meaning of other things. The body is no longer a visual end in itself but a means to an end, which is consumption.

The instrumentality of the body on display is further illustrated by the use of mannequins—another strategy that the bureau did not anticipate.

4-36. "Patterns" (CPC 1971, Print and Picture Collection, Free Library of Philadelphia).

Exhibitors put them with cradles, ice skates, and even artist's materials, but, for obvious reasons, they were most likely to be found with clothing or things used to make clothing. Here we find a spectrum of completeness, ranging from the truncated forms in a display of French and English corsets and dresses (fig. 4-35), to the fully modeled wax figures in an exhibit by a French pattern-maker (fig. 4-36). The latter was quite elaborate and included a pair of easels bearing framed fashion plates; a cut-out, two-dimensional representation of a fashionably dressed child; and a desk for a female attendant. This proliferation of bodies, represented or otherwise, increased the ambiguity about who or what was supposed to be on display. This would have been especially true if the observer were male, and the attendant were wearing clothing made from the company's patterns.

The proliferation of bodies at the Centennial was not confined to commercial exhibits, nor to displays of the human figure. A display of American reaping machines, probably in Agricultural Hall, included a pair of full-size horses in harness (fig. 4-37). The Swedish section of the Main

4-37. "Reaping Machine" (CPC 1965, Print and Picture Collection, Free Library of Philadelphia).

Building contained male figures in military uniforms; a similar exhibit could be found in the U.S. Government Building.[38] More to the point, in both the Swedish and Norwegian sections, there were some very important displays of Scandinavian folk life—"correct and lifelike representations of their soldiers, their weddings, their watchmakers, their hunters, and scenes in their home life"—which consisted of accurately dressed wax figures arranged in realistic settings. According to one account, the most striking depicted a peasant family mourning a baby's death (fig. 4-38).[39] This seems to have been the same tableau that Artur Hazelius exhibited at the 1878 Paris fair as part of a sensational collection of thirty "living pictures." This particular display was in fact based on a real painting, making it a relation to the genuine tableau vivant, a type of popular spectacle in which costumed performers, usually amateurs, reenacted scenes from well-known works of art.[40]

Hazelius was the founder of the Museum of Scandinavian Ethnography, established in Stockholm in 1873. His presence at the Centennial indicates a significant blurring of the institutional boundaries between stores, museums, and exhibitions. In the U.S. Government Building, for example, there was an impressive exhibit of animal resources, organized by two Smithsonian curators, Spencer F. Baird and George Brown Goode. The exhibit included a display of 408 painted plaster models of American fish,

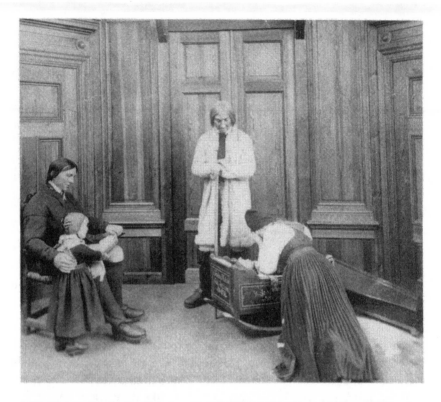

4-38. "Baby's Death. Swedish Sec: M. B." (CPC 1495, Print and Picture Collection, Free Library of Philadelphia).

mounted on freestanding partitions (fig. 4-39). This was a three-dimensional catalog, analogous to the printed catalog that Goode had prepared for the whole exhibit. As in all catalogs, an abstract, artificial order—a grid in the case of the partition, the Linnaean system in the case of the publication—substituted for an organic one.[41]

Compare this exhibit to a celebrated display of animal specimens known as Mrs. Maxwell's Rocky Mountain Museum (fig. 4-40). These were arranged in a naturalized setting, which occupied one whole wall of the state building shared by Kansas and Colorado. The display may not have been scientific, but it was visually more sophisticated than the Smithsonian exhibit. It was comparable not only to Hazelius's ethnographic tableaux but also to the dioramas or habitat groupings that were then being created in museums of natural history. In this context, we should remember that the Rocky Mountain Museum was not the work of a professional scientist. Most

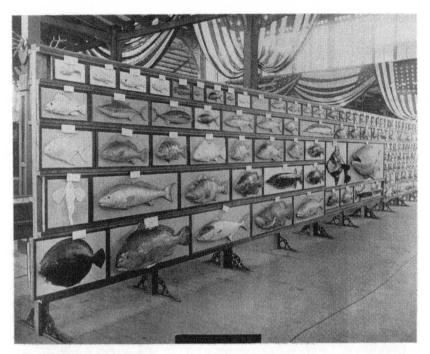

4-39. "Government Building" (CPC 510, Print and Picture Collection, Free Library of Philadelphia).

of the two hundred mammals and three to four hundred birds on display were killed or captured and then prepared by Mrs. Maxwell herself. The exhibit thus illustrates the continuing importance of the amateur scientist, at least in the United States, at a time when the authority of the professional had supposedly been established.[42]

Significantly, Mrs. Maxwell insisted on being photographed with her animals. The result was predictable: she was perceived as part of the display.[43] In the photograph, Maxwell appears fully dressed, of course, in a seated position, hands in lap, holding what appears to be a bird. She is a figure out of a polite Victorian parlor, and yet she seems strangely at home in her museum. Maxwell's position may be an expression of craftsmanlike pride in her work, but it is also, like every collection, a statement of self, of her perceived position in the world and the place of human beings in nature. This paralleled contemporary scientific developments; with the collapse of the camera-obscura model of seeing and knowing, man had lost his unique position as the observing subject and had himself become an observed ob-

4-40. "Mrs Maxwell's Rocky Mountain Museum Series, Colorado Building" (CPC 1085, Print and Picture Collection, Free Library of Philadelphia).

ject of scientific scrutiny.[44] Similarly, at the exhibition, new forms of display allowed the position of the human body to change from outside to inside the exhibit, and back again.

THE EXHIBITION AS A SPECTACLE

The exhibition appears to have been a relentlessly visual experience, which was designed to promote the primacy of the eye, that defining feature of modernity. It was a spectacle in the most literal sense, that is, "capital accumulated to such a degree that it becomes visible," to use Guy Debord's well-known formulation.[45] The French theorist seems to have dated the onset of spectacular society to the 1920s, with the development of various forms of mass communication and the rise of what he called the "concentrated" spectacle of totalitarian states, in which the image of the dictator reigned supreme. This was in contrast to the "diffuse" spectacle of democratic states, with its surfeit of goods forming many centers of distraction.[46]

As a spectacle, the exhibition was both diffused and concentrated. It was diffused in the very real sense that it represented a distracting surfeit of goods. It was concentrated in the more literal sense that it represented a crude form of mass communication, in which a mass of people and a mass of goods were brought together in one place. This was obviously a very cumbersome process, and the exhibition (at least in the object-oriented form of the nineteenth century) was in short order made virtually obsolete by more efficient forms of marketing.

Some form of spectacular display seems to have been what the organizers of the Centennial were after all along, whether it was in the form of the vista or the overview. As we have seen, architecture played a crucial role in shaping these ways of seeing. Pettit recalled the particular impact of the Main Building's skeletal iron frame: "There were no walls of partition dividing the building into distinct departments; the slender columns alone obstructed the vistas in every direction. The only lines of division between the Foreign sections were those formed by the passage-ways ten feet wide. Thus uninterrupted views were obtained from one Foreign section into another, and the interest of the Exhibition as a spectacular display was greatly enhanced."[47] *American Architect and Building News* made a similar point, comparing the cluttered interior of the industrial palace at the 1873 Vienna fair to the open space of the Main Building: "In the former the central rotunda effectually cut off from one wing the vista of the other, while the multitude of small transepts, like so many *culs-de-sac,* existed for themselves and not for the spectacle as a whole. Here the sweep of vision is unobstructed from end to end, not only through the central nave of 120 feet, but also through both side-naves of 100 feet span."[48] As communicated in photographs, this constructed view is both striking and misleading. Like

4-41. "Main Building." Nave looking west (CPC 580, Print and Picture Collection, Free Library of Philadelphia).

the vitrines, these pictures privilege sight and deny the totality of the human senses. Their stillness is exaggerated by the fact that they are relatively unpeopled, either because of the time required to make an exposure—occasionally the film is fast enough to catch the ghost of a figure (fig. 4-41)—or because the photographs were taken at an early hour, before the arrival of the crowd. In some cases, the floors are still wet from mopping.

To begin to understand the full, phenomenal reality of the exhibition, we must remember that it was more than just a visual experience. We must imagine the fragrance of exotic goods, the din of the crowd moving about a large space, and the nearly continuous sound of music emanating from various stations—the bandstand in the center of the building, the displays of instruments in the American section, the organs in the north and east galleries.[49] Surprisingly, the cavernous hall of the Main Building was supposed to have remarkably good acoustics—the Centennial Commission *Reports* described it as "resonant without reverberation"—and Pettit made reference to continuous concerts at the bandstand (fig. 4-42). In the American section, piano recitals averaged nearly ten a day, while the organs, the most

4-42. "Music Pavilion, Central Transept, Main Building" (Wilson, *Masterpieces* 3:civ, University of California Library, Berkeley).

popular of the building's musical attractions, recorded a combined total of well over six hundred performances.[50]

Taken in small doses, these concerts provided a pleasant source of background noise, an early form of Muzak, even an aural antidote to what we would call museum fatigue. But the effect of overlapping performances could also prove irritating, as the writer in the *Atlantic* peevishly explained:

> I have not yet been able to discover whether there is a stated time for music, or whether some melodious yet diabolic influence impels the performers at one and the same moment to rush to their different stools, so that as one listens absently but with pleasure to the organ rolling out the overture to the Huguenots the ear is tormented as by a gust with the persistence of "Il segretto per esser Felice" from a thin piano . . . ; and moving off to be out of reach of this, one comes within the range of another organ, and the soul swells and sinks with the chords of the funeral march from Beethoven's Sonata Eroica. Gradually the notes of the garden-duet from Faust steal through the sublime sorrow of the lament for a hero, and, disgraceful to say, it is not intolerable; but when "motives" from Martha begin to come in at the ear, Babel and Bedlam get possession of the senses and brain, and one takes to flight.

The crowd, the cacophony, the sheer visual pressure of the exhibition—it was all enough to make visitors want to flee this space for the relative peace of the park-like grounds. "I have noticed," said the same writer, "that people grow cross in the Main Building more easily than in other parts of the Exhibition; the want of homogeneousness in the array at once distracts and fatigues the attention."[51] Clearly, even the most serious audience had its limits, as Pettit acknowledged in his final report to the Centennial Commission:

> It is a mistake to suppose that the average visitor can be so effectually entertained by the surrounding display as not to be induced away from the exhibits. Most people, if they meet with some unexpected incidental pleasure, as for instance a musical concert, will invariably stop to observe and enjoy it as they pass by, and when so doing will endeavor to avail themselves of the opportunity to take a seat and rest. They find that visiting a large exhibition systematically, in a limited time, is extremely fatiguing. Hence all those facilities that can be offered for resting and yet sustaining the interest and attention, are acceptable, [sic] and should be judiciously introduced.

Revealingly, he went on to recall the precise behavior of the people in attendance: "A careful observer of the individuals composing the moving crowd in the Main Building would have noticed two things: First, that although rare industrial art and opportunities for instruction were present in the exhibits on all sides, yet, nevertheless, under all ordinary conditions of mind, 'the *most* interesting thing to the people was the people themselves'; and, second, that to the majority of visitors the next greatest attraction was presented by an effective musical performance."[52]

Pettit's remarks illuminate several important points about the nature of the exhibition and its audience. First, the concentrated study of a large collection of artifacts, no matter how systematically organized, was an exhausting, mind-numbing experience. The exhibition promised useful knowledge, but what it really provided was a surfeit of information, abstracted from any meaningful context. (The wisdom to know the difference is something that we have yet to acquire.) Second, the static conception of the exhibition as a table, as a well constructed array of objects, was in sharp contrast to the dynamic character of the audience, which constituted an urban crowd in the most restless, modern sense.[53] Such a crowd could not begin to focus on, let alone decipher, a meaningful arrangement of displays. Third, this audience did not constitute a passive surface on which the organizers could inscribe their own intentions. It brought its own agenda to the exhibition, which included entertainment as well as education, pleasure, and instruction. Now, there should be no doubt that the design of the Centennial reflected the preoccupations of an elite group of people. Yet Pettit's remarks remind us that the hegemony of this group, if we can call it that, did not go uncontested, not even by members of its own class.[54] His comments, which recall his own report on the behavior of visitors to the 1873 Vienna fair, suggest again that consumption is more than an economic function; it is a profoundly social act.[55] As Pettit observed, people came to the exhibition primarily to see and be seen by other people. This suggests that among the exhibition's spectacular functions was the promotion of a certain kind of social solidarity; it allowed a largely middle-class audience to view and understand itself as an emerging class of consumers. The exhibition permitted these subjects to contemplate not only the innumerable objects of desire that were on display but also *themselves* as objects and sources of desire.[56]

THE AMERICAN
SYSTEM OF AWARDS

Every given commodity fights for itself, cannot acknowledge the
others, and attempts to impose itself everywhere as if it were the
only one. The spectacle, then, is the epic poem of this struggle, an
epic which cannot be concluded by the fall of any Troy. The
spectacle does not sing the praises of men and their weapons, but of
commodities and their passions. In this blind struggle every
commodity, pursuing its passion, unconsciously realizes something
higher: the becoming-world of the commodity, which is also the
becoming-commodity of the world. Thus by means of a ruse of
commodity logic, what's specific in the commodity wears itself out
in the fight while the commodity form moves towards its absolute
realization.

—Guy Debord, *The Society of the Spectacle*

In retrospect, it is always the physicality of the exhibition that speaks to us
most strongly, through drawings, photographs, and, in some cases, extant
structures. We should not forget, however, that the principle function of the
exhibition was the systematic evaluation of goods. As the *Journal of the
Franklin Institute* reminded its readers shortly after the closing of the Centennial, "Throughout those miles of passages every object on display was
there, not alone for admiration, but for comparison, for selection."[1] In other
words, the exhibition was more than a collection of things; it was a vast
apparatus of distinction, a carefully designed system for working out the
relative value of commodities in a global market.

At the Centennial, the centrality of evaluation was expressed by the
location of Judges' Hall (see fig. 3-2). The primary economic functions of
production and consumption were symbolized by Machinery Hall and the

5-1. "Judges' Hall" (CPC 237, Print and Picture Collection, Free Library of Philadelphia).

Main Building, respectively. These were the two largest structures of the exhibition, located on either side of the "grand plaza" on Elm Avenue. As the symbolic heart of the fair, Judges' Hall was appropriately situated at the head of the plaza, on axis with the main gate. Covering little more than a third of an acre, the hall was tiny by comparison to its neighbors but no less important. As designed by Herman Schwarzmann, it was made of wood, like most of the fair's smaller buildings (fig. 5-1). The exterior walls were paneled and plastered to suggest half-timbering, while the porch, balconies, and belvedere were detailed in a structurally expressive manner. This was "modern architecture," according to the Centennial Commission; for us, it exemplifies the Stick style, which became fashionable after the Civil War and was evident in the design of other buildings at the exhibition.[2]

The interior of Judges' Hall was "elegantly paneled and decorated," in keeping with the importance of its program. The center of the hall was a large, truss-covered assembly room, where many of the exhibition's most important ceremonies took place (fig. 5-2). These included the final distri-

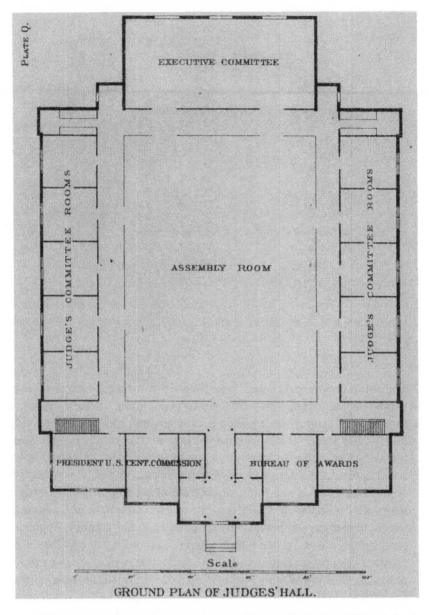

5-2. "Ground Plan of Judges' Hall" (USCC, *International Exhibition, 1876,* vol. 9, pl. Q, University of California Library, Berkeley).

bution of awards to exhibitors, held on September 27, 1876, as a well as a daily round of meetings by "patriotic, scientific, industrial, and other associations."[3] In fact, Judges' Hall was the equivalent of a small convention center; behind the assembly room, there was a meeting room for the Executive Committee, and the intervening walls could be removed to create a single, large space, 60 feet wide by 106 feet long—a surprisingly flexible arrangement. For their part, the judges gathered in small committee rooms on either side of the assembly room, and in a chamber on the second story. This was when they were not actually walking the floors of the other exhibition buildings, inspecting the goods on display.[4]

THE JURY SYSTEM

In addition to securing a design for Judges' Hall, the organizers of the Centennial had to devise a method for evaluating the goods on display. In this, they faced the dilemma of whether or not to adopt some version of the existing jury system.[5] This implied a large international body with hundreds of members, subdivided into specialized groups that examined the goods and made anonymous recommendations for graded awards—gold, silver, and bronze medals, honorable mentions, and so on.[6]

The defects in the system were numerous. First, the juries tended to favor the countries with the most floor space, since these appointed the largest number of members. Second, the most qualified candidates could often not afford to serve as members, since the positions were honorary, not paid. Third, the juries tended to shrink with the passing of time; since the positions were not paid, the members felt no compunction in quitting when it suited them. Fourth, the juries tended to be chauvinistic; the members felt it was their duty to secure as many medals as possible for their own countries. Finally, the awards were made anonymously and without any explanation. "The medals, when distributed, were as silent as the verdicts," observed N.M. Beckwith, the Centennial commissioner from New York and U.S. commissioner-general at the 1867 fair in Paris; "moral responsibility for the decisions attached to no one, and the awards thus made conveyed as little useful information, and carried as little weight, as anonymous work usually carries."[7]

Beckwith's concern for the exhibition as a source of "useful information" was typically American in its pragmatism.[8] His concern was shared by General Francis A. Walker, a statistician, a veteran of the Civil War, and, at the time of his appointment as chief of the Centennial's Bureau of Awards, a Yale professor of economics and history.[9] Walker put the problem in an explicitly commercial context:

> The radical defect of the medal system is that it conveys no practical information. The bronze medal, or the cross of the Legion of Honor, even if given with discrimination, merely signifies that the product awarded is good; but it does not answer the question with which Socrates was wont to confound his adversaries: Good for what? On the contrary, it may easily become the means of misleading the public and the body of purchasers, through the failure to state the uses to which the product may be best applied, or the conditions under which alone its use may be advantageous.

As an example of the ways in which the purchasing public could be misled, Walker provided the "familiar illustration" of the New England farmer comparing two prize-winning mowing machines: the "Triumph," the recipient of a gold medal at the Paris fair, and the "Farmer's Pride," the recipient of a silver. On the basis of this information, the farmer orders the Triumph. "When it arrives, he finds it an instrument of a high perfection of parts, great reach, and rapidity of operation; but, to his sorrow, he also finds that it is unsuited to this rough, side-hill farm, all hummocks, stumps, and stones, and it is knocked to pieces in a month." Alternatively, if the jurors had all been from areas like New England, and given the gold to Farmer's Pride, farmers in Illinois would have made similarly bad decisions, purchasing a machine that was poorly adapted to the soil or terrain of the prairie.[10]

Walker's anecdote helps to explain why the form of the jury system was so critical to the organizers of the Centennial or any other exhibition. The awards had an economic value; they were expected to help shape demand in a large and complex market, functioning as the nineteenth-century equivalent of *Consumer Reports*. In spite of all the piety about education, the organizers understood the exhibition in terms of trade, as an environment that provided vendors with direct physical access to a large body of potential customers.[11] This was at a time when the instruments of mass persuasion were just beginning to develop; the market was national, but the media were still largely local, and the basic forms of advertising—broadsides, trade cards, and classified advertising—had remained unchanged since before the Civil War. A prize-winning exhibitor could make the award a part of the display (see fig. 6-1); the exhibitor could also incorporate the image of the award into the design of trade cards and product labels, where

5-3. John McCann Oatmeal as honored at the Centennial Exhibition (Photograph by author).

it functioned as a sign of value and quality, as determined in an international context and under expert circumstances. Until recently, Campbell's Soup was the most familiar example of this practice, which dates back to the time of the Great Exhibition, at least. John McCann Oatmeal still uses pictures of medals and facsimiles of award certificates to illustrate how its excellence was established at exhibitions in London, Philadelphia, and Chicago (fig. 5-3).[12]

In the dissemination of useful information as a form of advertising, we see the commercial edge of what Jürgen Habermas has called "the unfinished project of modernity." In the eighteenth century, the unitary body of knowledge that had existed before the Enlightenment was rationalized into specialized realms, which Habermas identifies as science, morality, and art. These were institutionalized in the form of expert professions, which mediated between their particular realms and the everyday life of the public. The international exhibition was a case in point: it represented a market-oriented form of knowledge, embodied in goods and metastasizing into ever more specialized realms. (Remember that the Centennial's original system of classification provided for ten departments, a hundred groups, and a thousand classes.) These realms were institutionalized in the form of a jury, which rendered expert judgments that were expected to inform the everyday life of the consumer.[13]

THE AMERICAN SYSTEM

Habermas has called modernity an unfinished project because everyday life has not been transformed by critical reason, at least not as anticipated by eighteenth-century philosophers. Whether the specific project of the exhibition was similarly unfinished is a good question; certainly the organizers of the Centennial believed that there was room for improvement in the jury system. In their search for an alternative, they consulted people with experience of previous fairs, whether as exhibitors, commissioners, or members of the jury.[14] From these people, the organizers learned that the defects in the jury system had become known as early as 1851, at the Great Exhibition in London. By 1855, when the French held their first Exposition universelle in Paris, the system had become so contentious that Prince Napoléon, the president of the fair, recommended the abolition of both the juries and the awards. His proposal was ignored, and similar systems were adopted at the 1862 London and 1867 Paris fairs. After the closing of the 1867 fair, a number of commissioners published a report recommending that the awards be replaced by signed reports. In a sense, this was the policy adopted at the annual exhibitions held in London between 1871 and 1874. However, the organizers of the 1873 Weltausstellung in Vienna reverted to a system of graduated medals, while abandoning the principle of international competition. In Vienna, the main building consisted of a series of courts opening off a long central nave, and each country mounted its own separate exhibit, which was evaluated by its own national jury. The result was much criticized by Goshorn and others who visited the fair.[15]

The system adopted by the Centennial Commission was a conscious reaction to this experience. It was, in Walker's words, "intended to substitute for the anonymous verdict of a jury the personal decision of a responsible Judge, and for the vague language of gold, silver, and bronze medals, and order of the first class or the second class, a full and precise statement of the merits of each exhibit."[16] As outlined by the Executive Committee, the first article specified that the awards be granted on the basis of signed reports. The second called for a group of two hundred expert judges, half American and half foreign. The third provided a stipend of one thousand dollars for each of the judges.[17]

The system was supposed to be "judicial rather than representative," which meant that each country did not need to have its own judges in every group.[18] Great Britain, for example, was represented in only eighteen of twenty-eight regular groups; Germany, in twelve; France, in fourteen. As a result, the jury was supposed to be smaller and the process more equitable than had been the case at previous exhibitions.[19] Nevertheless, the total number of judges had to be increased to 250 when it became apparent that 200 would not be enough. This made it necessary to reduce the compensation of the American judges to six hundred dollars.[20]

The fourth article required that the reports and awards be made on the basis of "inherent and comparative merit," the criteria being "originality, invention, discovery, utility, quality, skill, workmanship, fitness for the purposes intended, adaptation to public wants, economy, and cost." The omission of aesthetics from this list of factors is telling, suggesting as it does the awkward position of the art object in an industrial fair. The fifth article specified that the completed reports be submitted to the Centennial Commission; the sixth, that the commission make the final decision on the award. This was to consist of a diploma, a standardized bronze medal, and a certified copy of the judge's report. The seventh article guaranteed the exhibitor's right to reproduce the report, ostensibly as advertising, but preserved the commission's right to publish the report in an appropriate manner.[21]

The Centennial Commission approved a design for a four-inch-diameter bronze medal, "very chaste in appearance, and the largest of the kind ever struck in the United States," according to James D. McCabe, the author of a popular history of the exhibition. Engraved by Henry Mitchell, a Boston artist, and struck at the Philadelphia Mint, the medal depicted a seated female figure representing this country (fig. 5-4). Dressed in classical drapery and crowned with laurel, the figure held the Great Shield of the

5-4. "Centennial Award Medal" (McCabe, *Illustrated History,* 844–45, University of California Library, Berkeley).

United States with one hand; with the other, she bestowed a second laurel crown on the symbols of art and industry crowded at her feet. This image was in turn surrounded by four small medallions that contained figures representing America, Europe, Asia, and Africa.[22]

In the new system, this medal was "only a token," and its allegorical design was informed by conventional notions of art, honor, and patriotism. The "real award" was the judge's report, which was supposed to disseminate useful information to producers and consumers.[23] Echoing Walker, McCabe explained, "The medal simply declares that an article is good; the report tells what it is good for, and how good."[24] As a group, the collected judges' reports were perceived to have a historical significance; they were expected to serve as a kind of time capsule in which the "ephemeral vista" of the exhibition and the world it represented could be immortalized in literary form. Writing before the Centennial opened, the Executive Committee looked forward to "reports which will be a record of the industrial, artistic, educational, and social progress of the nations and will preserve to future times the Centennial Exhibition of the 'form and pressure' of the present age."[25] Period libraries seemed to agree that these were important documents, and the reports, which varied in individual significance, were widely distributed.

THE GROUPING FOR THE JUDGES' WORK

All in all, this was a radical departure from the old jury system, and Goshorn recalled that the judges responded with "lively discussion" when the new system was first presented to them.[26] The Executive Committee's account suggests that the situation was a bit closer to open revolt: "The system of awards adopted by the Commission[,] being an innovation upon the usages of former Exhibitions, met with opposition on the part of a number of the foreign Judges, who made a formal protest against it, which was respectfully considered by the committee, but there appeared to be no sufficient reason for making any change. After a conference of the Judges with a special committee of this body, and a full discussion of the subject, in which some of the ablest foreign Commissioners sustained your rules, there was a general approval of what will hereafter be known as the American System of Awards."[27] This was obviously a reference to the American System of Manufactures, as it had been known since the 1850s.[28] What it meant to the judges is suggested by the report on an award made to the American Watch Company: "The movements made by this company are constructed upon what is known as the 'American system,' with interchangeability of parts for the several grades manufactured, and by the use of machinery devised and perfected in their factory, and by them first brought into use for the purposes of watchmaking." (See chapter 4 for more on the American Watch Company and the American System of Manufactures.)

From this account, it is apparent that the two systems of awards and manufactures both implied a faith in the power of rationalization. Both relied on the introduction of more specialized components—new machines and skilled workers on one hand, expert judges on the other—and on the employment of more sophisticated forms of organization. Both were designed to create a more standardized product, whether it was a clock, gun, or bronze medal. Both were perceived as characteristically American; echoing de Tocqueville, one French critic read the system of awards as a symptom of the American "love for uniformity, and the equality of democracy."[29] In the case of manufactures, this love was expressed by the use of interchangeable parts. Finally, the two systems both emerged in relation to a mass market of global dimensions. In the spectacle of the exhibition, this market was supposed to be revealed as a rationally known and consciously ordered place. The basis for this disclosure was the dual system of classification, which organized things according to geography and typology, that is, according to the object's place of origin and its affinity with like objects. As originally conceived, this system represented a progressive ideology and a hierarchical view of the world of goods; it was also decimal, having the potential to accommodate ten departments, one hundred groups, and one thousand classes.

The whole history of the Centennial can be seen as an attempt to reify this order in the form of the exhibition. As with other early world's fairs, the organizers aimed to create a transparently organized, classified landscape of commodities in which knowledge could be mapped and experienced in three dimensions. This ambitious project failed in many ways and for one reason: inspired by an Enlightenment-era confidence in their ability to know and order the world, the organizers consistently underestimated the complexity of the exhibition and the world it was supposed to represent. They had to revise the original system classification when it became apparent that the entire fair would not fit into a single, forty-acre building, as they had originally planned. Later they had to replace even the revised system of classification with the Grouping for the Judges' Work, when the classification failed to serve as a workable guide to the evaluation of goods.

Dorsey Gardner, who eventually became chief of the Publications Department and assistant secretary of the Centennial Commission, provided the only direct explanation for the adoption of the new grouping: "In the examination of objects for the distribution of awards by the Judges, it became necessary to associate exhibits classified in separate groups and installed in different buildings."[30] Apparently, the organizers had once again failed to describe the real order of things. The installation of displays was at odds with the evaluation of goods; products that had to be examined by a single group of judges were not adjacent to each other. According to Walker, the commission was also to blame for approving an overly elaborate system: "The Commission appear [sic] to have taken somewhat too literally the injunction of the Act of 1871—to prepare a *complete* plan for the classification of articles intended for exhibition. During the sessions of 1872–74 the subject received no small share of the attention of this body. The many discussions and the voluminous reports thereon finally issued in a system of classification of a wholly impracticable degree of minuteness and complexity."[31] Ostensibly, the new grouping represented a simplification and reorganization of the revised system. In place of the 7 departments, 52 groups, and 739 potential classes of the revised system, the grouping substituted 28 groups and 453 subgroups, based largely on the original structure of the classification. The chief improvement seems to have been the reconfiguration of some classes to form new constellations of goods and the subdivision of others to form more specific categories. The most striking change was the reclassification of products with processes—cotton, linen, and other fabrics, for example, with the machines used to make them. Apparently, the organizers had come to realize that production and consumption were not entirely separate domains, as suggested by the map of the fairground.

Even with these modifications, the Grouping for the Judges' Work made it difficult to locate certain classes of goods. Some still defied classification, while others could be classified in more than one way. A more striking defect was the exclusion of thirty classes that had been present in the revised system. In some cases, this required the creation of additional new groups; for Classes 630–36, "those relating to live-stock," the Centennial Commission formed Groups 30 to 35 and appointed a special body of judges representing the principal exhibitors—the United States, England, and Canada. In other cases, the missing classes were reassigned to surviving groups; Classes 345–49, "those relating to commercial systems and appliances; systems of government; institutions of benevolence, co-operative associations; religious organizations and systems, art and industrial exhibitions," were allocated to the judges in Group 28, Education and Science.[32]

Ironically, it was this last series of classes, associated under the label of "Physical, Social, and Moral Condition of Man," that had been preeminent in the original system of classification. Their neglect is significant, since it suggests a rejection of the social tradition of French fairs. This emphasized "the ultimate products" of the industrial economy—what I have called social goods.[33] Walker explained that the Centennial Commission was reluctant "to deal with the profound and difficult questions in moral, social, and economical philosophy which they involve."[34] Apparently, the commission had become reluctant to judge these goods like commodities. Or else it had concluded that they could only play a small and compromising part in an industrial fair.

GROUP 27

Judicial independence was an important principle of the American System of Awards, and both the Centennial Commission and the Bureau of Awards professed to take a hands-off approach to the judges. The decision to make an award rested with the commission, of course, but the judge's report was accepted or rejected in its entirety, with the exception of some editing by the bureau. Once a group of judges had adjourned, their conclusions were to be considered final unless there was good reason to believe that an exhibit had been overlooked, or unless the group itself agreed to reconvene.[35]

The judges were supposed to assemble on May 24, 1876, and submit their reports to the Centennial Commission by July 31.[36] In reality, they continued to work until the middle of September, the one exception being Group 27 on the Fine Arts. The judges in this group began on May 25, finished one month later, and then returned home. After receiving a complaint, the Bureau of Awards examined the records and discovered that the Committee on Painting had ignored the rules of the American System. According to Walker, the committee had decided to recommend awards on the basis of majority vote, allowing each member to nominate one work. This was in conflict with the principle that an award be based on the written recommendation of an individual judge and approved by a majority of the group. Furthermore, the committee had apparently set a limit to the number of awards it would recommend before seeing all the work. Upon reaching this limit, the committee refused to consider any other entries, even if they had not been examined. In response, Goshorn attempted to reconvene the committee in Philadelphia. A reduced number of judges met and added 128 names to the 85 originally recommended for awards.[37]

A year later, this incident sparked a surprisingly sharp debate in the pages of the *Nation,* between the magazine and three correspondents: George Ward Nichols, the secretary of Group 27, Frank Hill Smith, one of the judges, and Francis Walker himself.[38] The magazine began by praising the American System, and describing its operation with an anecdote illustrating the significance of the awards as a form of advertising:

> If three sewing-machines were selected for commendation, the judges would not say that one was the best, another the second best, and the other the third best, but would give an award to one because of its adaptability to the whole range of domestic work, to another (of high cost) as working perfectly in cambric, cloth, or leather, and to the third because, although less effective than either of the others for their special purposes, it was sufficiently good for ordinary family use, and could be furnished at a price within the reach of very poor people. So, through the whole range of the Exhibition, and in every department, the good qualities of the selected exhibits were to be authoritatively described, and this was supposed to constitute a value, especially for advertising purposes, far beyond the mere statement that an exhibit had received the "first" prize—no reasons being stated.

The magazine concluded that the American System had been a success, with the exception of Group 27 on the Fine Arts, whose judges had chosen to ignore their instructions. These allowed each group to set its own standard of quality but required every object meeting this standard to receive an award. The article further reported that the judges had telegraphed the president of the Royal Academy in London, suggesting that the older members forego their medals in favor of the younger, less established painters. As a result, the awards in the English department went to second-rate work, in spite of the fact that the department was reputed to contain the best paintings.[39]

George Ward Nichols responded by recounting how the judges had come to the conclusion that the American System was inapplicable to painting and sculpture. "It was found," he wrote, "that no two of the judges could agree in all respects in a criticism of a work of art, while it was not difficult to agree as to its *general artistic character.*" To paraphrase Walker, the judges could agree that a painting was good, but not what it was good *for.* As a result, the Committee on Painting had decided to make the awards on the basis of majority vote, the reports reading, simply, "For artistic excellence."[40]

For his part, Frank Hill Smith explained that the judges on the Fine Arts had only limited the number of awards given to painting. He denied any official communication between the judges and the president of the Royal Academy, and he insisted that, if their actions had been subversive, it had been because the system forced them to evaluate a work of art like a sewing machine. Each individual reaction was subjective, he argued, and could therefore not be rationalized in a report approved by a majority of judges—what amounted to a form of criticism by committee.[41] The debate concluded with Nichols disavowing the general report of Group 27 as published and accusing Walker of suppressing the judges' original report. Walker responded by accusing the group of submitting a forty-page manuscript, "of which not more than nine full pages, in the aggregate, were devoted to description or discussion of the Fine Arts Exhibition."[42]

This debate reveals something significant about the status of the artifact and the character of the exhibition. In rejecting the American System of Awards, the judges in Group 27 were attempting to secure a privileged position for their own area. This is what had been suggested by the original system of classification, in which "Plastic and Graphic Arts" had occupied the penultimate position, just below "Objects Illustrating Efforts for the Improvement of the Physical, Intellectual, and Moral Condition of Man," that is, social goods. But the sense of hierarchy among things was lost in the revised system. In its place, there was an apparent attempt to express the character if not the status of the different departments in the architecture of the exhibition: agriculture in an aggrandized barn; horticulture in an exotic "Moorish" greenhouse; machinery and manufactures in factory-like sheds.

With the exception of photography, which had its own building, and some exhibits that overflowed into the annex, the arts were displayed in the purpose-built museum of Memorial Hall. This had been designed as a permanent monument in a neoclassical style, which should have been a source of some distinction, but Memorial Hall was only one of five thematic buildings at the Centennial, and a relatively small one at that. As a result, the landscape suggested a certain equivalency between the different areas of the exhibition—a lack of hierarchy in which English painting was as important and worthy of attention as processed foods, a specimen palm, a sample of wrought-iron tubing, or a Renaissance Revival bedroom suite. The sameness of these things was stressed by the organizers' attempts to classify, install, and evaluate them all according to a single, comprehensive system.

In this situation, the authenticity and authority of the work of art, what

Walter Benjamin called its "aura," was in danger. The threat came not so much from the process of mechanical reproduction as from an environment and a system that celebrated this process.[43] The Centennial was, after all, an *industrial* fair; the work of art displayed in the hushed atmosphere of Memorial Hall was ultimately embedded in a larger context devoted to the factory and the machine. The fact that the exhibits in Memorial Hall contained both original works of art and mechanical reproductions only made the situation of the original that much more precarious, even if we admit that reproductions enjoyed more legitimacy in the nineteenth century than they do now.

The behavior of the judges in Group 27 can be seen, then, as an attempt to protect the aura of the art object, to secure its position in a culture whose values were becoming more and more commercial. Like the Centennial commissioners, who had declined to evaluate social goods like industrial products, the judges were drawing a line on commodification. They were attempting to define the boundaries of a process that was threatening to draw everything into the market, and that, by doing so, threatened to make everything the same. This is, of course, a problem that we still struggle with today.

THE COMMITTEE ON APPEALS

In addition to the rebellion of the judges on the Fine Arts, there was one other significant breakdown in the American System of Awards. The Centennial Commission was forced to establish a special Committee on Appeals to consider complaints from exhibitors whose products had been overlooked, or who felt otherwise wronged.[44] The five members of this committee nearly succeeded in subverting the entire system of awards, as recounted by the *Nation:* "At the 11th hour—after the better members of Commission had gone finally to their homes, and after the judges had dispersed to the four quarters of the globe—these persons succeeded in reopening the whole question and in securing certain rulings, which, but for the firmness and the honest indignation of Gen. Walker, Chief of the Bureau of Awards, and of Mr. Goshorn, the Director-General, would have defeated the whole scheme." As an example of what brought about this intervention, the magazine related the committee's success in securing an award for a particular western vintner, notwithstanding the conclusion of the regular judges that "the California product was not wine, or at least not such wine as could be properly recommended for public consumption."[45]

This behavior threatened the legitimacy of the entire system, based as it was on orderly, predictable, and transparent procedures. To restore some accountability to the system, the Centennial Commission was forced to appoint a second Group of Judges on Appeal to regulate the actions of the Committee on Appeals.[46] This new arrangement called for the committee to serve as a clearinghouse, examining and referring cases to the judges; they would make the actual recommendations for awards, which would be approved by the committee and adopted by the commission.[47] In spite of the arrangement, the appeals process resulted in 628 additional citations, many going to exhibitors whose products had already been rejected by the regular judges.[48]

For Walker, the appeals process was the single most important scandal of the exhibition. He allowed that the regular judges may have made some mistakes and overlooked some products, most likely because the exhibitors did not do their paperwork, but he insisted that the system of awards was basically fair, and he estimated that there were no more than a dozen exhibitors who, through no fault of their own, had not been visited by the judges. Worst of all, the Committee on Appeals had ignored its own policy of not accepting the cases of exhibitors whose products had already been fairly examined. Walker observed that "the Committee referred cases by the hundreds to the Judges on Appeals, without either consulting the Bureau of Awards or searching the records of the original groups to ascertain whether due examination had been made of the submitted; and, in some more flagrant instances, the Judges on Appeals were directed to take up cases where the Committee were distinctly advised by the Bureau of Awards that the products had been rejected for want of merit by the former groups."[49]

Walker also objected to the total number of awards, which had exploded to more than thirteen thousand (out of a total of some forty thousand exhibitors) as a result of the Centennial Commission's decision not to restrict the goods submitted for evaluation.[50] The decision meant that the judges were forced to consider what Walker called "petty exhibits"—"a can of maple syrup," "a pint of beans," "an embroidered bookmark"—things that we would expect to see at a county fair. In the competitive environment of an industrial fair, such artifacts were as compromised as a work of art. Some things were more equal than others in the museum of the exhibition, as Walker explained: "Now, it appears to me that a watch-maker, . . . who with great care fashions with his own hands two or three watches—to be displayed in an Exhibition—of a kind perhaps which he does not ordinarily make, may indeed be entitled to recognition for his skill and care and pains, but is not entitled to the same kind and degree of commendation as an [e]stablishment which turns out 200 watches a day, with absolute interchangeability of parts, and which ships its goods to every quarter of the globe."[51] This remark, which contains an oblique reference to the American System of Manufactures, is significant as a statement of industrial culture. It indicates an early privileging of the typical over the exceptional, the standardized over the singular, the products of the factory over those of the farm, house, and workshop. It is also significant because it calls for a policy of discrimination among things, and it was a comparable lack of discrimination that so upset the judges in Group 27.

REACTIONS TO THE AMERICAN SYSTEM

The explosion in the number of awards produced a concomitant swelling in the size of the collected judges' reports; the six volumes of the 1880 edition ran to 4,322 pages, not counting a 101-page index. Each part followed a standard format, consisting of a list of the judges assigned to that area of the exhibition, an appropriate excerpt from the Grouping for the Judges' Work, a general report summarizing progress in that area, the specific reports for each product receiving an award, another list of judges with the reports they had written, and a supplement describing the awards granted on appeal. Some of the general reports were quite short; others were major surveys, running to hundreds of pages and having some historical significance. A number were illustrated with precise technical engravings. Most of the specific reports on award were terse, single-sentence descriptions, not very different from the ones made by the judges in Group 27. In a few cases, the judges in other groups were inspired to write more extended justifications of their decisions.

An early edition of these reports was published in 1877–78 by J.B. Lippincott of Philadelphia. The company made them available by mail, at prices ranging from $.25 to $1.50 for each group. A complete set could be had for $20.00, with discounts of 10 to 30 percent provided to those who ordered in quantity; there was even a convenient order form.[52] The success of this venture is difficult to measure, since Lippincott's records burned in an 1899 fire.[53] But the demand was sufficient to justify a later edition, published by the Government Printing Office. A search of the catalogs (RLIN and OCLC) shows a surprisingly wide distribution of both issues: one hundred locations in twenty-seven states. Clearly, the reports were considered an important reference, something to be acquired by any major library, but it is difficult to imagine who actually read them, since the average person could turn to much livelier accounts in popular magazines, histories, and exhibition catalogs. This leaves an audience of specialists, which suggests that the Centennial was to some degree an "incomplete" project, at least as far as its direct impact on everyday life was concerned.

The evident shortcomings of the judges' reports helps to explain the mixed reaction to the American System of Awards. Walker considered it a success, as we would expect, but the Franklin Institute *Journal* regretted the abandonment of a system of graduated medals to recognize products of "special merit." As far as the *Journal* was concerned, "it is a prize and not a commendation that all competitors seek."[54] This argument continued to play out at future exhibitions. At the 1878 and 1889 fairs in Paris, the French reverted to a familiar system of graduated awards and elaborate juries, which was little changed from their earlier fairs. In contrast, the American organizers of the 1893 World's Columbian Exposition in Chicago adopted what they explicitly called the American System of Awards. This was after consulting Walker's and Goshorn's official reports on the Centennial Exhibition and involving William P. Blake in the development of the Chicago fair's system of classification.[55]

In crafting their own version of the American System, the organizers of the World's Columbian Exposition made two significant decisions. First, they incorporated the text of the award into the design of the certificate, suggesting that even the recipient could not be counted on to read the report. Second, they followed the precedent of the Centennial and other fairs in allowing the exhibitors to declare their displays *hors-concours,* that is, out of competition. This proved to be a mistake; once again, the American System provoked a revolt of the foreign commissioners, which was larger, more explicit, and ultimately more damaging than the one that had occurred in Philadelphia. Austria, Belgium, France, Germany, Great Britain, Italy, and Russia made a formal statement of their preference for a more conventional system of juries and awards. After Goshorn was called to testify, and the organizers affirmed their commitment to the American System, seventeen different countries, comprising most of the industrialized world, withdrew their exhibits from competition and refused to participate in the work of the juries. The organizers made some unspecified concessions, which lured most of these countries back into the system, but France and Norway maintained their boycott.[56] The president of the fair's board of directors summarized this sorry episode in terms both global and local:

The experience of expositions is that the subject of awards is not suscep-
tible of dignified and satisfactory treatment. Persons familiar with great
expositions have expressed the hope that a day may come when there shall
be no more judges, awards, medals, or diplomas. Whether this is the solution of the problem, or whether the feature of awards will some day attain
to a better a status, we can not tell. Two years after the close of the World's
Columbian Exposition the medals had not been distributed nor the reports
of the judges compiled. Should these reports be properly published by the
Government, and should they be found intelligent and impartial, they may
constitute a valuable landmark in the development of science and industry.
Otherwise nothing will have occurred in this branch of the World's
Columbian Exposition to give the subject of awards a better position than
it has hitherto occupied.[57]

That day did come, but not until forty years later. The occasion was the
1933 International Exposition in Chicago, dubbed "A Century of Progress"
after the city's first one hundred years. The organizers of the exposition
repudiated the jury system in whatever form, stating that "the competitive
idea of other fairs is not in the modern spirit."[58] As a result, there were no
prizes, and the exposition, which had as its philosophy "the service of science as applied in that industry for the comfort of man," emphasized the
display of industrial process as much as the product itself.[59] This was a
decisive historical moment, which marked the transition between an earlier
phase of object-obsessed exhibitions and a later phase of image-oriented
world's fairs.[60]

THE SAMENESS OF THINGS

Coleman Sellers was one of the Judges on Appeals, in addition to being a
mechanical engineer and the author of an article about the American System of Awards, which was published in the Franklin Institute *Journal*. In
addressing the tedium of the judges' reports, he admitted that the authors
had undoubtedly "been compelled to use the same language in commenting
on many similar objects, but in so doing they simply say that these exhibits
are of equal value."[61] Whether consciously or not, Sellers was acknowledging the power of the exhibition to disable difference, not only between goods
of the same class but also between different classes of goods. In part, this
was simply an aspect of commodification, but it was also an inherent feature of a universalizing project like the exhibition, in which everything was

present and accounted for in the same way.[62] In such a collection, there were really no masterpieces, in spite of the claims made by the title of a prominent illustrated catalog of the Centennial.[63]

So it is that the exhibition was at cross-purposes with itself. It was an enemy of cultural distinction, of the kind that it was set up to make, as well as of the kind that the judges in Group 27 took for granted. But it was also an enemy of national distinction, which formed the ultimate basis of the fair, whatever its design. Looking back on the Centennial, Walker observed that "international exhibitions are doing a work in which good is not accomplished. . . . I refer to the leveling influence exercised by the close juxtaposition and comparison of the products of different countries."[64]

This perception of a "leveling influence" suggests a contrarian explanation for the dramatic expansion of American art that took place in the late nineteenth century. The Centennial has long been considered an instrument of the expansion, which resulted in the founding of so many new museums, schools, and art associations.[65] There is some truth to this perception; the exhibition was certainly associated with the founding of a museum and school in Philadelphia and with the construction of a Frank Furness–designed gallery for the Pennsylvania Academy of Fine Art, also in Philadelphia, as well as the Smithsonian's Arts and Industries Building in Washington, D.C. But the expansion of American art as a larger and more general phenomenon had begun some time before the Centennial and is more properly viewed as being associated with the end of the Civil War, however much it was stimulated by the exhibition.[66]

The best that can be said about all these establishments is that they formed part of a network of display-oriented institutions, which was growing in response to the growth of the material world. This kinship was recognized by the Centennial classification, which put museums and exhibitions in the same category of "social goods." In the museum, the status of the art object as a commodity is obscured; acquisition suggests a kind of apotheosis in which the artifact passes beyond the realm of the market. In the museum, the object's value appears to be established and its circulation discontinued, even though we know that it may be returned to the market, and that, until then, it continues to influence the value of other objects still in circulation. In the exhibition, where consumption may have been deferred but was never denied, and the status of every thing flickered back and forth between commodity and object lesson, the situation of the art object was considerably more volatile. It is this volatility that the organizers of the Centennial were attempting to suppress with their classification, and that the judges in Group 27 were opposing with their rebellion against the American System of Awards. In the same sense, it is possible to give the new art institutions of this period a collective interpretation: they were a bid to stabilize the value of a specialized realm of knowledge, to state its meaning in terms at once public and concrete, in an environment where the art object was in danger of losing its aura and becoming just another commodity. From this point of view, the institutions can be seen not as signs of cultural maturity, as some historians have presented them, but as symptoms of a deep cultural anxiety about the value of things in the modern world.[67]

6

THE EXHIBITIONARY COMPLEX IN PHILADELPHIA

> Whether for display or for adjudication, a classification, instead of being a matter of exquisite and refined theory, is the most purely practical thing in connection with an exhibition of arts and industries. The disposition to refine and multiply distinctions is one which will always be strongly felt, but it should be stoutly resisted. A few score of broad natural divisions are all that are required. Whatever is more than this comes of the great enemy of all world's fairs. It took the Commission somewhat more than four years to find out that classifications are made for exhibitions—not exhibitions for classifications.
>
> —Francis Walker, "The Philadelphia Exhibition"

In trying to explain the complex character of the exhibition, period observers like Patrick Geddes resorted to a variety of institutional analogies. In *Industrial Exhibitions and Modern Progress* (1887), the Scottish biologist and sociologist wrote that an upcoming Glasgow fair could take shape "as an extended shop-window, music saloon, and refreshment bar of unparalleled lustre and magnificence." Alternatively, the fair could develop "as a true museum, somewhat less partial and confused, of real material and social progress in the immediate past, and a school, somewhat more effective and inspiring, of these in the immediate future." Competitive display must be a factor in the design of the fair, he argued, "for unless our ultimate products are brought here together to be criticised and compared, they have come simply to be sold, and our incipient museum can never be more than the mere bazaar it is at present." He repeated this dichotomy in other places, stating, for example, that "40 bazaars will never make one museum."[1]

The meaning of the term *bazaar* may not be entirely clear in this context. According to the *Oxford English Dictionary*, it derives from the Persian language, its oldest sense dating back to the fourteenth century: "An Oriental market-place or permanent market, usually consisting of ranges of shops or stalls, where all kinds of merchandise are offered for sale." A second sense came into use at the beginning of the nineteenth century: "A fancy fair in imitation of the Eastern bazaar; *esp.* a sale of useful and ornamental articles, in behalf of some charitable or religious object. Also used of a shop, or arcade of shops, displaying an assortment of fancy goods."[2] For someone like Geddes, then, a bazaar was a kind of market, a store or complex of stores selling fancy or ornamental fabrics, such as ribbons, silks, and laces.[3] It had connotations of the commercial, the exotic, the ephemeral, and the female, which accounts for his concern about the character of the exhibition.

The dichotomy of the bazaar and the museum was a symptom of anxiety about the market, mainly, as evidenced in the previous chapter by the rebellion of the judges on painting. It was also a symptom of anxiety about the exhibition itself, which was an exceedingly ambiguous institution—not quite museum and not quite market. William Blake had addressed this condition in 1872 in his report as executive commissioner. Here he acknowledged the economic impact of world's fairs, while stressing their broad educational benefits for the entire population: "We are accustomed to recognize the value of such exhibitions for the immediate effects in the promotion of industry and the arts, but the vast aggregate of instruction given by them, not alone to citizens, but to all classes of the people, is a phase of their utility which is too often overlooked or is not sufficiently recognized."[4]

Like the museum, but even more so, the exhibition was an institution of popular education. The Pennsylvania state commissioners, for example, called the Centennial "a school of incomparable excellence."[5] But what kind of lessons did this school provide? In general, the people who visited the exhibition learned about new inventions in a variety of areas, but also about the idea of progress and their relationship to other people—all races, nations, and cultures. They learned about themselves as defined against these others. In a more fundamental sense, they learned about the market— what was available, what was desirable. As anthropologist Burton Benedict has succinctly observed, "People were to be educated about what to buy, but more basically they were to be taught to want more things, better quality things and quite new things."[6] At the same time, they learned that the world was a much bigger place than they had ever imagined it to be, acquiring imperial tastes at a time when consumption was still relatively local.

In this sense, the exhibition represented a global market in which the goods that were on display were also, in some way, for sale. Many of these things—fabric samples or lumps of coal, for example—were of little intrinsic value and were merely suggestive of exchanges that might occur at another place and time. But many of the more expensive things were actually there to be sold, so that the impact of the exhibition can be at least partly explained by the direct transfer of goods from the hall to the home. After the Centennial had closed, a correspondent to *American Architect and Building News* described this phenomenon precisely and intimately: "It is very interesting in many of our private houses to fall in with numerous objects which in the Exhibition we had grown to regard and admire as old friends; and then, too[,] it is not unfrequently quite as amusing to observe the knowing way in which their present possessors talk of them, when one considers that, prior to the opening of the Exhibition, many of these same good people were not aware that such objects were manufactured."[7]

The acquisitive fever induced by the display of so much desirable stuff turned the simplest transaction into a spectacular event, which drew a rapt, even aggressively curious, crowd, as described by a writer in the *Atlantic Monthly:*

> The interest taken in any purchase by the by-standers is so intense as to be painful to the purchaser; a ring forms immediately round the latter and the vendor, which increases momentarily until the transaction is over, all hanging speechless on the dialogue between the two. . . . A lady acquaintance told me that just as her purchase was concluded and the article replaced in the case, so that it became indistinguishable among its fellows, a stranger of her own sex arrived on the scene, and seeing that it was too late, dogged her until they reached a secluded spot in one of the less frequented departments; then she accosted her in a low voice: "You bought something just now." "Yes." "What was it?"

If viewing a purchase could cause this kind of impertinence, the mere prospect of a sale could impel an observer to cross the boundary of display. This is what happened at an English exhibit, where the young male attendants were failing to properly demonstrate the use of an Indian shawl to a potential customer. One of the more aroused onlookers was moved to show her own female competence: "a very nice-looking middle-aged woman with an ardent gaze stepped from the circle, took it from their hands, gave it in a trice the proper twist, and then turning about deftly threw it over her own shoulders and stood there on exhibition until everybody concerned or not concerned was satisfied."[8] Thus, the observer became the observed.

Whether museum or market, the exhibition provided a powerful and historically significant lesson in looking. It was part of a "vast system of eye education," as one source put it, which instructed visitors in the gaze of the modern consumer.[9] To the extent that markets have always existed, there was nothing new about this kind of desiring, devouring, discriminating looking. Yet the exhibition acquainted people with new strategies of display, signifying new grounds of knowledge. These strategies implied a new kind of relationship between subject and object, a relationship of projection and intimacy that sits at the heart of our commodified culture. The simple surfeit of things called forth the consumer's greedy eye, infatuated with things but never truly satisfied, even as the same surfeit promised the illusory satisfaction of every desire. This was truly the phantasmagoria, the ancestor of Debord's displacing, distracting spectacle.

The institutional ambiguity of the exhibition was expressed by an extended debate over price tags. At the Great Exhibition, there was considerable disagreement about whether exhibitors should be required to indicate the cost of their goods, whether they should be merely permitted to provide such information, or even prohibited from doing so. The organizers eventually decided that the jurors should consider cost in making awards. Significantly: "They were not, however, prepared to call upon Exhibitors in all cases to affix prices partly because they were unwilling that the Exhibition should bear the appearance of a bazaar for the sale of goods."[10] The specter of value continued to loom at later fairs; at the 1855 Exposition universelle, the French permitted exhibitors to indicate cost, leading one English critic to conclude that the exposition had been reduced to the level of an "immense bazaar."[11] At the 1873 Weltausstellung, the Austrians permitted exhibitors to specify price along with other useful information "on labels attached to each article."[12] As we have seen, the organizers of the Centennial adopted the same policy.

Clearly, there was a certain amount of buying and selling going on at the exhibition, although observers disagreed about its propriety. Geddes disapproved, as did our unnamed English critic, but Francis Walker endorsed the practice, arguing that it enhanced the experience of visitors and defrayed the expenses of exhibitors. He feared, however, that the proper function of the fair might be overwhelmed by an excess of commercial activity:

But where the prime object of the individual exhibitor is the sale of goods, the true end of an exhibition is likely to be soon lost sight of; and this may easily be carried so far as to lower the tone and impair the effect of the entire exhibition. The so-called bazaars outside the Exhibition buildings at Philadelphia, in which thinly disguised Germans or Irishmen sold sacred relics or the characteristic wares of various oriental countries, . . . were perhaps well enough in the same view which tolerates the peanut-stand and the soda-fountain; but it was hard to have patience with the traffic which, from opening to close of the Exhibition, went on, through a great part of the Italian and not a little of the French sections of the Main Building, in the pettiest and cheapest wares. The amount of rubbish thus "unloaded" upon the American public was enormous.[13]

Walker's commentary speaks of a familiar but not misplaced anxiety. In addition to functioning as a bazaar in the metaphorical sense, the Centennial accommodated a number of quite literal markets. Anna Baker, a Philadelphia woman who kept a diary of her experiences at the exhibition, recalled visiting the Turkish and Japanese bazaars, which took the form of freestanding pavilions.[14] Similar attractions included a Tunisian coffee house as well as three small wooden structures—"Eastern bazaars on a small scale"—for the sale of sponges and religious souvenirs.[15] The evidence demonstrates that commerce was not restricted to such specialized structures; a photograph of the Spanish section in the Main Building shows a typical vitrine with two signs, one announcing the receipt of a prize medal, the other advising customers to apply at the section office (fig. 6-1). Baker herself made a number of purchases, including a set of china from an exhibitor in the English department.[16] She was not alone; *Atlantic Monthly* reported that Americans had "bought . . . from the costly enamels and porcelains of China and Japan to the coarse pottery of different nations," and that "all the best objects of bronze, brass, terra-cotta, china, and embroidery" had "long been sold, and ordered in duplicate, sometimes 20 times over."[17] Such transactions did not escape the scrutiny of customs officials. Congress had provided for the free importation of goods displayed at the Centennial, but anything sold or consumed at the exhibition was subject to the normal tariff, which averaged 40.6 percent in 1875. Anything donated to the government or to public, educational, or charitable institutions was exempt from the tariff.[18] This policy must have had something to do with the vast quantity of material—twenty-one freight cars worth, in addition to the twenty-one cars originally sent to the exhibition—which the curator, George Brown

6-1. "Damascene Ware—Spain. Northwest view of Elkington and Company's exhibit" (CPC 2227, Print and Picture Collection, Free Library of Philadelphia).

Goode, sent back to the Smithsonian Institution in Washington, D.C. To deal with this increase in the size of the Smithsonian's collections, Congress appropriated funds for a new museum, the Arts and Industries Building, next door to the institution's existing home on the Mall.[19]

As the Smithsonian case illustrates, there was a real and intimate relationship between the museum and the exhibition. This was an effect of the exhibition's own collection—the arguments it made, the opportunities it provided, the habits it engendered. London's Victoria and Albert Museum had its origin in a group of objects obtained at the 1851 Great Exhibition, some donated and others purchased with the aid of a forty-five-thousand-dollar grant from the British Parliament.[20] Furthermore, the museum's home in South Kensington was built with surplus funds from the exhibition.[21] Similar connections can be drawn between the 1873 Weltausstellung and the Technische Museum in Vienna; the 1893 World's Columbian Exhibition, the Field Museum of Natural History, and the Museum of Science and Industry in Chicago; the 1893 fair and the Commercial Museum in Philadelphia; the 1894 Midwinter Exhibition and the De Young Museum in San Francisco; the 1901 Pan-American Exposition and the Albright Art Gallery in Buffalo; the 1915 Panama-California Exposition and the Museum of Man in San Diego.[22] Finally, there was a direct connection between the Centennial and the Pennsylvania Museum and School of Industrial Art. The latter was established in Memorial Hall, with a collection of objects purchased at the exhibition.

Again, the relationship between these institutions is evident in the language of the period. *American Architect* declared the Centennial "a museum par excellence."[23] The Board of Finance called it "a museum of the products of the world."[24] Expanding on this analogy, the *Philadelphia Press* described the exhibition as "a popular museum, a training school, an academy of design, a vast study for the common people."[25] Inversely, Blake cited a reference to museums as "Permanent Exhibitions," implying that one was the outcome of the other.[26] Such language recognized a growing network of spectacular institutions, which included the museum, the exhibition, and the department store, in addition to the arcade and the panorama. This network, which Tony Bennett has termed the "exhibitionary complex," emerged between the late eighteenth and mid-nineteenth centuries, at the same time as the "carceral archipelago," as Foucault called it, and its disciplinary institutions—the prison, the factory, the barracks, the school, and the hospital.[27]

The roots of the exhibitionary complex in Philadelphia are deep, reaching back to a cabinet of mechanical models, scientific specimens, and historical artifacts, which the American Philosophical Society had begun to assemble by 1768.[28] Charles Willson Peale established what was probably the first American museum, probably dating to 1786, in which he displayed portraits of famous men and natural history specimens.[29] Later institutions became more specialized. The first American art museum and school, the

Pennsylvania Academy of Fine Art, was founded in 1805; the Academy of Natural Sciences, claiming to be the oldest institution of its type in the Western Hemisphere, followed in 1812.[30] The Franklin Institute, established in 1824, organized its own cabinet of mechanical models and mineral specimens and began a series of competitive exhibitions that continued over the next fifty years.[31] The merchant, William Wagner, founded his Free Institute of Science in 1855, and John McArthur designed the institute's new building (1859–65), which contained a museum of natural history.[32] Even the Civil War proved to be no obstacle to the expansion of the city's exhibitionary complex. In 1864, a group of temporary buildings in Logan Square (now Logan Circle) housed the largest of the fairs held to raise money for the U.S. Sanitary Commission, an organization caring for sick and wounded soldiers.[33] By the time of the Centennial, Philadelphia could also boast what was supposed to be the beginnings of a national museum in Independence Hall, in addition to a mile-long market on Girard Street; a thirty-three-acre zoo, the oldest in the country, which was located in the western part of Fairmount Park, not far from the exhibition; and a medical museum at the College of Physicians, which included Dr. T.D. Mutter's infamous collection of anatomical specimens.[34]

It is evident that the Centennial provided some kind of a boost to this complex of institutions. The anniversary of American independence inspired both the Academy of Natural Sciences and the Academy of Fine Arts to build substantial new homes for their collections.[35] As we saw in the previous chapter, many have credited the exhibition with propelling a national movement that included the creation of new art associations, museums, and schools. Since the Centennial's reach beyond Philadelphia is difficult to substantiate, this chapter will focus on the real, demonstrable impact of the exhibition on three local institutions that emerged in its wake—the International Exhibition Company, the Pennsylvania Museum and School of Industrial Art, and the Grand Depot, John Wanamaker's department store. What follows is a brief account of their origins, their relationships to the exhibition and to each other, and the ways in which the problems of the exhibition—order, architecture, installation, display, and evaluation—were articulated across the entire complex of institutions.

THE PERMANENT EXHIBITION

The Centennial, like all good things, had to come to an end. The commission was asked to prolong the exhibition, but it decided to close the fair as planned on November 10, 1876.[36] After six months in which the Centennial had absorbed the attention of the entire city, if not the whole country, it must have seemed incredible that the entire landscape of the exhibition could just disappear. In fact, it would have a lasting impact on the fabric of Fairmount Park, as had always been planned. The improvements made by Herman J. Schwarzmann—the draining, grading, and planting of the fairground—had permanently changed the appearance of the park's western area. The elaborate fountain erected by the Catholic Temperance Union would remain, as would other works of public art and several structures—Memorial and Horticultural Halls; the Queen Anne–style British commissioner's building; the Ohio state pavilion, consisting of twenty-one different kinds of Ohio stone and probably too difficult to take down.[37] Many other buildings were auctioned off, removed from the fairground, and reconstructed in other locations.[38] But the Centennial's principal feature, the 1,880-foot-long Main Exhibition Building, seemed doomed by size alone. "Everyone is well satisfied," reported *American Architect and Building News,* "that the cost of keeping the Main Building in repair must preclude the possibility of keeping it standing for either public or private purposes, even if there were any enterprise that would need so large a building." Undaunted, the Franklin Institute contacted similar organizations in New York, Baltimore, and Boston, hoping to form an association to sponsor annual exhibitions of American industry in the building—an expansion on the series that the institute had been holding since 1824.[39] Some still feared that this enormous structure would be sold, dismantled, and reerected in another, competing city. For a time it seemed that a New York company would do just that.[40]

Into the breach stepped a group of men led by merchant and philanthropist Clement M. Biddle; many had previously been involved with the Centennial.[41] Toward the end of October 1876, this group formed the International Exhibition Company (IEC), with the intention of establishing a permanent exhibition in Fairmount Park.[42] As described in the IEC's *Official Bulletin,* the company was a public-spirited venture; the exhibition would be an improved version of the 1876 fair.[43] In fact, what the company was trying to create was the kind of popular attraction that had already been established at the reconstructed Crystal Palace at Sydenham—a winter park set in a pleasure garden, providing "light education packaged as entertainment."[44]

The IEC purchased the Main Building at auction for $250,000—considerably less than its original cost of $1.76 million.[45] The commissioners of Fairmount Park, in their eagerness to clear the fairground, had originally intended to tear everything down as soon as possible, but they eventually allowed the Main Building to remain standing.[46] The commissioners granted a license to the IEC, which specified that the company use the building and the surrounding grounds only to hold an exhibition "for the pleasure and instruction of the public"—learning and leisure combined. The license forbade the sale of goods in the building "except such as may be necessary for carrying out the design of said Exhibition Company under their charter"— an ambiguous provision that brings to mind the previously discussed anxiety about the market. Finally, it allowed the company to charge admission to the exhibition but limited revenues to an amount equal to "all needful expenses, additions, repairs and maintenance," plus 6 percent interest paid to investors and another, unspecified percentage contributed to a "sinking fund" to pay off the debt.[47] At the time, 6 percent was considered a reasonable rate of return for a profit-making but public-spirited venture.

Like the 1876 fair, the permanent exhibition was supposed to be financed by the sale of stock. Several meetings were held at city hall to drum up public support, but the main subscribers turned out to be Philadelphia's "large wholesale business men"—the merchants who might be expected to have an interest in this new project.[48] In fact, much of the capital was recycled from the Centennial itself. In April 1877, *American Architect* reported that the IEC had raised a nominal sum of $630,000, consisting of $130,000 in cash and $500,000 in stock that had originally been issued by the Board of Finance. Unfortunately, the value of this stock had been reduced by a decision of the U.S. Supreme Court, which found that a $1.5 million appropriation by Congress was a loan to the exhibition, not a gift. The Board of Finance was thus required to reimburse the Treasury before making a return to the stockholders, and the actual value of the sum raised by the IEC was significantly reduced to $280,000.[49]

In spite of this setback, the Permanent International Exhibition opened as scheduled on May 10, 1877. According to *Harper's Weekly,* the people of Philadelphia responded with an enthusiasm that recalled the opening of the Centennial exactly one year earlier. A huge crowd, estimated at one point to number twenty-five thousand people, packed the Main Building to hear President Rutherford B. Hayes open the permanent exhibition. The afternoon ceremonies included performances of Handel's *Hallelujah Chorus* and the *Centennial Hymn* written by John Greenleaf Whittier and John K. Paine for the opening of the 1876 fair. A.T. Goshorn, the fair's director-general, and John Welsh, the highly regarded president of the Board of Finance, both spoke, thus lending their support to the project.[50]

An engraved view of the ceremonies shows some of the alterations that had been made to the Main Building under the direction of Henry Pettit, the new head of the IEC's Bureau of Management (fig. 6-2). During the Centennial, the building had functioned as something of a concert hall, with performances taking place in various locations—at the bandstand, on the organs in the mezzanines, in the exhibits of musical instruments in the American section. Pettit's alterations created a more formal arrangement that accommodated the large musical spectacles of the period, while reminding visitors of the reconstructed Crystal Palace at Sydenham. A stepped orchestra gallery had been built in the north end of the transept, accommodating twenty-five hundred performers and linking the existing Roosevelt organ with the floor of the hall. Arcades connecting the organ with the north towers provided additional overviews and framed an eight-thousand-seat auditorium. Light was provided by five "colossal chandeliers"—significant additions, given the fact that, although the Main Building was originally provided with gas jets, the 1876 fair had not been open at night for fear of fire.[51]

In spite of these alterations, the architecture of the permanent exhibition was basically unchanged; the order, however, had undergone signifi-

6-2. "The Permanent Exhibition, Philadelphia—Opening Day," by F.B. Schell (*Harper's Weekly* 21, no. 1065 [26 May 1877]: 413, Library of Congress).

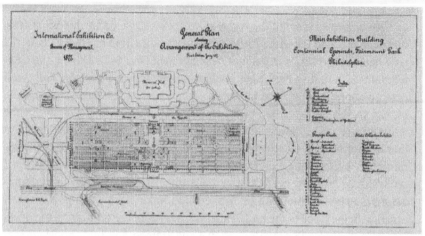

6-3. "General Plan showing Arrangement of the Exhibition. International Exhibition Company. Autograph: "Diagram showing how the different 'departments' and exhibits were rearranged after the Centennial, for the new Exhibition of 1877" (Pettit, "Centennial Exhibition," 1:63, Historical Society of Pennsylvania architectural drawings collection on loan to the Athenaeum). *Enlarged plate appears on page 242 of the appendix.*

cant revision. Instead of the Centennial's decimal classification, the organizers of the permanent exhibition had adopted a new system of thirty categories. This might seem to recall the classification of the Great Exhibition; in fact, it was based on a system used at the smaller 1872 Polytechnic Exhibition in Moscow, which the Committee on Classification had once consulted.[52] The significance of this revision is not clear. The permanent exhibition was not competitive; the organizers had also abandoned the American System of Awards, so the classification did not have to serve as a guide to the judges. Nor did it provide a blueprint for the installation, since the arrangement of displays reflected not the order of the exhibition but its bureaucratic structure in eight administrative departments: Education, Publication, Musical, Art, Industrial, Machinery, Agricultural, and Public Comfort.

The Centennial's dual system survived only in the sense that the plan of the permanent exhibition combined administrative departments with national courts (fig. 6-3). These were vestiges of the 1876 fair, which had been donated by foreign governments and reassembled in the nave. This arrangement, again similar to the one at Sydenham, was supposed to be a boon for those unable to travel, while providing pleasant mementos for the veteran of the Grand Tour: "The display of Austrian bent-wood furniture will take the traveled beholder in memory back to the Ringstrasse and the *shoene blaue Donau,* the Russian malachite will transport him back to the Isaac Cathedral at St. Petersburg, while the Italian glassware, mosaics, and jewelry will recall the Lido, the Doge's Palace, and the 'Piazza.'"[53] Like all souvenirs, these mementos were intended to awaken the memory, to bridge the interval between past and present. But unlike the relatively worthless souvenirs of nature—shells, stones, pressed flowers—these mementos were goods, things for the house and body, that equated travel and consumption. In the displays of furniture, malachite, glassware, mosaics, and jewelry, travel not only was verified by consumption, as tourists do with souvenirs, but also was, in some sense, obviated by it. Thus, travel became a form of consumption—of objects and experiences. Inversely, consumption became a form of travel in which one experienced the world through its objects.

In this form, the permanent exhibition became the subject of some familiar educational metaphors. The *Bulletin* described it as an encyclopedia, as a "Universal Museum," and as "the natural outcome of our Centennial," just as the Victoria and Albert Museum was the outcome of the Great Exhibition.[54] Publisher and politician John W. Forney's inventory of the exhibits—"all enclosed in an edifice so light, harmonious, and comprehensive, as to constitute one great school in itself"—completes this list.[55] It should come as no surprise, then, to find that the Education Department was promoted as one of the main features of the permanent exhibition. Among its other attractions, the department included a number of fully furnished model school rooms, comparable as examples of contextual display to the dioramas and model rooms of the Centennial.[56] This emphasis on learning may have been a reflection of Biddle's own interests—he had helped to found Swarthmore College, and in 1877 was establishing the first kindergarten in Philadelphia[57]—or perhaps it institutionalized what people already understood to be the mission of the exhibition.

In spite of all this rhetoric, the permanent exhibition was clearly not a school in any conventional sense. It was an institution of popular education, which combined learning and leisure. In a speech before a crowd of people in the Main Building, John William Wallace, author, legal scholar, and president of the Historical Society of Pennsylvania (1868–84), described the exhibition as "a school of instruction and a place of rational recreation."[58] The *Bulletin* for its part assured readers that "amusement will be blended with instruction."[59] The Centennial, of course, had had its amusement zone, the so-called Centennial City, but this was located outside the fairground, beyond the control of the organizers. With Elm Avenue serving as a *cordon sanitaire,* the 1876 fair was beyond the reach of the amusement zone and was therefore free of its taint. In contrast, the permanent exhibition was a promiscuous combination of these two Centennials, which helps to explain why it was in perpetual danger of becoming something less edifying than its organizers proposed. *American Architect* had warned of this possibility before the exhibition started. While noting its advantages for a manufacturing city like Philadelphia and citing its value as "a school of instruction to our manufacturers and workmen," the magazine cautioned against following too closely the example of the reconstructed Crystal Palace:

> It is said that the president of the new exhibition has been studying carefully the scheme of the Crystal Palace Exhibition at Sydenham. We have read a saying of Byron's, that when he would write a poetical romance he read all the others that he could find, so as to know what not to introduce into his own. It may be hoped that a similar forethought guards the president's study of that rather seedy establishment, which has degenerated into little else than a place of cheap popular amusement. It is to be hoped too, that the Philadelphia exhibition will be preserved from the danger of becoming a mere bazaar for the exhibition of wares on sale, a danger which besets all great exhibitions, and becomes serious when they are made permanent.[60]

In fact, the *Bulletin* was quite frank in defining the original purpose of the permanent exhibition as "creating a bazaar for the exposition and sale of goods and a place for refined amusement"—commodities linked to the commodification of leisure. In spite of the restrictions imposed by its license, the IEC not only allowed business to take place in the Main Building but also took a cut on the proceeds—5 percent on orders for future delivery and 10 percent on the sales of goods on display.[61]

What the *Bulletin* meant by "refined amusement" is amply illustrated by the other attractions of the permanent exhibition: the proposed fifteen-thousand-square-foot aquarium; the New England Log Cabin, a well-known feature of the Centennial, now amplified by an Indian encampment; the diorama of Washington reviewing the troops at Yorktown; Dr. Charles Hoffnagle's collection of Indian and Chinese curiosities, including relics from Washington's house at Germantown; Professor M.W. Dickenson's "microcosm of the Arts and Sciences," consisting of "200,000 specimens of medals, minerals, fossils, coins, shells, relics of the Mound-builders, etc.," not to mention "a small case illustrating botany by conchology, flowers of all kinds made from shells," which was the handiwork of Dickenson's sisters.[62] In addition to these attractions, there were a series of extravaganzas like the one held on July 5, 1880. The program for this event included a trumpet salute from the four towers of the crossing; a bicycle parade; a series of military exercises; a formal ceremony in honor of Independence Day; a "carnival" or procession of people in Chinese costume; a number of organ recitals; an "illumination" of the building, first by gas, then by "prismatic lights" producing colored effects; and, finally, a demonstration of interior and exterior lighting by the United States Electric Lighting Company.[63]

Such fare may have been popular with the crowd, but it was not enough to save the permanent exhibition. The exact chronology of failure is difficult to establish, but it is clear that the exhibition was plagued by financial problems from the start. In August 1877, only months after the opening, the IEC was forced to make an appeal for public support, in the form of fifty thousand dollars in new subscriptions.[64] By December, the *New York Times* was reporting that the directors were struggling to keep the exhibition from falling into the hands of the sheriff.[65] Their creditors eventually agreed to exchange stock for debt, and the Board of Finance wrote off the mortgage on the Main Building. (A report to the IEC's stockholders states that the board actually received the sum of forty thousand dollars, contributed by "four of Philadelphia's most liberal and enterprising citizens" in exchange for another mortgage on the building.[66]) By January 1879, the company's finances appear to have improved, and the exhibition, which had been closed for refurbishing, reopened in May.[67] But the *Times* reported in August that "the Permanent Exhibition has received a blow from the effects of which it is staggering and must, at no distant day, fall dead." For reasons that went unexplained, the Fairmount Park commissioners had rescinded the IEC license and had notified the company that it would have two years to remove the Main Building and its contents from the park.[68] The commissioners reversed this action the following April, again for unexplained reasons.[69]

Wallace's 1881 speech appears to have been the swan song of the permanent exhibition. He alluded to organizational problems and the difficulty of forming a coherent collection from the flotsam of the 1876 fair: "Of course, in the first moments of a suddenly made purchase . . . everything could not be either planned or administered exactly as everyone wished, or as the managers designed. A little time, some consideration, and some experience were indispensable in order to translate what remained of a great body of things which had been brought together for the Exhibition of a season, into a system quite different, and which should be of use for enjoyment continuously and for years." Brandishing a copy of the latest *Bulletin,* and rising to his full rhetorical stature, Wallace added this peroration on the autonomy of objects and the authority of a well-ordered collection: "Shall this majestic edifice, so charmingly harmonious, so richly filled with objects of beauty and of use, stand? Shall this comprehensive plan of education in art, in science, and, greater still, in what assists domestic comfort and the happiness of homes, have in this our city its full effect? Need I ask such a question here? Where is the man that will dare to lay his rude and ruthless hand—to scatter and to destroy them—upon the collections before us; classified with skill, so clearly and with such impressiveness; themselves explaining their purpose, their connexion and dependencies." The three hundredth anniversary of Philadelphia was fast approaching, and Wallace proposed to celebrate this occasion in the Main Building, but to no avail.[70] In January 1881, the *Times* reported that "the Directors of the Permanent Exhibition have decided to recommend to shareholders that the show be closed, the exhibits removed, the building sold, and the affairs of the concern wound up."[71] The Main Building was sold to a B.C. Mitchell for a sum of ninety-seven thousand dollars, and demolition began by December.[72] The affairs of the IEC were settled, however slowly.[73] It was not until March 1883 that the stockholders decided to dissolve the company, at what appears to have been their last meeting.[74]

THE PENNSYLVANIA MUSEUM

In an odd way, the destruction of the Main Building after the failure of the permanent exhibition brought the design of the Centennial to completion, since Memorial Hall was finally visible from Elm Avenue. The center of the art department at the 1876 fair, Memorial Hall had been conceived as a monument to the country's anniversary and as a permanent addition to Fairmount Park (see fig. 3-5). In contrast to nearly all the other buildings of the fair, the 365-foot-long structure with its 150-foot-high dome had been constructed in permanent materials—granite, glass, and iron. It had also been given a prominent site on Lansdowne Terrace but had remained concealed from the street as long as the IEC continued to operate its bazaar in the Main Building. This forced the museum that came to occupy Memorial Hall into a surprisingly complicated relationship with the bazaar.

John Maass made some large and largely unsubstantiated claims for the design of Memorial Hall in his biography of Schwarzmann, who was responsible for the design.[75] It is really quite conventional, recalling the

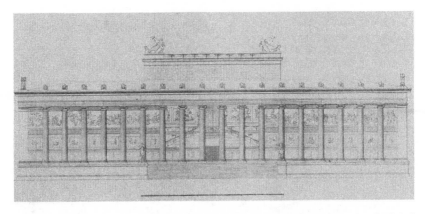

6-4. Altes Museum, front elevation, by Karl Friedrich Schinkel (Karl Friedrich Schinkel, *Sammlung Architektonischer Entwürfe* [Berlin: Ernst & Korn, 1866], 37).

form of Schinkel's Altes Museum in Berlin (1822–30), with a symmetrical, figure-eight plan and a projecting stair leading through a vestibule into a central rotunda; the resemblance is heightened by the use of monumental sculpture as points of emphasis. The two buildings vary primarily in style; the Altes Museum is Greek Revival, while Schwarzmann designed Memorial Hall in what he called the "Modern Renaissance"—a term associated with the late neoclassicism of the École des Beaux-Arts (fig. 6-4, 6-5, and 6-6). Again in contrast to the Altes Museum, the main spaces of Memorial Hall were all arranged on one story, obviating the need for a grand interior staircase; the corners and midpoints of the long facades were emphasized by projecting pavilions; the "rotunda" was squared and domed; and the colonnade and open courtyards of the museum were replaced by the arcades, pavilions, and enclosed galleries of the hall. But the basic organization remained the same.

Whatever its pedigree, critical reaction to Memorial Hall was tepid, if not entirely negative.[76] William Dean Howells damned it with faint praise, observing that the building, although disfigured by two large bronze statues of Pegasus on either side of the main entrance, was "otherwise conventionally well enough."[77] Explaining the purpose of the building, a writer in *Canadian Monthly* sniffed, "The gallery was erected by the state of Pennsylvania as a memorial to the event, and is intended to be a permanent ornament of Fairmount Park. It is certainly massive enough to be permanent, but cannot by any interpretation be accounted an ornament."[78] A correspondent to *American Architect* went even further, describing Memorial Hall as "a building which almost from the outset has been among educated people regarded

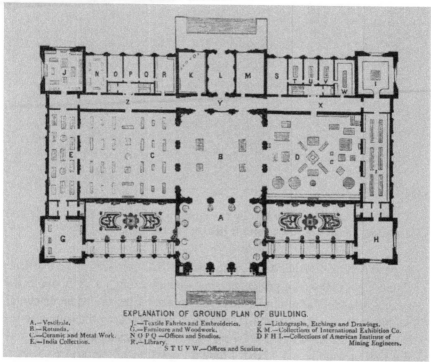

EXPLANATION OF GROUND PLAN OF BUILDING.

A.—Vestibule.   J.—Textile Fabrics and Embroideries.   Z.—Lithographs, Etchings and Drawings.
B.—Rotunda.   G.—Furniture and Woodwork.   K M.—Collections of International Exhibition Co.
C.—Ceramic and Metal Work.   N O P Q —Offices and Studios.   D F H I.—Collections of American Institute of
E.—India Collection.   R.—Library   Mining Engineers.
             S T U V W.—Offices and Studios.

6-5. "Explanation of Ground Plan of Building." Pennsylvania Museum and School of Industrial Art (Pennsylvania Museum, *First and Second Reports*, n.p., Library of Congress).

as so far from being a success, that it is beginning to be very generally regretted that such a work should stand any chance of going down to posterity as representative of the architecture of the period." He cited poor construction, bad ornament, and misrepresented structure; he was particularly disturbed by the consoles in the rotunda, which appeared to support the dome but were in fact hung from it. By contrast, the forthright design of the hall's admittedly temporary neighbors provided a more admirable example of American building: "It is hardly too much to say that Mr. Petit's [*sic*] frank, honest, and masterly construction, open and apparent to everyone, in the Main Building and Machinery Hall, seem even with their transient character to be far more representative work than what is beginning to be regarded an absurd sort of elephant on the hands of—well, probably the State as much as any one may be considered the owner."[79]

This writer correctly perceived that Memorial Hall was the antithesis of the Main Building. One was "architecture"; the other was "engineering."

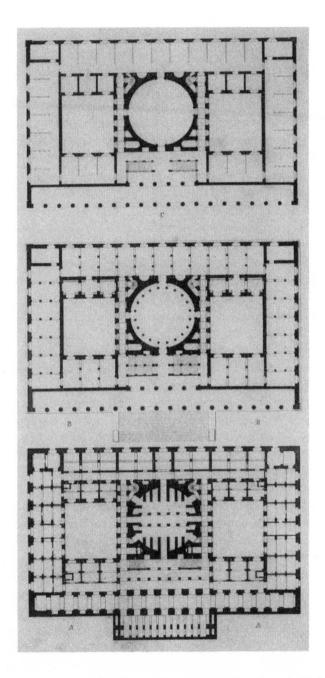

6-6. Altes Museum, by Karl Friedrich Schinkel (Schinkel, *Sammlung Architektonischer Entwürfe*, 38).

One had the enclosed, well-defined rooms of a masonry structure; the other, the open, undifferentiated space of an iron frame. This was all to be expected; Memorial Hall had been designed as a museum in accordance with appropriations made by the city of Philadelphia and the state of Pennsylvania.[80] In comparison to the Main Building, the hall had to bear a heavier burden of representation. It had to express the museum's cultural authority by deploying all the rhetorical devices of a traditional monument—the dome, the decorative sculpture, the neoclassical style, the use of heavy, permanent materials, and a compositional form based on axial symmetry and pyramidal massing.

The origins of the museum date to the summer of 1875, when it became apparent that the coming exhibition would provide "unparalleled opportunities" for establishing such an institution. A meeting was held as early as July 20, in the offices of James L. Claghorn, president of the Commercial Bank in Philadelphia. This resulted in the formation of the Provisional Committee, which was charged with preparing a plan of organization and applying to the authorities in charge of Memorial Hall—the Board of State Centennial Supervisors, the Fairmount Park Commission, and the city of Philadelphia. The committee received permission to use the building and adopted a plan calling for the establishment of a corporation known as the Pennsylvania Museum and School of Industrial Art.[81]

To understand the character of this institution, we need to consider the meaning of the term *industrial art*. This implied the literal application of art to industry, of artistic taste (in the form of decoration) and artistic skill (in the form of drawing) to the creation of industrial artifacts. In this sense, industrial art represents the origins of what we would call industrial design, if not the design ethos itself. Its development acknowledged the divergence of theory and practice, of the idea of the thing and its making, which proceeded from the decline of craft and the rise of industry. The ideas of industrial art were similar to those of period art and architecture. Nature and history were considered appropriate sources of form; this explains the significance of the museum as a study collection of scientifically organized and historically authenticated models. The use and production of the artifact were acceptable factors in design, but the artist's primary concern was the iconographic problem of decoration. Thus, we see at this time the development of a theory of ornamental design, based on the knowledge of nature and history, on the application of simple geometry, and on the notion of "fitness" or appropriateness of decorative form to function.

Finally, industrial art was a response to French hegemony in matters of taste, French leadership in the production of "artistic" goods. Industrial art recognized the economic significance of an attractive design, as evidenced by the Provisional Committee's application to use Memorial Hall: "The development of our Art industries is a matter especially important, for the commercial value of a great number of manufactured products which we use depends upon the Art character of the work more than upon either the raw material or the cost of production. . . . In very many instances, the taste displayed in the design really forms almost the whole value."[82] With the emergence of a visually oriented consumer culture, the look of things—their display value—was becoming an increasingly important factor in their reception as goods. This helps to explain why the original charter of the Pennsylvania Museum, filed on February 25, 1876, stated the aim of the institution in explicitly commercial terms: "The purpose for which the corporation is formed is to establish for the State of Pennsylvania in the City of Philadelphia, a Museum of Art in all its branches and technical application[s] and with a special view to the development of the Art Industries of the State, to provide in connection therewith means of instruction in Drawing, Painting, Modelling, Designing et cetera, through practical schools, special libraries, lectures and otherwise. The institution to be similar in its general features to that of the South Kensington Museum of London."[83] This reference is significant; already one of the most important art museums in the world, the South Kensington (now Victoria and Albert) was the seat of a national system of art education, which included a library and normal school in London, as well as professional schools of design in many British cities. The system was instrumental in the transformation of British design, from its embarrassing state in 1851, when the host country had made a poor showing at its own exhibition, to a position of world leadership twenty-five years later. American advocates of industrial art were clearly hoping for a parallel development in the United States, as evidenced by this passage in *American Architect:*

> The first exhibition in Hyde Park justified itself to the English people by the disclosure it made of their very secondary position in all those works of the hand and brain into which the element of art or taste entered as an essential feature. What they have since accomplished to remedy these defects, under the spur of the painful contrasts then first presented to them, constitutes perhaps the most remarkable chapter in the history of art. In ornamental fabrics, wall-papers, pottery, decorative metal-work, wood and stone carving, furniture, and stained glass, they are already exceeded by no

other nation; in some of these respects they are without a rival. If we could in the same way make a good use of our evident deficiencies in the education of art, as shown in the instructive contrasts at Philadelphia, we too might accomplish a new renaissance.[84]

The core collection of the South Kensington Museum consisted of artifacts that had been purchased at the Great Exhibition, and American advocates of industrial art recognized a similar opportunity at the Centennial.[85] As early 1872, when the organizers were just beginning to plan the exhibition, William Blake had argued for the establishment of a museum like the one in London. He cited the organic relationship between the two institutions, the exhibition and the museum, which was based on the visual habits engendered by the display of precious things:

> A most valuable result which may be made to grow out of the exhibition in 1876, would be the establishment of a permanent museum of decorative art similar to the very useful and attractive museum at South Kensington, in England. Such museums seem naturally to grow out of great exhibitions. The treasures of highly ornamented and carefully wrought objects, the production of the best artists in all countries, displayed on such occasions, beget a desire to have them kept constantly in view for the benefit of all classes. . . . The opportunity for acquiring such objects at exhibitions is excellent, and has been availed of extensively abroad at each succeeding international exhibition. Our exhibition will give a most favorable opportunity, and we should not lose sight of it, but rather resolve at the outset that such a museum of art in its applications to industry shall be established permanently in Philadelphia.[86]

Walter Smith, himself a product of the South Kensington Museum and the director of art education for the state of Massachusetts, wrote a letter to the Provisional Committee explaining how this end was to be accomplished: "The works of private exhibitors can be bought, and on more favorable terms than will ever be possible in this century again, and the exhibits of governments (except in the case of historical works) may doubtless be secured, if the proper influences can be brought to bear; thus, that which cannot be bought may be given, and the private displays which would not be given can be purchased; and if this be accomplished, the Centennial Exhibition, besides being a record of a great historical fact, will be also the commencement of a great industrial future for the whole country."[87] To secure this future, an acquisition fund was formed, and a Committee of Selection appointed to spend $25,000 at the exhibition. This was half as much as the British had spent in 1851, but still a good sum of money—approximately $363,000 today. The committee made daily visits to the fairground, where it had first choice of the goods on display.[88] A small sign identified its purchases, advertising the new institution and making the goods that much more distinctive. "Visitors to the Centennial can hardly have helped noticing," recalled *American Architect and Building News,* "what a surprising number of attractive things bore the placard, 'Purchased for the Pennsylvania Museum School of Industrial Art,' and thinking that the school would have rather a magnificent collection when it was finished."[89] In addition, as Smith had predicted, the committee received a number of gifts from foreign commissioners and private exhibitors, in addition to making contacts with museum professionals from abroad. These included P. Cunliffe Owen, British Centennial commissioner and the South Kensington director, who helped to arrange a loan of Indian artifacts, as well as a gift of work from the museum in London.[90] Thus, the exhibitionary complex in Philadelphia was brought into contact with a larger network of institutions.

The Pennsylvania Museum opened in Memorial Hall on May 10, 1877, exactly one year after the inauguration of the Centennial and on the same day as the permanent exhibition.[91] The museum had taken possession of the hall right after the close of the 1876 fair, but the building needed repairs, so the museum held its first show at the Academy of Fine Arts during the first three months of the year. Consisting of objects purchased at the Centennial or borrowed from private collections, the show lost money but attracted some fifteen thousand visitors; the Board of Trustees judged it a success. At the time of the May opening, the collection consisted of material taken from the first show; artifacts that had been in storage at Memorial Hall; three private holdings of European glass, pottery, and porcelain, loaned through the agency of P. Cunliffe Owen; and a group of Persian art objects that Owen had purchased for the museum.[92] The plan published one year later (fig. 6-6) shows how this collection was arranged, with ceramics and metalwork in the large central gallery west of the rotunda, prints and drawings in the halls to the north, the India Collection in a gallery to the west, textiles and embroidery in the northwest corner of the building, furniture and woodwork in the southwest.

From the beginning, the order of the museum and the arrangement of its displays ranked high among curatorial concerns. "After the preliminary arrangements for the opening day," stated the Board of Trustees' *Reports,* "attention was given to the systematic distribution and classification of the collections, grouping together, so far as practicable, objects of similar character, and perfecting the plan of labelling, in order that visitors might be informed of the exact character of each object, and be enabled to study them more intelligently."[93] The language of this account is familiar, with its emphasis on the systematic, that is, scientific, grouping of things, based on object type or, in the case of the India Collection, country of origin. This is the Classical mentality that we encountered at the Centennial, minus the ambition of the dual system. The emphasis on "perfecting the plan of labelling" would seem to be in contrast to the exhibition, where the naming of things was a haphazard affair, the job of an admittedly imperfect catalog. But it speaks of a concern for nomenclature that was characteristic of early modern science in its taxonomic form.

Well into the twentieth century, the curators of the Pennsylvania Museum were still trying to organize the collection on a scientific basis, although there was some disagreement about whether this implied typology or geography. By 1911, the conflict between these two approaches was resolved in favor of typology, and the museum announced a "systematic" reorganization of what apparently did not even deserve to be called a collection. Looking back, the *Bulletin* ruefully declared, "Until this work had been completed the policy of the Museum had been one of accumulation only, with no attempt at proper attribution or classification." Whatever the reality of this observation, the institution had been clarifying its mission as an art museum since the turn of the century, exporting nonconforming objects—gemstones, archeological and anthropological artifacts—and removing fakes and duplicates from display.[94] Apparently the museum was more like the exhibition than we would have imagined, at least as regards the heterogeneity of its collection.

Three early photographs tell very different stories about the installation of this collection in Memorial Hall. They were all produced by the Centennial Photographic Company, which had received the franchise to document the exhibition and which stayed in business long enough to also document the early years of the museum. The first photograph (fig. 6-7) is a view from the rotunda, looking toward the west into the large central gallery devoted to ceramics and metalwork. In this room, there is an array of vitrines, as we would expect to see in a museum at this time, all built to a standard design. The grid of the gallery's translucent ceiling seems to be at odds with the classical architecture of the building, and yet it is entirely consistent with the essential rationality of the exhibit below, which is more rigorously

6-7. "Memorial Hall" (CPC 3044, Print and Picture Collection, Free Library of Philadelphia).

ordered than anything we have seen at the Centennial. The second photograph (fig. 6-8) is a view from the entrance back into the rotunda, which
suggests that the collection was more loosely organized than either the first
photograph or the *Reports* would have us believe. The exhibit here includes

6-8. "Memorial Hall" (CPC 2881, Print and Picture Collection, Free Library of Philadelphia).

a model of Independence Hall, a painted crucifixion in a Gothic Revival frame, probably an altarpiece, and displays of ceramics. One of these is installed in an Oriental vitrine that was part of the Chinese section in the Centennial's Main Building.

These two images show the use of a conservative, Cartesian form of display, in the sense that the vitrines impose a visual relationship between subject and object that is distant and therefore "objective." The third photograph (fig. 6-9) illustrates a space identified as the Moore Memorial Room. This held a collection of objects that Mrs. Bloomfield H. Moore had acquired in the course of her travels, and that she gradually donated in memory of her husband, beginning in 1882.[95] The photograph indicates that, early in the history of the Pennsylvania Museum, the curators had begun to employ a more progressive, contextual form of display, with paintings, tapestries, furniture, ceramics, and what appear to be metal artifacts all shown together in a manner recalling the Centennial's model rooms. Although the numbered cards seem to refer to a catalogue, the aim is not to name and sepa-

6-9. "Moore Memorial Room—S.E. Angle." Memorial Hall (CPC 3136, Print and Picture Collection, Free Library of Philadelphia).

rate, as in a Classical table, but to risk the confusion of the world by creating a meaningful assemblage of things. The result is not exactly a period room, with its mixture of artifacts and architecture creating an "authentic" interior; that would not become common in American museums until the 1920s.[96] But, remarkably, it does suggest the *kunsthistorische* arrangement of the Kaiser Friedrich (now the Bode) Museum in Berlin, with its combination of painting, sculpture, and furniture evoking the zeitgeist.[97]

During the museum's early years, the artifacts illustrated in these photographs took up only the center and western half of Memorial Hall. The four galleries in the building's east wing were occupied by a collection of mineral specimens belonging to the American Institute of Mining Engineers, while the two rooms on either side of the north vestibule contained the overflow from the IEC's Art Department in the Main Building. The presence of this material was the result of an unusual arrangement between the museum and the permanent exhibition, which helps to explain the synchronization of their openings. Because Memorial Hall was still hidden behind the Main Building, the museum had agreed in essence to serve as an annex to the bazaar. In exchange for display space and the receipts from admissions to Memorial Hall, the IEC had offered to pay the Pennsylvania Museum six thousand dollars a year in quarterly installments. If the museum remained open through the winter, this would increase to eight thousand dollars. The museum accepted the proposal of a guaranteed income, rather than trust "the entrance fees of such persons as might accidently visit the Museum, the communication with the street cars being practically cut off by the Main Building."[98]

Unfortunately, this mutually beneficial arrangement fell victim to the IEC's financial troubles. By 1878, the company had paid the museum only a small fraction of the agreed-upon sum, and the trustees were considering a lawsuit.[99] After a series of financial difficulties, the company failed, as we have seen, but the museum survived to spawn its own small branch of the exhibitionary complex. The School of Industrial Art was founded in 1877; for the duration of the century, it probably was more prominent than the museum itself. Originally established in its own building on Spring Garden Street, the school moved in 1893 to a Greek Revival structure on South Broad Street, the former Pennsylvania Institution of the Deaf and Dumb (John Havilland, 1824–26; William Strickland, 1838). It still operates there as the University of the Arts.[100]

Meanwhile, the museum in Fairmount Park "languished," according to the trustees, who considered moving nearer the school, closer to the center of town. A serious campaign to abandon Memorial Hall began in the 1890s. The building had its detractors, who complained that its condition was deteriorating, that its location was too remote or too difficult to reach by carriage, and that its galleries were "cavernous" and unsuitable for painting. After the donation of the Wilstach Collection in 1892, they could also argue that the building had become too small to accommodate the crowds that were coming to see the collection's three-hundred-plus paintings.[101] The campaign eventually led to the construction of a new and more monumental complex (Trumbauer, Zantziger, and Borie, 1916–28) on Fairmount Hill itself, at the head of the new Benjamin Franklin Parkway. The museum moved to its new home in 1928 and changed its name a few years later to the Philadelphia Museum of Art.

Stephen Conn has rightly interpreted the significance of this move as a repositioning of the institution away from the ideal of industrial art and the South Kensington model and toward the fine-arts ideal as represented by the Louvre and its American representative, the Metropolitan Museum in

New York. This process, which had already begun with the donation of the Wilstach paintings, accelerated after 1925 with the appointment of architectural historian Fiske Kimball as director of the museum. Kimball proceeded to reorganize the collection in a radical fashion, essentially creating two museums in the new building. The best examples of painting, sculpture, and architecture were exhibited to the general public on the main floor, in a series of period rooms and *kunsthistorische*-style displays. Known as "Main Street," these rooms and displays surveyed the history of art—the Renaissance through the eighteenth century in the north wing, Asia and medieval Europe in the south. Everything else—both minor objects and the minor arts—was consigned to study collections for specialists on the ground floor.

In addition, Conn has asserted that Kimball was replacing science with history in the organization of his museum, but that is really too simple; we could just as well say that Kimball was replacing one kind of science with another. Looking back on the museums of the nineteenth century, Kimball criticized his predecessors for being too scientific in their approach to things, yet his own humanism was imbued with science. Main Street was a metaphor for evolution—the origin of the art object being analogous to the origin of the species—which Kimball equated with historical progress. The organizers of the Centennial had made a similar equation, which was a feature of the Victorian mind: the observation of natural progress as a support to theories of cultural evolution.[102]

Finally, Conn has faulted poststructurally inspired scholars like Bennett for being more interested in criticism than history—a false dichotomy if there ever was one. He has dismissed Foucauldian interpreters of the museum for being too obsessed with operations of power, inclining toward explanations that are either "conspiratorial" or "catachismic" (*sic*).[103] This is a shame, for Michel Foucault's account of epistemic change in *The Order of Things* sheds a light on the transformation of the Pennsylvania Museum, just as it provides a context for understanding the changing design of the Centennial. The basic project of knowledge in the Classical age was to name things and to locate their representations on a great table of identities and differences. This table represented a static order that could not accommodate change within itself, but could only be moved whole, in cataclysmic leaps, from one place to another. In contrast, the characteristic figure of modern knowledge was the series; its great theme was development—of life, labor, and language; of man himself. All modern knowledge was historical in the sense that History—with a capital H, as distinguished from ordinary history as "an empirical science of events"—was "the fundamental mode of being of empiricities."[104] The exhibition was still grounded in the tabular order of the Classical age, although that order was already bending to the pressure of history, in the sense that the classification was supposed to be both systematic and progressive. One form of knowledge was giving way to another; if the Pennsylvania Museum in Memorial Hall was more of a table, Main Street in the Philadelphia Museum of Art constituted an explicit historical series. Similarly, the transition between different forms of display at the exhibition and the museum implied a shift from one way of seeing to another, as the analytical, objective sorting of things in rooms and vitrines was gradually displaced by the promiscuous mixing of objects and media in contextual displays.

THE NEW KIND OF STORE

Given what we have learned so far, we can imagine the exhibitionary complex as a kind of gradient. At one end would be situated those institutions, like the museum, in which consumption is more or less denied. Nothing is supposed to be for sale in the museum; the collected artifact has been removed from the commercial context of use and exchange and resituated in a rarified environment of pure display. The consumption that is denied in the gallery is deferred to the museum store, where we can satisfy our visually stimulated appetites by acquiring souvenirs of the collection—books, posters, postcards, "museum-quality" collectibles. Furthermore, the artifact is preceded by its reputation as a commodity; we thrill to view the "priceless" work of art, while ignoring the fact that its special status is only temporary. The object can always be deaccessioned, that is, sold, whereupon it resumes its interrupted status as a commodity. Until then, it continues to exercise an influence on the market by diminishing the supply of comparable goods (by the same artist, of the same type, period or culture), and by adding to the distinction of such goods that are still in circulation.

At the other end of this gradient would be situated those institutions, like the department store, in which consumption is more or less affirmed. The exhibition, as an institution in which consumption was both mystified and celebrated, in which things were perceived as both serial commodities and singular object lessons, would lie somewhere in the middle; the bazaar would lie somewhere between the exhibition and the department store. The Centennial gave rise to a full range of these institutions—a bazaar, a museum, and a department store founded by John Wanamaker. The exhibition's connection to the department store was admittedly more tenuous than the ones tying it to the bazaar and the museum, but Wanamaker did participate in the management of the Centennial, and he did exploit the special circumstances of the exhibition in the establishment of his own store.

Wanamaker began his business life humbly enough. In 1861, he and his brother-in-law, Nathan Brown, opened a small clothing store for men and boys. Known as Oak Hall, the store was located in a six-story commercial building at the corner of Sixth and Market Streets in Philadelphia (fig. 6-10). The building itself was known at McNeill's Folly, which seems appropriate; the beginning of the Civil War may not have been the best time to start such a business. Yet Oak Hall thrived, in no small part because of the "New System," which Wanamaker introduced in 1865, and which he described as "one price and goods refundable." Within ten years, the store had grown to become what was supposedly the largest business of its kind in the United States, covering nearly two acres.[105]

Brown's death left Wanamaker free to establish another store under his own name, which he did in 1869. The store, known as John Wanamaker and

6-10. "View of the Largest Clothing House in Philadelphia." Oak Hall exterior, 1862 (Print Collection, Historical Society of Pennsylvania).

6-11. "Interior View of the Finest Clothing House in America. John Wanamaker & Co., 818 and 820 Chestnut Street" (Historical Society of Pennsylvania).

Company, was situated on the 800 block of Chestnut Street, next door to the Continental Hotel, where the Centennial Commission would meet in the 1870s. The design of the store, with its "luxurious fittings and artistic decorations," was intended to match the pretensions of its new, more upscale location.[106] A view of the interior shows a gas-lit, through-floor space, bisected by a domed rotunda, with some kind of patterned floor covering, paneled walls, a molded cornice, and a coffered ceiling (fig. 6-11). The merchandising of this space looks more accessible than we might expect at this time, with coats displayed on dress forms, vests hung from walls, ties (?) on revolving racks, and pants stacked on long tables. Some things were still kept in glass cases or in boxes behind counters, but customers could examine these articles while seated comfortably on rotating stools. The boundaries of display were being lowered here, just as in other parts of the exhibitionary complex.

Wanamaker's retail innovations even extended to the public space of the street. Here he challenged traditional business practices by making a direct, visual appeal to the customer on the sidewalk. According to Herbert A. Gibbons, an early biographer, "The show windows, the upper part of which were of mediaeval stained glass, were the sensation of the day; for the old conservative tailors of Philadelphia were opposed to display of any sort." Gibbons did not provide any details, but a view of the store's exterior shows two large windows at ground-floor level, with the suggestion of a display behind the glass in each one (fig. 6-12). Over time, in response to

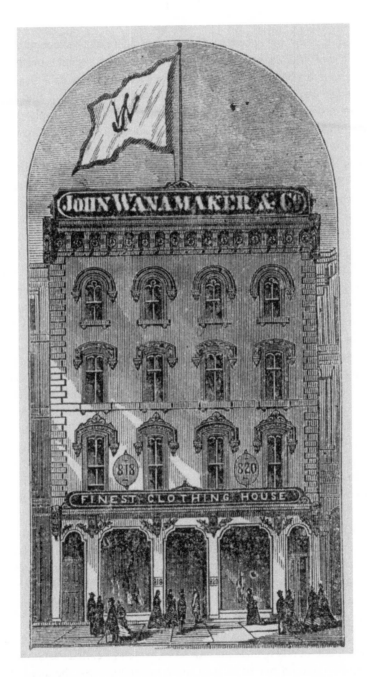

6-12. "812 and 820 Chestnut Street." John Wanamaker and Company (Campbell Collection, Historical Society of Pennsylvania).

changing tastes, the appearance of the store's interior became more under-stated, and Wanamaker began to focus increasing attention on the rooms catering to his bespoke clientele. Gibbons's account makes it clear that the merchant owed much of his success to the arrangement of these spaces: "Here customers had to wait, and here piece goods were displayed, not in cases under glass and presided over by an alert salesman, but thrown out on tables with artistic carelessness. On the walls were paintings. . . . On the tables Wanamaker placed suitings that he thought would sell themselves better than they could be sold to the particular clientele he was studying. The result exceed his hopes. John Wanamaker & Co., by sheer merit of goods and by adroit display in the windows and within the store, were win-ning customers every day."[107] Greater openness to the street, greater access to the goods inside, greater emphasis on the seductions of visual display— the Chestnut Street store does not appear to have had the hyperventilated atmosphere of Emile Zola's *Au Bonheur des Dames,* with women swoon-ing over waterfalls of fabric, but it was introducing Philadelphia to modern standards of display. As we have seen, these were characterized by a lower-ing of the boundary between subject and object.

Some time before 1873, in a quest for more space to house his growing business, Wanamaker attempted to buy the building next door to Oak Hall, but the owner refused to sell. Wanamaker then turned his eye to a freight depot that had been abandoned by the Pennsylvania Railroad after the con-struction of city hall made the depot impossible to reach by rail. Located at the corner of Thirteenth and Market Streets, just east of Center Square, the depot consisted of a small brick office building, a two-hundred-foot-wide enclosed shed, and some open, ancillary structures (fig. 6-13). This com-plex was somewhat historic, having been a staging area for men and mate-riel during the Civil War. In 1874, just before Wanamaker purchased the property, it had also housed the last and largest of the Franklin Institute fairs, held in honor of the institute's fiftieth anniversary. In 1875, having no immediate use for the depot, Wanamaker loaned it to the organizers of the Moodey and Sankey revival meetings, taking place from November 21 to January 28. During this time, the truss-covered shed was made to serve as an auditorium for more than ten thousand people (fig. 6-14).[108]

On May 6, 1876, just four days before the opening of the Centennial, Wanamaker finally opened his new store, which he called the Grand Depot. The timing could not have been more auspicious, for the store stood to benefit from its association with the exhibition. The store's own literature made this clear, using the language of the exhibition itself:

6-13. "The Site of the John Wanamaker Store, Philadelphia." Old Pennsylvania Railroad freight depot (Wanamaker Papers, box 50, file 1, Historical Society of Pennsylvania).

6-14. "The old Railroad Station as used by Moodey & Sankey in 1875, before it was altered to the Wanamaker Store" (Wanamaker Papers, box 50, file 1, Historical Society of Pennsylvania).

In no point of wonder the new store was second only to that international group of buildings, and during the summer it was a sort of Centennial "annex."

The Centennial celebrated liberty for the American colonies in 1776.

The Wanamaker Store celebrated "freedom from the shackles of old, burdensome customs of business."

The Centennial lasted six months, pleasing and instructing ten million visitors.

Wanamaker's has kept on pleasing, instructing and serving countless millions,—an ever-growing exhibition of products of soil and skill from every land under the sun and an exposition of Service without parallel in the mercantile world.[109]

These parallels were more than forced or fortuitous. Speaking in 1900, Wanamaker explained that his department store and the reorganization of life that it represented were both reflections of the exhibition, which had pictured a world of goods under one management: "The Centennial of 1876 was, in my judgement, the moving cause of a departure toward business by single ownership. The rising tide of popular desire to assemble under one roof articles used in every home with freedom to purchase was a constant suggestion in 1876, not alone because of its convenience, but because to some degree it would form a permanent exhibition company which succeeded the Centennial." Thus, the department store was a cognate of not only the 1876 fair but also its supposed successor, the permanent exhibition in Fairmount Park. The latter had failed because of its remote location and bad management, according to Wanamaker. Alluding to the spectacular character of all these institutions, he went on to declare: "The Centennial opened a new vision to the people of the United States. It was the corner stone upon which manufacturers everywhere were rebuilding their business to new fabrics and fashion, and they became more courageous by reason of the lessons taught them from the exhibits of the nations of the world."[110]

In spite of these parallels, the Grand Depot was at an early stage in its development. At first, Wanamaker was still only selling clothing for men and boys, but he soon added departments for women and girls. It was not until March 12, 1877, however, that he officially opened what he described as "the New Kind of Store."[111] Wanamaker had developed the New System into a set of eight Rules of Business, which included the necessary combination of high volume and low prices.[112] Defying retail boundaries, he had expanded his merchandise to include more than dry goods: shoes and hats, in addition to fabrics, notions, and ready-to-wear clothing.[113] This mix of goods and practices is the hallmark of the department store, and the Grand Depot was one of the earliest and most important examples in the United States. Significantly, Wanamaker called it "the First American System Store"—an allusion to that other modern project of rationalization, the American System of Manufacturing, if not the Centennial's System of Awards.[114]

As significant as this development may be in terms of business history, it is the physical transformation of the Grand Depot that concerns us here. The exterior (fig. 6-15) had been extensively remodeled for the opening of the 1876 store, presenting itself as a Moorish fantasy that evoked the image of an oriental bazaar and recalling either Schwarzmann's Horticultural Hall or, in the Main Building, Furness's Brazilian court. More important, the interior design of the 1877 store exploded the open, rectangular space of the depot in a new and rather remarkable way (fig. 6-16). The display counters were arranged in concentric circular blocks, with aisles radiating out from the center, in defiance of the building's rectilinear structure. The merchandising would have been familiar; the counters were surrounded by stools, enough to seat fourteen hundred customers, and much of the stock was displayed in the open, with fabric stacked in neat bolts or draped "with artful carelessness," as in the Chestnut Street store. But the idea of the plan represented a leap from the narrow, vertically organized confines of both

6-15. Grand Depot, 1906, by W.N. Jennings (Wanamaker Papers, box 50, file 1, Historical Society of Pennsylvania).

6-16. Grand Depot interior (Wanamaker Papers, box 50, file 1, Historical Society of Pennsylvania).

the Market and the Chestnut Street buildings. Essentially, Wanamaker had accomplished in his 1877 store what manufacturers would not achieve in their factories until the beginning of the twentieth century—literally, a horizontally integrated business. This was one of the reasons that the store "created such a sensation," according to Wanamaker.[115]

At the time, there was another local institution with a comparable form. This was the Mercantile Library, located in the old Franklin Market on Tenth Street, not far from the Grand Depot. (Philadelphia's Eastern State Penitentiary has a radial plan with a central point of control, but a fundamentally different, cellular system of space.) The focus of the library was a circular reference desk, around which the bookshelves were arranged in a radial plan, which was awkwardly inserted into the rectangular space of the old market building (fig. 6-17).[116] The antecedent for this design and others like it (the Library of Congress, the original library of the University of California in Berkeley) was the reading room of the British Museum in London (Sydney Smirke, 1852). Here the head librarian occupied the nucleus

6-17. "Interior View of the Mercantile Library" (*Philadelphia and its Environs*, 101, Free Library of Philadelphia).

of a knowledge system consisting of the concentric circles of the catalog, the radiating arms of the readers' tables, and the triple-tiered drum of the reference collection. The goal was maximum visibility and control, with the librarian's gaze penetrating from the room's center to its periphery. The reading room was a variation on the theme of the panopticon, but it was a "weak" one, since the readers were mobile and could easily return the librarian's gaze.[117]

The panopticon was invented by Jeremy Bentham, the English philosopher, jurist, and political theorist. As interpreted by Foucault, it was both a building type and a technology of vision. As a building type, the panopticon consisted of a ring of individual cells surrounding a central observation tower. The interior was illuminated in such a way that the occupants of the cells remained visible to the overseer in the tower; the overseer, on the other hand, could not be seen by the occupants. As a technology of vision, then, the panopticon reversed the principle of the spectacle, as exemplified by the public execution of criminals during the Classical age: it manifested power not by making the few visible to the many but by making the many visible to the few. The panoptican rendered the bodies of its occupants both docile and useful, by separating them into individual cells and subjecting them to the controlling gaze of an invisible overseer. It democratized the "eye of power" in the sense that anyone could assume the overseer's position—anyone, that is, who was not already an occupant. It internalized this eye in the sense that the occupants, not knowing who might be watching or when, learned to watch over themselves.[118]

Like the reading room of the British Museum, the Grand Depot was weak in its design. The open space of the store did not exactly promote the radial visibility and lateral invisibility of the panopticon, but the wheel-like arrangement did represent the centripetal movement of power, with the employees as spokes and Wanamaker as the force turning the wheel (fig. 6-18). Furthermore, the employees were somewhat isolated in the cell-like blocks of the display counters, which rendered them more docile and more useful. Thus the store's design served to fix the employees in space, subjecting them to the demands of their customers; it shattered the traditional boundaries of business, while dividing the resulting mass of merchandise into coherent departments; it created a higher level of social organization, while promoting greater efficiency in the circulation of goods. This all suggests that the department store can be appropriately ranked with the other institutions of the disciplinary society, an argument supported by Forney's intriguing interpretation of the store's success: "The watchwords of the business are Veracity, Courtesy and Accommodation, and these are made effec-

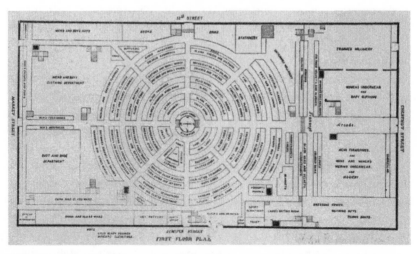

6-18. "First Floor Plan." Autograph: "John Wanamaker's Grand Depot, 1887" (Library Company of Philadelphia). *Enlarged plate appears on page 243 of the appendix.*

tive throughout the establishment by means of Organization, Order and *Discipline*" (my emphasis).[119]

Like the installation of the Main Building, however, the arrangement of the Grand Depot created only an illusion of power by suggesting a central point of control. The surveillance function was not really concentrated at the center of the building but dispersed throughout the store in the form of Wanamaker's employees, who watched the customers, the merchandise, and, to a certain degree, each other. Judging from the evidence, what was really at the center of the Grand Depot changed from time to time. As described in a 1911 guide, the store's nucleus was oddly blind and inward-looking, consisting of a circular counter for the display of silks and a gas-lit "dark room" used to show evening-gown fabric in the correct light.[120] It was an elite woman, then, who stood at the heart of Wanamaker's diagram of ordered consumption—an appropriate symbol given the fact that the store's most important customers would have been female.

Wanamaker had to be familiar with the design of the Mercantile Library, but more likely it was an exhibition—specifically the 1867 Exposition universelle in Paris—that inspired the plan of the 1877 store. As we have seen, the exposition was installed in an "elliptical" building according to the dual system of classification, with departments in concentric galleries and countries in radial sections. Later, the success of this scheme induced the organizers of the Centennial to try their own rectangular version of the dual system. The Grand Depot did not have the systematic organization of the exhibition, but the store was divided into an ever-increasing number of lettered departments, which were given physical form in the plan of the building. Furthermore, the literature of the period shows that customers did see the store as a kind of fair. A man attending the opening exclaimed that it was "just as if the Centennial had come to life again." Four years later, Forney described the store in similar terms: "As is very commonly remarked, a view of the main floor from the antique gallery west of the Chestnut street entrance strikingly recalls the Centennial Exhibition. There is the same width of display extending about as far as the eye can reach, the riches of the world brought together from all lands, and representing all departments of art and industry, tastefully arranged to be shown with advantage. There is the same sense of spaciousness and, what is specially noticeable, the same ample illumination, the whole place being light, bright and cheerful."[121] So it is safe to say that, for Wanamaker's customers, the interior of the Grand Depot evoked the space and light of the Centennial's Main Building. But it should also be noted that Forney was conflating two different ways of seeing the exhibition—the surveying look of the overview, with its "width of display," and the penetrating look of the vista, "extending about as far as the eye can reach."

Wanamaker's own biography supports this interpretation of the store as a kind of fair. In fact, he was a one-man exhibitionary complex, having helped to organize the 1864 Sanitary Fair. He also was a member of the Centennial Board of Finance and a director of the permanent exhibition that opened in Fairmount Park not long after his 1877 store.[122] Furthermore, Wanamaker's stores were represented as fixtures of public life. One early piece of advertising announced that "Oak Hall is now an acknowledged institution."[123] According to a 1926 guide, the Grand Depot "gave full expression to its place as something more than a trading mart, by keeping open one evening for the sole purpose of letting people see its sights—no business being allowed."[124] Established around 1880, this policy was the retail equivalent of keeping the museum open at night for the benefit of working people. Finally, in 1911, the successor to the Grand Depot was inaugurated in a style that recalled the opening of the Centennial. Thousands of guests crowded the courtyard of the new building, and a platform of dignitaries—"eminent Federal, State and City officials, foreign Ambassadors, representatives of the Army and the Navy, well-known bankers, merchants and professional men, and others distinguished in various capacities"—lent their support to the occasion. President William Howard Taft gave the dedication, and the five hundred voices of the Wanamaker Chorus sang two odes especially written for the occasion.[125]

The prominence of the store must have had something to do with its size and location next to Philadelphia's city hall. The Grand Depot had expanded gradually, filling the whole block between Market, Chestnut, Thirteenth, and Juniper Streets by 1883. This necessitated the construction of an arcade-like connection between a new entry on Chestnut and the existing wheel of the Grand Depot. All in all, it was an untidy group of buildings, which did not project the unified, dignified, *classical* image required of a public institution after the construction of the Boston Public Library (McKim, Mead, and White, 1887–98) and the architectural success of the 1893 World's Columbian Exposition in Chicago. An entirely new structure, erected in stages between 1902 and 1911, supplied the necessary image. As designed by the Chicago firm of Daniel H. Burnham, the architectural director of the 1893 fair, the two-million-square-foot store was a palazzo of consumption, a Renaissance-style block filling the site and rising to a height of twelve stories (fig. 6-19). Typologically, the store was an office building,

6-19. John Wanamaker's Department Store, D.H. Burnham and Co. with John T. Windrim, Philadelphia, 1902–1911. Second building from the left (Photograph by author).

a steel-framed structure with a granite curtain wall. But it was a classical variant of this type, with the three-part arrangement of base, shaft, and capitol that Burnham's firm helped to popularize in works like the 1893 Land Title Building in Philadelphia and the 1902 Flatiron Building in New York.[126] Ironically, the new store marked a return to the vertically organized business of Oak Hall. The seven public floors were joined by fifty passenger elevators and by a dramatic, skylit court (fig. 6-20). This was a truly spectacular space that provided a unified interior image for the store, as well as an auditorium for daily recitals on the great organ installed in a second-floor loft. The organ and the large bronze eagle that was perched in the middle of the ground floor had been purchased at the 1904 Louisiana Purchase Exposition in St. Louis.[127]

These giant souvenirs reinforced the old connection, but the Wanamaker store was already being positioned less like an exhibition and more like a museum. In effect, it was being nudged onto a different part of the institutional gradient. This was in keeping with the architectural pretensions of

6-20. John Wanamaker's Department Store, enclosed central court (Photograph by author).

the building and with Wanamaker's own activities. He was on the board of directors for the Pennsylvania Museum, graduating to the position of vice president by the time of his death. He helped to found Philadelphia's Commercial Museum, a.k.a. the Permanent Exhibition of Manufactured Products, with objects obtained at the 1893 Chicago fair. He had similarly close relations with the University of Pennsylvania museum, establishing the archeological section, financing expeditions, and displaying the collected artifacts in his store.[128] It is probably no accident, then, that in 1881 the Grand Depot opened an art gallery specializing in "the best modern painting."[129] Or that parts of the 1911 store were organized like a museum of art and archeology, with rooms decorated according to culturally specific themes—an Egyptian Hall, Greek Hall, Moorish Room, Byzantine Chamber, and Empire Salon. The furniture department, which showed antique furniture and tapestry, as well as the store's own art furniture, had pretensions that clearly went beyond mere trade. "To visit its displays," claimed the guide, "particularly the superb collections grouped in effective settings at the Chestnut Street end of the Fifth Floor, and the rare importations and unique bits to be found in the Little House (Sixth Floor, Juniper) is like wandering through a museum of fine furniture."[130] This reference to contextual displays is notable; it encompassed model rooms and two entirely furnished model apartments in the "Little House" on the sixth floor. In 1876, then, the Grand Depot could be represented as an annex to the Centennial Exhibition. By 1921, in contrast, Wanamaker could explain the store's success with the recollection that "the vast area of space allotted to the many kinds of merchandise displayed made it seem more like a museum than a store."[131]

CONCLUSION

Throughout this work, I have been deliberately vague in my use of the term *exhibition.* This is because I wanted the reader to understand that my conclusions apply both to the Centennial Exhibition in particular and to a generation of international exhibitions in general. These early world's fairs formed a classified landscape traversing time and space, from the 1851 Great Exhibition in London to the 1915 Panama-Pacific Exposition in San Francisco and the Panama-California Exposition in San Diego. But these were merely milestones; the boundaries of this landscape were elastic, extending as far back as the first French national fairs at the end of the eighteenth century, when we begin to see the characteristic features of the exhibition, and as far forward as the 1933 Century of Progress in Chicago, where the organizers self-consciously rejected the competitive, object-oriented tradition of earlier fairs. In this chapter, I have expanded the boundaries of the classified landscape in a different dimension, by considering its institutional outposts—the bazaar, the museum, and the department store. These formed a network in which the temporary landscape of the exhibition and the design problems it represented—order, architecture, installation, display, and evaluation—were made permanent in the landscape of the modern city.

As we have seen, the organizers of the exhibition were preoccupied with the problem of order. To a certain degree, this was a pragmatic response to the nature of their project—the size and complexity of the collection, the emphasis placed on the display of the thing itself—but it was also a reflection of mind. The organizers were still looking at the world with the idealized eye of the Enlightenment. The design of the exhibition implied a stable gaze that was nevertheless being disturbed by the movement of history, such that the systematic and tabular order of the Centennial had to represent evolutionary progress. This it pretended to do by modeling the mechanical development of materials into manufactures, from raw to cooked, as a basis for the production of social goods.

The people who visited the exhibition did not share this preoccupation. They looked at the world with different if equally disturbed eyes—the glance of the restless modern subject. In accommodating this audience, the organizers had to adapt themselves and their project, which turned out to be much more difficult to manage than they had ever imagined. They discovered that the exhibition was an extremely wicked problem that demanded its own set of compromises. In the case of the Centennial, these included the first revision of the system of classification in response to the site plan; the replacement of a systematic and tabular arrangement of displays by the so-called installation by races; and the second revision of the classification as the Grouping for the Judges' Work, after the failure of the second system to properly indicate the boundaries of evaluation. In this light, the exhibition represents a significant historical moment, when the limitations of the modern professions, based on specialized, scientific knowledge and rational, instrumental problem-solving, begin to become apparent.

We have seen a similar concern for taxonomic order in the other institutions of the exhibitionary complex—in the half-hearted attempt to classify objects at the IEC bazaar; in the continuing priority given to the order and arrangement of the Pennsylvania Museum's collection, not just after the opening but throughout the institution's residency in Memorial Hall; in the departmentalization of Wanamaker's Grand Depot. In general, however, order posed a less significant problem for the managers of these projects; they seem to have learned the lesson of the exhibition, as stated by Walker: "A few score of broad natural divisions are all that are required." By comparison, the exhibition represents an extreme case. Yes, its collection was larger and more complex, but there were also different problems of architecture and evaluation.

The architectural problem of the Centennial exhibits a tension between two design professions—architecture and engineering—and between two corresponding ways of building—the representational and the rational. This tension was inherent in the program of the 1873 competition, which called for a permanent monument and a temporary exhibition hall, conjoined in a single design. After considering the alternatives, the organizers concluded that the demands of the permanent and the temporary were irreconcilable, and they restated the program to produce two separate structures: Memorial Hall and the Main Building. Eventually, these were joined in the fairground by three other large halls and a host of smaller buildings. In the struggle for professional authority, the Centennial represents a short-lived victory for engineering, in the sheer volume of rationalized space contained by the larger structures and in the sense that engineers designed so much of the exhibition—site and buildings. There were attempts to reconcile this tension in professional partnerships like Calvert Vaux and George Radford, and their design for the temporary exhibition hall, the Pavilion Plan, itself denotes a significant reconciliation between the rational and representational. Their design was rational in the standardization of space and structure, in the systemization of construction, and in the distinction made between universal and functionally specific space. It was representational in the use of a Gothic style and a vaulted structural system signifying rationality.

Once again, the organizers' expressed preference for rational building represents an extreme case, and the other institutions of the exhibitionary complex show a drift toward representation in architecture. The bazaar inherited the relatively uninflected space of the Main Building, but the center of this structure was reconfigured as a more functionally specific concert hall. The museum opened in Memorial Hall, the most representational building of the exhibition, designed by an engineer, but it eventually moved into more monumental and archaeologically correct quarters designed by architects. Finally, the department store occupied a former railroad depot, whose open space and panoramic arrangement of merchandise brought to mind the space and arrangement of the exhibition. As the store was repositioned as a museum, however, the engineer's depot was eventually supplanted by the architect's palazzo. In much the same way, the modest practicality of the Centennial landscape was eventually displaced by the cultural ambition of the Court of Honor at the 1893 Chicago fair.

At the Centennial, the rational space of the Main Building threw the burden of representation onto the arrangement of displays. The systematic and tabular order of the exhibition had to be made transparent in the installation; in the first plan, then, individual exhibits were located by type and country in a grid of knowledge. But it was geography that predominated as a principle of organization in the second plan of installation, with national sections arranged to form a map of the world, projected to form four spheres of industrial influence. What was left of the systematic ideal receded into the American section as a modest gradient of displays. Even this limited bid for transparency was undermined as the need to make the exhibition attractive trumped the desire to render it meaningful.

As a compact version of the Centennial, shrunk to the size of the Main Building, the bazaar could have replicated the exhibition in miniature. This seems to have been the intention, yet the managers lacked a real commitment to the ideal of transparency. As a result, the systematic order of the bazaar, whatever its real significance, was not apparent in the haphazard arrangement of displays by national courts and administrative departments. In contrast, the museum curators displayed an early and continuing concern for the twin projects of classification and arrangement. The curators approached their collection with much the same systematic attitude as the organizers of the exhibition, yet the problems of the museum never reached the same magnitude as those of the exhibition. The museum collection was smaller, simpler, and more stable, and a traditionally monumental building bore much of the burden of representing the museum's place in the cultural order.

Ironically, it was the consumption-oriented department store that came closest to embodying the original ideals of the exhibition. The Grand Depot provided a unitary display, in the sense that the space of the building afforded a panoramic view of all the merchandise. The organization was transparent and systematic, in the sense of there being an apparent fit between the order of the store in departments and the arrangement of the merchandise. But the arrangement was not tabular, although it seemed to recall the dual installation of the 1867 Paris fair. The wheel was supposed to be a diagram of power relations in the store, but it could be read for little else, beyond suggesting a centered vantage point that does not ever seem to have existed. Still, by all accounts, the interior of the store presented an attractive spectacle of consumption that, in its power to distract and displace the world, recalled and rivaled the spectacle of the exhibition in the Main Building.

The Centennial shows us that bewilderment and disorientation were typical responses to this spectacle. The organizers wanted to present a single clear picture of the world, but what the audience really perceived was a series of blurred impressions. This disjunction signifies a conflict between two ways of seeing and knowing, as denoted by the gaze and the glance, and as was evidenced by the two principles of installation, with their respective emphases on the vista and the accent. This conflict was further reflected in a shift between two "schools" of display: the Cartesian and the contextual. The first is represented by the vitrine, which imposes a distant and purely visual relationship between subject and object; the second, by the mannequin and model room, which lowers the boundaries of display and resituates the object in a meaningful relationship to other things. Although both of these schools privilege the visual, the organizers understood that the exhibition was an experience in which seeing existed in a symbiotic relationship with hearing, and in which the diffuse spectacle of objects on display was matched or even surpassed by the equally diffuse and distracting spectacle of other people.

Based on the short histories presented in this chapter, it would be difficult to gauge the audience's experience of the other exhibitionary institutions. But we can imagine that it was less acute, given the fact that these institutions all represented smaller, more local problems of collection and display. The bazaar and the department store shared the same rational architecture as the exhibition—the bazaar in the literal sense of the Main Building; the department store in the analogous sense of the railroad depot, whose open space made it possible to give the store "the same width of display" as the exhibition, a view that could only be properly understood from above. The museum also shared the architecture of the exhibition, but it was in the representational mode of Memorial Hall. The space of the museum was thus more structured, more hierarchical, and therefore less disorientating than we would expect to have found elsewhere in the complex.

In any case, the deracinated condition of the displayed object was much the same in these institutions as at the exhibition, so that the observer would have been likely to perceive the object as similarly distanced and estranged. This is evidenced by the fact that we see some of the same attempts to lower the boundaries of display, such as Wanamaker making his merchandise more accessible and appealing in his Chestnut Street store. We also see attempts, other than the classification itself, to create a meaningful context for the object. This could be the cultural context of *kunsthistorische* displays or the environmental context of model and period rooms. It could also be the context of the body, as in dress forms and mannequins, or the context of a developmental series, as in the Philadelphia Museum's Main Street.

The institutions of the exhibitionary complex were all articulated across the same set of design problems, but the exhibition remained a special case as a form of competitive display. It was not enough for the goods to be gathered together and arranged coherently; they had to be examined and ranked—good, better, best—to provide consumers with guidance in a strange new market. The order, architecture, and installation of the exhibition, as well as the strategic display of goods, were all means to the single great end of evaluation. This made the exhibition demonstrably different from the other institutions of the complex, although some form of evaluation played a part in each one. For example, an equivalent tradition of competitive display exists in the museum, as exemplified by various annuals and biennials, but it is only a vestige of an earlier academic practice that is no longer central to the institution's brief.

As a collection, the exhibition remained a relatively open, indeterminate affair, which took in everything and could never be complete; its ideal was the comprehensive view of the panorama. The organizers exercised some control over the admission of exhibitors, but this was not the museum curator's power to shape the collection. Although space was always at a premium, the exhibition was characterized by a great superfluity of objects, which visitors negotiated largely on their own terms. In contrast, the museum as a collection is relatively closed and determined. As Susan Stewart has observed, the ideal is Noah's ark—a representative sample of things, the parts that can generate the whole world.[132] In both the museum and the exhibition we can recognize some attempt to exercise cultural authority, to impose expert judgment between the audience and the artifact, to distinguish between "good" and "bad." In the museum, this happens at the outset, at the boundary between the collection and the world, or when the curator selects an artifact for display. In the exhibition, where the boundary was far more permeable, the exercise of authority happened after the fact, in the deep interior of the collection, when the judge selected among competing objects to award a prize.

The museum, then, is an institution with very strong boundaries. Curators patrol its borders, exercising much more control than the exhibition commissioners ever did. The twin gates of collection and display ensure that the visitor sees a selected and well-ordered representation of the world, or at least a portion of it—art, science, technology, history. In contrast, the boundaries of the other institutions appear relatively weak. The bazaar was practically gateless; it subsisted on the leavings of the exhibition and had no system of evaluation. It could not maintain the boundary between learning and leisure, which was the boundary between the exhibition and the world outside its gates, that is, the amusements of the Centennial City. In the department store, collection and display formed a single gate, in the sense that what was collected was invariably displayed. The buyer exercised some control over the admission of objects, but it was a weak authority, exercised in tandem with the customer, who acted like a judge in comparing things, ranking them in terms of price and quality and finally choosing the best for purchase. The exhibition functioned similarly, the commissioners exercising some power over the shape of the collection, the judges making the final selection.

Ironically, while the exhibition was clearly meant to function as an apparatus of distinction, creating differences between goods of the same type, it also had the unanticipated effect of disabling differences between distinct types of goods. The organizers' demonstrated passion for the systematic meant that everything had to be judged in exactly the same way. This provoked a strong reaction from the judges of the Committee on Painting, who sought to preserve the special status of their own area. Their issue was boundaries—between art and industry, between the sacred and profane, between the commodified and what is not. The tension between these areas went to the heart of the exhibition. As a form of universal knowledge, it posed the problem of a radically heterogeneous collection, which brought together things that were quite rightly kept apart. As a table, it was not always successful at maintaining identities and differences. This is what made the exhibition so precarious—even dangerous, in cultural terms—a project. It formed a panorama that was shifting, fragmented, dense, and therefore difficult to read from any one point of view—an appropriate picture of the modern world.

Appendix

ENLARGED PLATES

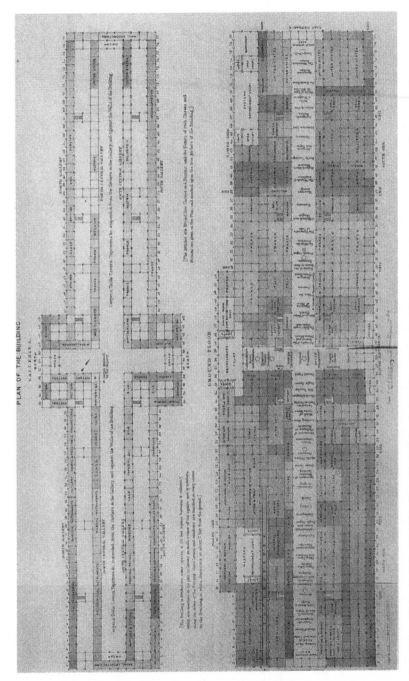

1-2. "Plan of the Building." 1851 Great Exhibition in London (Great Exhibition, *Official Descriptive and Illustrative Catalogue*, n.p., Library of Congress).

1-5. "Paris Universal Exposition 1867. Plan of the Building and Park" (United States, Commission to the Paris Exposition, 1867, *Reports*, vol. 1, n.p., University of California Library, Berkeley).

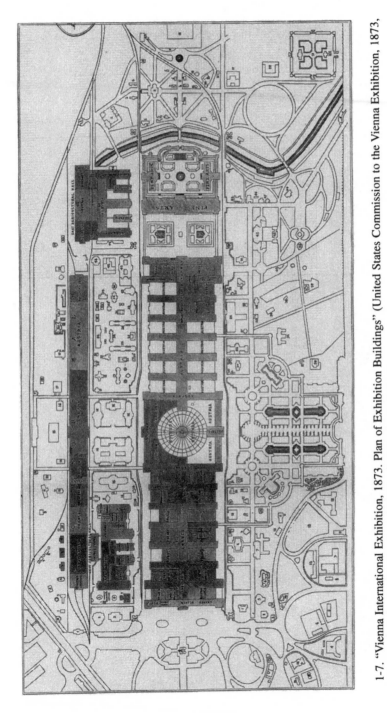

1-7. "Vienna International Exhibition, 1873. Plan of Exhibition Buildings" (United States Commission to the Vienna Exhibition, 1873, *Reports*, vol. 1, pl. 3, University of California Library, Berkeley).

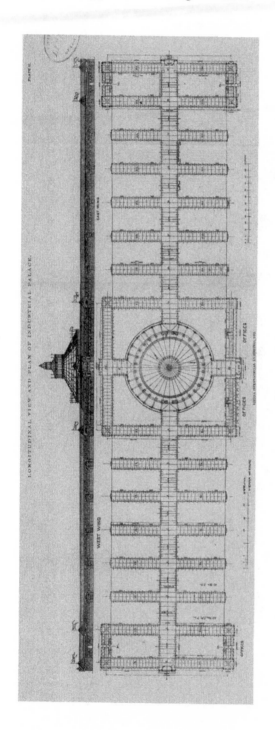

2-3. "Longitudinal View and Plan of Industrial Palace." 1873 Weltausstellung in Vienna (United States, Commission to the Vienna Exhibition, 1873, *Reports*, vol. 1, pl. 2, University of California Library, Berkeley).

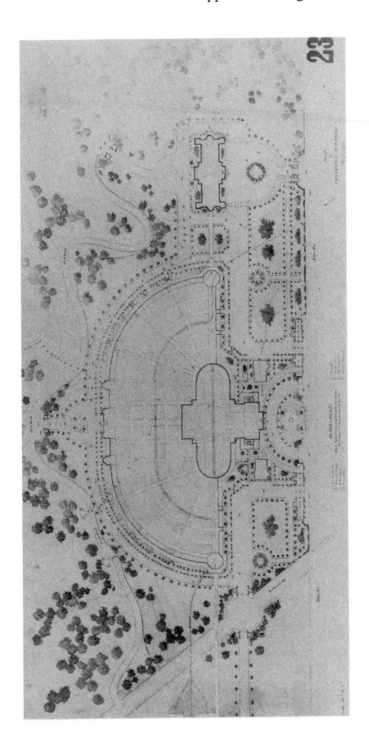

2-6. "Block Plan" (site plan), by Edward Collins and Charles M. Autenrieth (United States Centennial Commission [USCC], *Photographs of Plans for Centennial Exhibition Buildings* [albums, 1873], 3:73, Business Science and Industry Department, Free Library of Philadelphia).

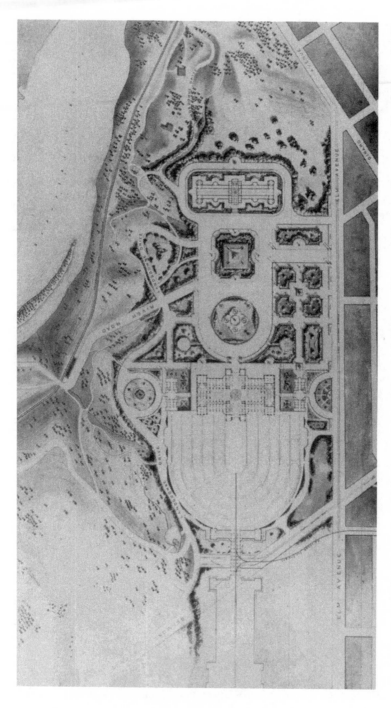

2-9. "Block Plan," by Samuel Sloan (USCC, *Photographs of Plans*, 3:34, Business Science and Industry Department, Free Library of Philadelphia).

2-24. "Main Pavilion. Interior View," by Calvert Vaux and George K. Radford (United States Congress, Senate, *National Centennial*, n.p., University of California Library, Berkeley).

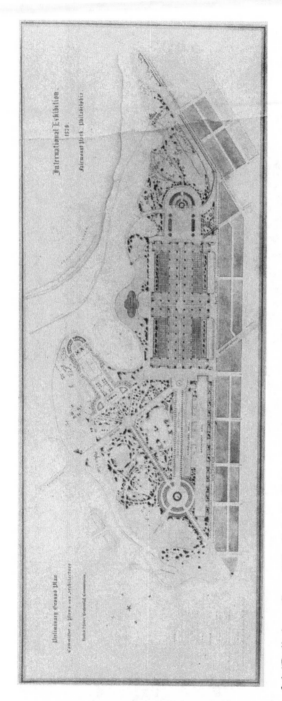

3-1. "Preliminary Ground Plan Submitted by the Committee on Plans and Architecture of the United States Centennial Commission" (Pettit, "Centennial Exhibition," 1:46, Historical Society of Pennsylvania [Philadelphia] architectural drawings collection on loan to the Athenaeum of Philadelphia, with the support of the Pew Charitable Trusts through its Museum Loan Program).

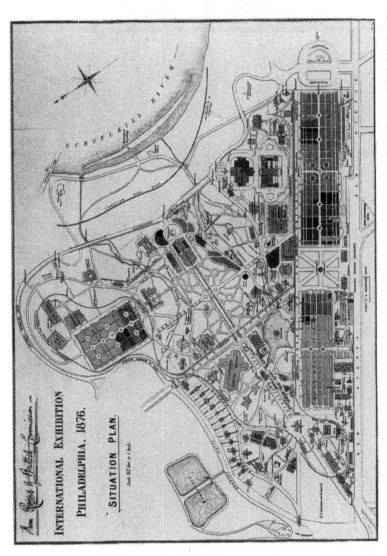

3-2. "Situation Plan." Autograph: "From Report of British Commission" (Pettit, "Centennial Exhibition," 1:53, Historical Society of Pennsylvania architectural drawings collection on loan to the Athenaeum).

3-8. "From the Reservoir" (CPC 2064, Print and Picture Collection, Free Library of Philadelphia).

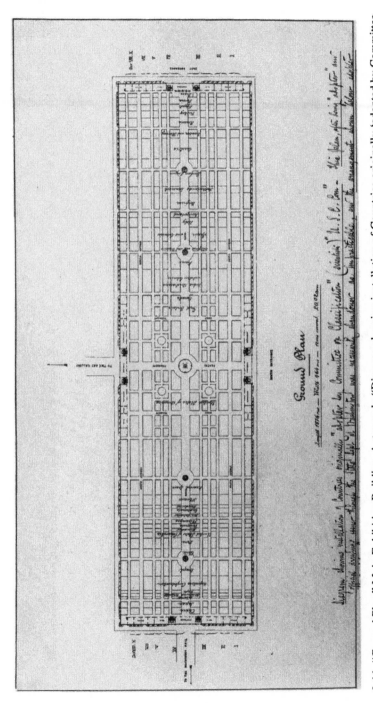

3-11. "Ground Plan." Main Exhibition Building. Autograph: "Diagram showing installation of Countries originally 'adopted by Committee on Classification' (scientists) 'U.S.C. Com.' This plan, after being 'adopted' and official drawings issued through the State Dept[.] at Washington was necessarily abandoned as impracticable, and the arrangement shown below adopted in its place" (Pettit, "Centennial Exhibition," 1:61, Historical Society of Pennsylvania architectural drawings collection on loan to the Athenaeum).

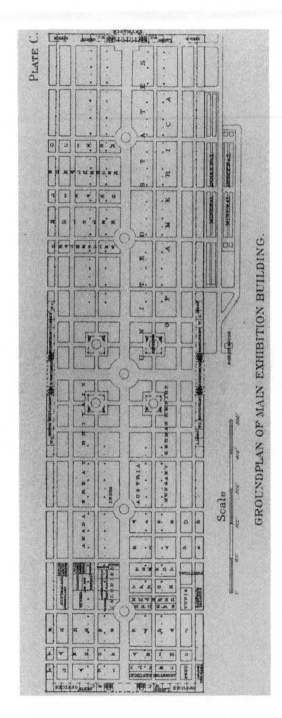

3-12. "Ground Plan of Main Exhibition Building" (USCC, *International Exhibition, 1876*, vol. 9, pl. C, University of California Library, Berkeley).

4-12. "The Centennial—Balloon view of the Grounds" (*Harper's Weekly* 20, no. 1031 [30 Sept. 1876]: supplement, Library of Congress).

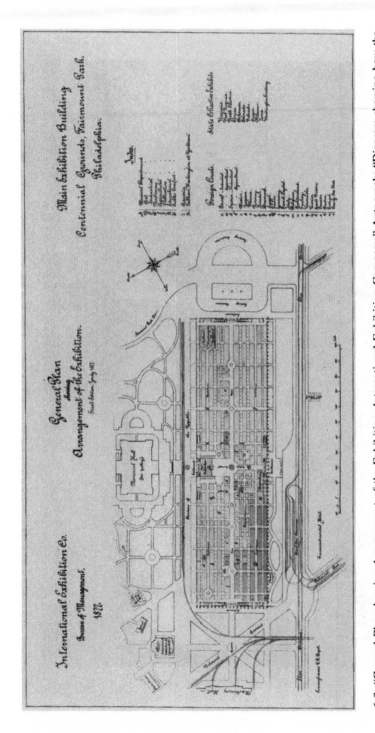

6-3. "General Plan showing Arrangement of the Exhibition. International Exhibition Company." Autograph: "Diagram showing how the different 'departments' and exhibits were rearranged after the Centennial, for the new Exhibition of 1877" (Pettit, "Centennial Exhibition," 1:63, Historical Society of Pennsylvania architectural drawings collection on loan to the Athenaeum).

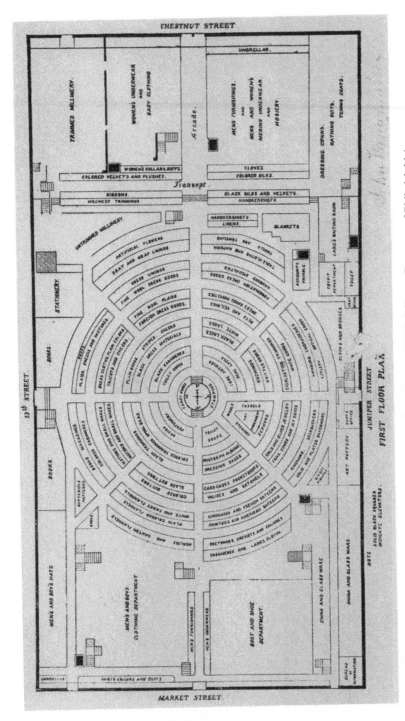

6-18. "First Floor Plan." Autograph: "John Wanamaker's Grand Depot, 1887" (Library Company of Philadelphia).

NOTES

CHAPTER 1

1. Susan Stewart, *On Longing: Narratives of the Miniature, the Gigantic, the Souvenir, the Collection* (Durham, N.C.: Duke University Press, 1993), 153–54.

2. Roland Barthes, "The Plates of the Encyclopedia," in *New Critical Essays,* trans. Richard Howard (New York: Hill & Wang, 1980), 24.

3. United States Centennial Commission [USCC], *International Exhibition, 1876* (Washington, D.C.: GPO, 1880–84), 1:56.

4. John Allwood, *The Great Exhibitions* (London: Studio Vista, 1977), 12; J.S. Ingram, *The Centennial Exposition, Described and Illustrated* (Philadelphia: Hubbard Brothers, 1876), 24–28; Kenneth W. Luckhurst, *The Story of Exhibitions* (London: Studio Publications, 1951), 73, 77–80; Nikolaus Pevsner, *A History of Building Types* (Princeton, N.J.: Princeton University Press, 1976), 243.

5. These numbers are taken from the official literature. There were 5,494 exhibitors in 1849, according to United States, Commission to the Paris Exposition, 1867, *Reports of the United States Commissioners to the Paris Universal Exposition, 1867,* ed. William P. Blake (Washington, D.C.: GPO, 1870), vol. 1, "General Survey," 13.

6. Exposition des produits de l'industrie francaise, 1834 (Paris), Jury central, *Rapport du Jury central exposé en 1834,* ed. Charles Dupin (Paris: Imprimerie Royale, 1836), viii–ix.

7. Patricia Mainardi, *Art and Politics of the Second Empire: The Universal Expositions of 1855 and 1867* (New Haven, Conn.: Yale University Press, 1987), 22.

8. Kenneth E. Carpenter, "European Industrial Exhibitions Before 1851 and Their Publications," *Technology and Culture* 13 (July 1972): 466.

9. Derek Hudson and Kenneth W. Luckhurst, *The Royal Society of Arts, 1754–1954* (London: Murray, 1954), 187; Luckhurst, *Story of Exhibitions,* 83–96.

10. Mainardi, *Art and Politics,* 22.

11. The section included "Sculpture as a Fine Art," "Works in Die-sinking, Intaglios," "Architectural Decorations," "Mosaics and Inlaid Works," "Enamels," "Materials and Processes Applicable to the Fine Arts generally, including Fine Art Printing, Printing in Colour, etc. etc.," and "Models." Great Exhibition of the Works of Industry of All Nations, *Reports by the Juries on the Subjects in the Thirty Classes into Which the Exhibition Was Divided* (London: Spicer Brothers, 1852), xxii.

12. Great Exhibition of the Works of Industry of All Nations, *First Report of the Commissioners for the Exhibition of 1851* (London: W. Clowes, 1851), xxxii–xxxiii.

13. Great Exhibition, *Reports by the Juries*, iii.

14. Great Exhibition of the Works of Industry of All Nations, *Official Descriptive and Illustrated Catalogue of the Great Exhibition of the Works of Industry of All Nations, 1851* (London: Spicer Brothers and W. Clowes, 1851), 22–26.

15. Henry Cole, "Report on the Management of the British Portion of the Paris Universal Exhibition," in Great Britain, Royal Commission to the Paris Exposition, *Reports on the Paris Universal Exhibition* (London: Eyre & Spottiswoode, 1856), 26.

16. Mainardi, *Art and Politics*, 26.

17. Ibid., 42–43.

18. Cole, "Report," 38–39.

19. Exposition universelle, 1855 (Paris) [Commission impériale], *Exposition des produits de l'industrie de toutes les nations, 1855. Catalog officiel publié par ordre de la Commission impériale*, 2d ed.(Paris: E. Panis, [1855]), xiii.

20. Cole, "Report," 25–26.

21. The same source refers to a dual system of classification at the 1855 fair, based on the use of the thing as well as the material and method of manufacture, but the official literature makes it clear that this was not the case. *The Exhibition of Art-Industry in Paris, 1855* (Paris: Stassin & Xavier; London: Virtue, [ca. 1855]), ii. Allwood repeated this claim in *Great Exhibitions*, 35.

22. Exposition universelle, 1855 (Paris), Commission impériale, *Rapport sur l'Exposition universelle de 1855 présenté à l'empereur par S.A.I. le prince Napoléon, président de la commission* (Paris: Imprimerie impériale, 1857), 133–36.

23. Ibid., 136, 138–40.

24. Ibid., 140. The prince admitted the practical necessity of separate structures for the fine arts, agriculture, and moving machinery in *Rapport*, 141.

25. William P. Blake, "Previous International Expositions," in USCC, *Journal of the Proceedings of the United States Centennial Commission at Philadelphia, 1872* (Philadelphia: E.C. Markley, 1872), 58.

26. United States, Commission to the Paris Exposition, 1867, *Reports*, 1:165.

27. USCC, Committee on Classification, "Report on the Classification," in USCC, *Journal of the Proceedings of the United States Centennial Commission at Philadelphia. Fifth Session: May, 1874* (n.p., [1874?]), app. no. 3, 36, booklet bound in USCC, *Journals and Reports of the United States Centennial Commission, Philadelphia, 1872-76*, Historical Society of Pennsylvania, Philadelphia.

28. Exposition universelle, 1867 (Paris), Commission impériale, *Rapport sur l'Exposition universelle de 1867, à Paris* (Paris: Imprimerie impériale, 1869), 16–20. The system of classification is explained in United States, Commission to the Paris Exposition, 1867, *Reports*, vol. 1, "Introduction," 165–81, and "General Survey of the Exposition," 15.

29. Sigfried Giedion, *Space, Time and Architecture: The Growth of a New Tradition* (Cambridge: Harvard University Press, 1976), 260-61.

30. This scheme is supposed to have had its origins in a plan by the English architect Edward Payne for the 1862 London fair. Allwood, *Great Exhibitions*, 42.

31. Exposition universelle, 1867 (Paris), Commission impériale, *Rapport*, 17.

32. William P. Blake, "Appendix C. Report to the United States Centennial Commission, upon the Organization, Administration, and Results of the Vienna International

Exhibition, 1873," in , U.S. Congress, Senate, *The National Centennial* (Washington, D.C.: GPO, 1874), 1580:169.

33. Philadelphia, Commission to Vienna, *The Vienna Exposition* (Philadelphia: King & Baird, 1873), 4–7.

34. Henry Pettit, "Appendix D. Report of Mr. Henry Pettit, Civil Engineer, Special Agent to the Vienna Exhibition," in U.S. Congress, Senate, *National Centennial*, 281.

35. Ibid., 282.

36. Black, "Report to the United States Centennial Commission," 169.

37. United States, Commission to the Vienna Exhibition, 1873, *Reports of the Commissioners of the United States to the International Exhibition Held at Vienna, 1873*, ed. Robert H. Thurston (Washington, D.C.: GPO, 1876), 1:59–60. Cf. Blake, "Report to the United States Centennial Commission," 165–68: "In addition to these groups, provision was made for special exhibitions and competitive trials of machines and methods, for the history of inventions, the history of industry, of prices, and an exposition of the commerce and trade of the world."

38. USCC, *International Exhibition*, vol. 2, app., 101–2.

39. Blake, "Previous International Expositions," 54–55.

40. Ibid., 61–62.

41. USCC, *Journal* (1872), 73–74.

42. USCC, *International Exhibition*, vol. 2, app., 1. The growing size and significance of this committee testified to the importance of order as an issue in the design of the exhibition. Established as a special committee with three members at the Centennial Commission's first session, it was made a standing committee with five members at the second session in May 1872 and enlarged to seven members at the fourth session in May 1873. USCC, Committee on Classification, "Report on the Classification," 45–47.

43. Michel Foucault, *The Order of Things: An Archaeology of the Human Sciences*, World of Man series, ed. R.D. Laing (New York: Vintage Books, 1973), 63–67; J.G. Merquior, *Foucault* (London: Fontana Press/Collins, 1985), 45–46.

44. With its innermost gallery of antiquities, the main building of the 1867 Exposition universelle was described as "an unwritten history of civilization which every one could read." United States, Commission to the Paris Exposition, 1867, *Reports*, 1:17.

45. *Oxford English Dictionary*, 2d ed., s.v. "systematic."

46. Foucault, *Order of Things*, 160–63.

47. Ibid., 131.

48. Harriet Ritvo, "Zoological Nomenclature and the Empire of Victorian Science," in *Victorian Science in Context*, ed. Bernard Lightman (Chicago: University of Chicago Press, 1997), 334–36; Barbara T. Gates, "Ordering Nature: Revisioning Victorian Science Culture," in *Victorian Science in Context*, ed. Bernard Lightman (Chicago: University of Chicago Press, 1997), 179; Foucault, *Order of Things*, 132.

49. Foucault, *Order of Things*, 74–75.

50. U.S. Congress, House, *The National Celebration of the Centennial Anniversary of the Independence of the United States by an International Universal Exhibition, to be Held in Philadelphia in the Year 1876*, report to Congress by the United States Centennial Commission, ed. Henry D.J. Pratt (Washington, D.C.: GPO, 1873), 1572:70.

51. Philip W. McIntyre and William F. Blanding, eds., *Men of Progress: Biographical Sketches and Portraits of Leaders in Business and Professional Life in and of the State of Maine*, comp. Richard Herndon (Boston: New England Magazine, 1897), s.v. "Nye, Joshua."

52. Ingram, *Centennial Exposition,* 746; Robert W. Rydell, *All the World's a Fair: Visions of Empire at American International Expositions, 1876–1916* (Chicago: University of Chicago Press, 1984), 17.

53. *Dictionary of American Biography* (1928, 1929, 1936); *National Cyclopaedia of American Biography* (1936); *The New-York Historical Society's Dictionary of Artists in America* (1957); all s.v. "Blake, William." Also USCC, *Journal* (1872), 146. Blake would also be active at the 1878 and 1889 Paris fairs, as well as at the 1893 exhibition in Chicago. John Maass, *The Glorious Enterprise: The Centennial Exhibition of 1876 and H.J. Schwarzmann, Architect-in-Chief* (Watkins Glen, N.Y.: American Life Foundation, 1973), 134.

54. USCC, *Journal* (1872), 129.

55. Ibid., 130–31.

56. William Whewell, "The General Bearing of the Great Exhibition on the Progress of Art and Science," in *Lectures on the Results of the Exhibition, Delivered before the Society of Arts, Manufactures, and Commerce, at the Suggestion of H.R.H. Prince Albert, President of the Society* (Philadelphia: A. Hart, 1852), 17.

57. USCC, *Journal* (1872), 130–31.

58. Ibid., 131–34. The similarity between this form of notation and the Dewey decimal system was not lost on John Maass. He recounted how the young Melvil Dewey first proposed a version of his system in 1873, while a student and library assistant at Amherst College. According to Maass, Dewey based his idea for the catalogue on the Centennial classification, which had been circulated in leaflet form to the nation's schools of higher education. Maass further asserted that Dewey based his form of notation on the one that had been proposed by the Committee on Classification, and that he "cunningly covered his tracks." Maass, *Glorious Enterprise,* 336, 338, 340.

59. U.S. Congress, House, *National Celebration,* 77.

60. Ibid., 83–84.

61. At the fourth session, for example, John Campbell described the proposed changes to the system of notation by explaining that "the figures attached to the classes designate accurately the *location* [my emphasis] of articles in departments, groups, and classes." U.S. Congress, Senate, *National Centennial,* 30.

62. Foucault, *Order of Things,* xxii.

63. USCC, *Journal* (1872), 131.

64. Howard Gillette Jr., "The Emergence of the Modern Metropolis: Philadelphia in the Age of Its Consolidation," in *The Divided Metropolis: Social and Spatial Dimensions of Philadelphia, 1800–1975,* ed. William W. Cutler III and Howard Gillette Jr., Contributions in American History series (Westport, Conn.: Greenwood Press, 1980), 85:11; Russell F. Weigley, "The Border City in Civil War, 1854–1865," in *Philadelphia: A 300-Year History,* ed. Russell F. Weigley (New York: W.W. Norton, 1982), 375. For an explanation of the system, see the *Centennial Guide to the Exposition and Philadelphia* (Philadelphia: Richard Magee & Son, 1876), 29–30.

65. Foucault, *Order of Things,* 131.

66. USCC, *Journal* (1872), 135.

67. Cf. Foucault, *Order of Things,* 146: "There must be continuity in nature."

68. USCC, *International Exhibition, Philadelphia. 1876. System of Classification* (Philadelphia, 1874), 16; U.S. Congress, House, *National Celebration,* 4.

69. USCC, *Journal* (1872), 124.

70. Ibid., 134.

71. Cf. Stewart, *On Longing,* 151: "In contrast to the souvenir, the collection offers example rather than sample, metaphor rather than metonymy. The collection does not display attention to the past; rather, the past is at the service of the collection, for whereas the souvenir lends authenticity to the past, the past lends authenticity to the collection. The collection seeks a form of self-enclosure which is possible because of its ahistoricism. The collection replaces history with classification, with order beyond the realm of temporality. In the collection, time is not something to be restored to an origin; rather, all time is made simultaneous or synchronous with the collection's world."

72. Ingram, *Centennial Exposition,* 21.

73. USCC, Committee on Classification, "Report," 35.

74. Ibid., 35.

75. See chap. 6, no. 119, and accompanying text.

76. Barthes, "Plates," 32.

77. USCC, Committee on Classification, "Report," 35.

78. Ibid., 41.

79. Ibid., 36.

80. Ibid., 36–37.

81. Ibid.

82. Ibid., 37–38.

83. USCC, *International Exhibition,* vol. 2, app., 1–2.

84. USCC, Committee on Plans and Architecture, *Report of the Committee on Plans and Architecture, to the U.S. Centennial Commission* (Philadelphia: J.B. Lippincott, [1873]), 11.

85. U.S. Congress, Senate, *National Centennial,* 94.

86. USCC, *International Exhibition,* vol. 2, app., 11.

87. Ibid., 1:57, 635.

88. Walter Benjamin, "Unpacking My Library: A Talk About Book Collecting," in *Illuminations,* ed. Hannah Arendt (New York: Schocken Books, 1968), 60.

89. Blake, "Previous International Expositions," 63.

90. USCC, *International Exhibition, 1876, Official Catalogue,* 2d ed. (Philadelphia: John R. Nagle, 1876), pt. 1, 25. A comparable system was used in the Crystal Palace.

91. I have been told that columns continued to be numbered consecutively into the twentieth century.

92. USCC, *International Exhibition,* 9:50–51.

93. The 1873 Vienna fair was a case in point; participating countries did not provide timely information about their exhibits, and Blake reported that the first edition of the catalogue was "very imperfect and incomplete." Blake, "Report to the United States Centennial Commission," 201.

94. USCC, *International Exhibition,* 1:635–37; 2:66–67. See 2:115–21 for more on the Board of Finance.

95. Ibid., 1:637–38. There were eventually fourteen editions of the catalogue.

96. Ibid., 1:638–39.

97. "The Catalogue, of course, was never complete," said Gardner, "though the revised edition is believed to be more nearly so than that of any previous International Exhibition." Ibid., 1:638.

98. "Arrangement of Great Exhibitions," *Nation* 21, no. 543 (25 Nov. 1875): 337.

CHAPTER 2

1. In France, the Académie royale d'architecture was established in 1671, the Académie royale des sciences in 1666, the Corps du génie in 1676, the École des ponts et chaussées in 1715, and the École spéciale d'architecture in 1795. Richard Michael Levy, "The Professionalization of American Architects and Civil Engineers, 1865–1917" (Ph.D. diss., University of California, Berkeley, 1980), 3–6.

2. Cf. ibid., 7–8.

3. Horst W.J. Rittel and Melvin M. Webber, "Dilemmas in a General Theory of Planning," *DMG-DRS Journal* 8, no. 1 (1974): 222; Donald A. Schön, *The Reflective Practitioner: How Professionals Think in Action* (New York: Basic Books, 1983), 21–30. My use of the terms "strong" and "weak" is based on Ignasi de Solà-Morales Rubió's idea of "weak architecture," which in turn reflects postmodern theorist Gianni Vattimo's idea of "weak thought." Ignasi de Solà-Morales Rubió, "Weak Architecture," in *Differences: Topographies of Contemporary Architecture,* trans. Graham Thompson, ed. Sarah Whiting (Cambridge: MIT, 1997), 57.

4. Cf. Le Corbusier, *Towards a New Architecture,* trans. Frederick Etchells (New York: Praeger, 1960), 7: "The Engineer's Aesthetic, and Architecture, are two things that march together and follow one another."

5. Women played an active part in fund raising for the Centennial, and they even built their own hall after being ejected from the exhibition in the Main Building, but that is not my story. See Mary F. Cordato, "Representing the Expansion of Woman's Sphere: Women's Work and Culture at the World's Fairs of 1876, 1893, and 1904" (Ph.D. diss., New York University, 1989).

6. What constitutes an architect or an engineer at this time is certainly an interesting question, as illustrated by the confusion over the biography of Herman J. Schwarzmann (1846–1891). Maass and others called him the "architect-in-chief" of the Centennial, but his official title was chief engineer of the grounds, and his previous occupation had been as an engineer for the Fairmount Park Commission. It is not known whether he ever had a formal architectural education, but he did study at the Royal Military Academy in Munich, which would imply an education as an engineer. He was clearly trying to establish himself as an architect; beginning in 1870, he advertised himself as such in the Philadelphia city directory, although by 1874 he had designed only two small park buildings. By Maass's count, Schwarzmann designed thirty-four buildings at the Centennial. After the exhibition, he attempted to practice as an architect in Philadelphia and in New York, but without much success. His career was cut short by sickness and an early death. Maass, *Glorious Enterprise,* 19, 20, 22, 34–35, 116–17, 135; Sandra L. Tatman and Roger W. Moss, *Biographical Dictionary of Philadelphia Architects: 1700–1930* (Boston: G.K. Hall, 1985), 703–4; USCC, *International Exhibition,* 9:20.

7. Henry Pettit, *Final Report to the U.S. Centennial Commission on the Structures Erected for the Vienna Universal Exhibition, 1873, and Previous Exhibitions in London and Paris* (Philadelphia, 1873), 5, Historical Society of Pennsylvania, Philadelphia.

8. USCC, *Journal* (1872), 116.

9. Ibid., 158.

10. Ibid., 205.

11. U.S. Congress, House, *National Celebration,* 184.

12. Allwood, *Great Exhibitions,* 52; Tatman and Moss, *Biographical Dictionary,* 605–6; U.S. Congress, Senate, *National Centennial,* 279.

13. USCC, *International Exhibition*, vol. 2, app., 8. These reports were also published as an appendix to U.S. Congress, Senate, *National Centennial*.

14. Also at the fifth session, the recently appointed secretary of the Centennial Commission, John L. Campbell, enumerated among his duties "the collection of information about International Exhibitions." USCC, *International Exhibition*, vol. 2, app., 10.

15. Joan Bassin, *Architectural Competitions in Nineteenth-Century England* (Ann Arbor: UMI Research Press, 1984), 63, 67; Eugene Ferguson, "Technical Museums and International Exhibitions," *Technology and Culture* 6, no. 1 (Dec. 1965): 35; Ingram, *Centennial Exposition*, 24, 28–29; Tom F. Peters, *Building the Nineteenth Century* (Cambridge: MIT Press, 1996), 226.

16. Allwood, *Great Exhibitions*, 18–19; Luckhurst, *Story of Exhibitions*, 110; Peters, *Building the Nineteenth Century*, 226–54; Pevsner, *History of Building Types*, 244–45. Sydenham Palace was destroyed by fire in 1937, according to Giedion, *Space, Time and Architecture*, 249; in 1936, according to Allwood, *Great Exhibitions*, 24.

17. Pettit, *Final Report*, 6, 26–27.

18. Blake, "Report to the United States Centennial Commission," 145.

19. Cf. Tony Bennett, "The Exhibitionary Complex," *New Formations* 4 (1988): 97: "Moreover, the ambition to render the whole world, as represented in assemblages of commodities, subordinate to the controlling vision of the spectator was present in world exhibitions from the outset." Bennett is concerned with the impact of the overviews that were also a feature of these fairs. See chap. 4 of this book.

20. Luckhurst, *Story of Exhibitions*, 132.

21. "In looking for the useful, one has, without wanting it, found the beautiful." *Moniteur universel*, no. 260 (17 Sept. 1867): 1214, in Pevsner, *History of Building Types*, 246.

22. Pettit, *Final Report*, 23. The epithet has also been credited to Napoléon III. Morford, *Paris in '67, or, The Great Exposition, Its Side-Shows and Excursions* (New York: G.W. Carleton, 1867). In *Library of American Civilization* (Chicago: Library Resources, 1970), microfiche 11799, 113; Ingram, *Centennial Exposition*, 38.

23. Eugene Rimmel, *Recollections of the Paris Exhibition of 1867* (London, 1868), 8, in Arthur Chandler, "Paris 1867: Exposition universelle," in *Historical Dictionary of World's Fairs and Expositions, 1851–1988*, ed. John E. Findling (New York: Greenwood Press, 1990), 36.

24. Pettit, *Final Report*, 23.

25. USCC, *Journal* (1872), 58–59.

26. Giedion, *Space, Time and Architecture*, 260.

27. Philadelphia, *Vienna Exposition*, 4–7; Henry-Russell Hitchcock, *Architecture: Nineteenth and Twentieth Centuries* (Baltimore: Penguin Books, 1968), 216.

28. Philadelphia, *Vienna Exposition*, 5.

29. Ibid., 7.

30. Pettit, "Report of Mr. Henry Pettit," 286–87.

31. Blake, "Report to the United States Centennial Commission," 142–43.

32. Pettit, "Report of Mr. Henry Pettit," 282.

33. "Arrangement of Great Exhibitions," 337.

34. Pettit, "Report of Mr. Henry Pettit," 284.

35. Blake, "Report to the United States Centennial Commission," 145.

36. Pettit, "Report of Mr. Henry Pettit," 284.

37. Blake, "Report to the United States Centennial Commission," 147.

38. Ibid., 142, 147.

39. Pettit, *Final Report,* 19. Blake and Goshorn made similar remarks. Cf. Blake, "Report to the United States Centennial Commission," 143; USCC, *International Exhibition,* 1:8.

40. Sarah Bradford Landau, "Coming to Terms: Architecture Competitions in America and the Emerging Profession, 1789 to 1922," in *The Experimental Tradition: Essays on Competitions in Architecture,* ed. Hélène Lipstadt, 54–61; Hilde de Haan and Ids Haagsma, *Architects in Competition* (New York: Thames & Hudson, 1988), 10; Leland M. Roth, *A Concise History of American Architecture* (New York: Harper & Rowe, 1980), 10.

41. Thomas Gordon Jayne, "The New York Crystal Palace: An International Exhibition of Goods and Ideas" (Master's thesis, University of Delaware, 1990), 49.

42. USCC, *Journal* (1872), 51.

43. USCC, *International Exhibition,* vol. 2, app., 1–2; Luckhurst, *Story of Exhibitions,* 188.

44. USCC, *Journal* (1872), 101–2.

45. Philadelphia Architects, "Instructions to Architects Competing for Plans for the Centennial Anniversary Building" pamphlet, [1872], in USCC, "Documentary Record of the Centennial," scrapbooks, 31 vols., plus 9 boxes, 1876-79, Centennial Collection, 1:87, Historical Society of Pennsylvania, Philadelphia. Hereafter cited as USCC, "Documentary Record," followed by volume and page number; *Suggestions of Architects of New York City,* pamphlet, [1872], in USCC, "Documentary Record," 1:91.

46. Charles A. Cummings, William R. Ware, and Samuel F. Thayer, *Suggestions of Architects of Boston to Committee on Plans and Architecture of Centennial Commission* pamphlet, [1872], in USCC, "Documentary Record," 1:89.

47. USCC, *Journal* (1872), 141–42.

48. Ibid., 141–45.

49. John Henry Hicks, "The United States Centennial Exhibition of 1876" (Ph.D. diss., University of Georgia, 1972), 16; Maass, *Glorious Enterprise,* 33; Joseph M. Wilson, *The Masterpieces of the Centennial International Exhibition,* vol. 3, *History, Mechanics, Science* (Philadelphia: Gebbie & Barrie, 1876), cii.

50. USCC, *International Exhibition,* vol. 2, app., 9; vol. 9, 29.

51. USCC, *Journal* (1872), 206–7.

52. Ibid., 211–12.

53. USCC, *International Exhibition,* 1:29–30.

54. USCC, Committee on Plans and Architecture, *Report,* 10.

55. Wilson, *Masterpieces,* 3:xcvi.

56. USCC, Committee on Plans and Architecture, *Report,* 3.

57. Ibid., 11–13.

58. These photographs and pamphlets, which form the basis of this discussion, can be found in the collections of the Historical Society of Pennsylvania, the Free Library, and the City Archives, all in Philadelphia.

59. USCC, Committee on Plans and Architecture, *Report,* 4.

60. Roth, *Concise History,* 145–46; *Macmillan Encyclopedia of Architects,* 1982 ed., s.v. "Vaux, Calvert." For more on Vaux, see William Alex, *Calvert Vaux: Architect and Planner* (New York: Ink, 1994), and Francis R. Kowsky, *Country, Park, and City: The Architecture and Life of Calvert Vaux* (New York: Oxford University Press, 1998).

61. Roth, *Concise History,* 150.

62. Tatman and Moss, *Biographical Dictionary,* 730–34.

63. Ibid., 510; Theo B. White, ed., *Philadelphia Architecture in the Nineteenth Century* (Philadelphia: Art Alliance Press, 1973), 29.

64. Condit counts three Broad Street stations, the first built in 1851–52. Carl W. Condit, *American Building Art* (New York: Oxford University Press, 1960), 2:190, 213, 215–16, 271; Carl W. Condit, *American Building: Materials and Techniques from the First Colonial Settlements to the Present* (Chicago: University of Chicago Press, 1968), 48, 132, 135–36; Henry Pettit, "Obituary Notices of Members Deceased. Joseph Miller Wilson, A.M., C.E.," *Proceedings of the American Philosophical Society* 42, no. 173 (Apr. 1903): i–vi; Tatman and Moss, *Biographical Dictionary,* 870–71; Wilson Brothers and Company, *Catalogue of Work Executed* (Philadelphia: J.B. Lippincott, 1885), 4–29.

65. Dorothy Gondos Beers, "The Centennial City, 1865–1876," in *Philadelphia: A Three Hundred Year History,* ed. Russell F. Weigley (New York: W.W. Norton, 1982), 420; White, *Philadelphia Architecture,* 30; Tatman and Moss, *Biographical Dictionary,* 724–25; Henry F. Withey and Elsie Rathburn Withey. *Biographical Dictionary of American Architects (Deceased)* (Detroit: Omnigraphics, 1996), 556.

66. Tatman and Moss, *Biographical Dictionary,* 17, 156–57.

67. Antoinette J. Lee, *Architects to the Nation: The Rise and Decline of the Supervising Architect's Office* (New York: Oxford University Press, 2000), 68, 82.

68. Francis W. Kervick, *Architects in America of Catholic Tradition* (Rutland, Vt.: Charles E. Tuttle, 1962), 134; Withey and Withey, *Biographical Dictionary,* 620.

69. Tatman and Moss, *Biographical Dictionary,* 614–15.

70. Ibid., 717–18.

71. My thanks to Pamela Scott and S. Allen Chambers Jr. for providing me with this information.

72. Tatman and Moss, *Biographical Dictionary,* 682.

73. USCC, Committee on Plans and Architecture, *Report,* 14.

74. Ibid., 4–5.

75. Landau, "Coming to Terms," 56.

76. Pettit, *Final Report,* 23–24.

77. [Edward] Collins and [Charles M.] Autenrieth, *Proposed Centennial Buildings,* pamphlet, [1873], 1–5, Centennial Collection, Historical Society of Pennsylvania, Philadelphia. Unless otherwise noted, the pamphlets describing these projects were printed in a standard format without any facts of publication, although they all must date to 1873, the year of the competition.

78. Samuel Sloan, *Description of Design and Drawings for the Proposed Centennial Buildings, to Be Erected in Fairmount Park,* pamphlet (Philadelphia: King & Baird, 1873), 5, 30–33, Centennial Collection, Historical Society of Pennsylvania, Philadelphia.

79. Carroll L.V. Meeks, *The Railroad Station: An Architectural History* (New Haven, Conn.: Yale University Press, 1956), 100.

80. John McArthur Jr. and Joseph M. Wilson, *Revised Design in Competition for Proposed Centennial Exhibition Building, for Exposition of Industry of All Nations, to Be Held in Philadelphia in 1876,* pamphlet (Philadelphia: King & Baird, 1873), 6–7, 12–13, Centennial Collection, Historical Society of Pennsylvania, Philadelphia.

81. McArthur and Wilson, *Revised Design,* 12, 14–17.

82. H[enry] A. Sims and J[ames] P. Sims, *Proposed Centennial Buildings,* pamphlet, [1873], 1–3, Centennial Collection, Historical Society of Pennsylvania, Philadelphia.

83. Thomas M. Plowman and B[artholomew] Oertly, *Proposed Centennial Buildings,* pamphlet [1873], 1–2, Centennial Collection, Historical Society of Pennsylvania, Philadelphia.

84. James C. Sidney, *Proposed Centennial Buildings,* pamphlet, [1873], 1, Centennial Collection, Historical Society of Pennsylvania, Philadelphia.

85. [Josse A. Vrydagh], *Proposed Centennial Buildings,* pamphlet, [1873], 1, Centennial Collection, Historical Society of Pennsylvania, Philadelphia.

86. Vrydagh, *Proposed Centennial Buildings,* 5.

87. Francis R. Gatchel and Stephen Rush Jr., *Proposed Centennial Buildings,* pamphlet, [1873], 1–2, Centennial Collection, Historical Society of Pennsylvania, Philadelphia.

88. J[oseph] S. Fairfax, *Proposed Centennial Buildings,* pamphlet, [1873], 1–2, Centennial Collection, Historical Society of Pennsylvania, Philadelphia.

89. USCC, Committee on Plans and Architecture, *Report,* 7.

90. Calvert Vaux and George Kent Radford, *Proposed Centennial Buildings,* pamphlet, [1873], 3–4, Centennial Collection, Historical Society of Pennsylvania, Philadelphia; Vaux and Radford, "Designs for the Proposed Centennial Exposition Building," *New-York Sketch-Book of Architecture* 1 (Sept. 1874): 2.

91. Vaux and Radford, *Proposed Centennial Buildings,* 1–2.

92. Vaux and Radford, "Designs for the Proposed Centennial Exposition Building," 2.

93. Pettit, *Final Report,* 14.

94. USCC, Committee on Plans and Architecture, *Report,* 5.

95. Ibid., "Appendix No. 5: Proposed Centennial Buildings," n.p.; USCC, *International Exhibition,* 1:31.

96. USCC, *International Exhibition,* vol. 2, app., 8.

97. USCC, Committee on Plans and Architecture, *Report,* 5–6, 9–10.

98. The state act, approved on March 23, 1873, stipulated that "a permanent fireproof building shall be erected in Fairmount Park as part of the Centennial Exhibition buildings . . . , which building shall remain in Fairmount park perpetually as the property of the people of this Commonwealth for the preservation and exhibition of national and State relics and works of art, industry, mechanism, and products of the soil, mines, et cetera, of this State." The city ordinance of February 22, 1873, stated that "a permanent building . . . shall be permitted to remain in said Park as the property of the City of Philadelphia, for the exhibition and preservation of such works of nature, art, and products of the soil and mine, and works of art applied to industry, copies of reproductions of articles of skill for the free education and enjoyment of the people of the nation." USCC, *International Exhibition,* vol. 2, app., 204, 242.

99. Ibid., 1:305.

100. USCC, Committee on Plans and Architecture, *Report,* 7–8.

101. In the future, designers would deal directly with the Executive Committee and the Board of Finance. The work of the Committee on Plans and Architecture appears to have been over, and it was formally dissolved at the end of the commission's fifth session in May 1874. USCC, *International Exhibition,* vol. 2, app., 10.

102. Wilson, *Masterpieces,* 3:c–ciii. Cf. Henry Pettit, "Report of Henry Pettit, Consulting Engineer,: in USCC, *Journal of the Proceedings of the United States Centennial Commission at Philadelphia, Fifth Session* (n.p., [1874?]), app. no. 1, 20-23.

103. Ibid., 3:ciii. The price of the Main Building was eventually reduced to $75,569.65 per acre. USCC, *International Exhibition,* 9:42.

104. Wilson, *Masterpieces* 3:ciii, cvi. Cf. Henry Pettit, "Report of Henry Pettit,

Consulting Engineer," in USCC, *Journal of the Proceedings of the United States Centennial Commission at Philadelphia*, Fifth session (n.p., [1874]), app. no. 1, 20-23.

105. Ibid., 3:cvi.

106. USCC, Committee on Plans and Architecture, *Report*, 7.

107. Levy, "Professionalization," 69, 71, 135, 242–44.

CHAPTER 3

1. USCC, *International Exhibition*, 9:32, 77, 80. The original Main Building, covering an area of eighteen acres, was enlarged by the addition of two-acre annex at the east end.

2. Ibid., 9:88, 93, 105, 107–8.

3. Ibid., 9:31.

4. Ibid., 9:150

5. *Visitor's Guide to the Centennial Exhibition and Philadelphia* (Philadelphia: J.B. Lippincott, 1876), 11.

6. Giedeon, *Space, Time and Architecture*, 264; James B. Jackson, *American Space: The Centennial Years, 1865–1876* (New York: W.W. Norton, 1972), 234; Richard R. Nicolai, *Centennial Philadelphia* (Bryn Mawr, Pa.: Bryn Mawr Press, 1976), 15; Thomas J. Schlereth, "The Material Universe of American World Expositions, 1876–1915," in *Cultural History and Material Culture: Everyday Life, Landscapes, Museums*, American Material Culture and Folklife series, ed. Simon J. Bronner (Ann Arbor: UMI Research Press, 1990), 267.

7. Paul A. Tenkotte, "Kaleidoscopes of the World: International Exhibitions and the Concept of Culture-Place, 1851–1915," *American Studies* 28 (Mar. 1987): 9.

8. USCC, *International Exhibition*, 9:43- 44.

9. Ibid., 9:42–44.

10. Wilson, *Masterpieces*, 3:cxxv.

11. Peters, *Building the Nineteenth Century*, 40.

12. The same concern led the organizers to close the exhibition at night, even though the building was illuminated by seven thousand gas burners. USSC, *International Exhibition*, 9:42, 45; Wilson, *Masterpieces*, 3:cxxiv.

13. USCC, *International Exhibition*, 1:110.

14. The largest was the Union Depot in St. Paul, Minnesota (1879–81), with a length of 640 feet and a span of 189 feet. Condit, *American Building Art*, 2:201–3.

15. Edward C. Bruce, *The Century: Its Fruits and Its Festival* (Philadelphia: J.B. Lippincott, 1877), 68; USCC, *International Exhibition*, 2:154; United States, Centennial Board of Finance, *Second Annual Report* (n.p., 1875), 3.

16. USCC, *International Exhibition*, 1:111.

17. Bruce, *Century*, 70; United States, Centennial Board of Finance, *Second Annual Report*, 3.

18. United States, Centennial Board of Finance, *Second Annual Report*, 4. Pettit calculated the total quantity of building material at 51,687,587 pounds or 25,843 tons. Henry Pettit, "Centennial Exhibition," scrapbook, vol. 2, p. 22, Athenaeum, Philadelphia.

19. USCC, *International Exhibition*, 1:111; Bruce, *Century*, 70.

20. Bruce, *Century*, 70.

21. Peters, *Building the Nineteenth Century*, 351.

22. Martin Jay, *Downcast Eyes: The Denigration of Vision in Twentieth-Century French Thought* (Berkeley: University of California Press, 1993), 57.

23. USCC, *International Exhibition,* 1:57.

24. Blake, "Report to the United States Centennial Commission," 169.

25. USCC, Committee on Classification, "Report," 37–38.

26. Luckhurst, *Story of Exhibitions,* 111, 135.

27. Blake, "Previous International Expositions," 61.

28. USCC, *Journal* [1872], 74.

29. USCC, *International Exhibition,* 1:634.

30. Ibid., 1:40, 53–54.

31. USCC, Committee on Classification, "Report," 38–39.

32. USCC, *International Exhibition,* 1:40; Pettit, "Centennial Exhibition," 1:61.

33. Pettit, "Centennial Exhibition," 1:59–60.

34. William Whewell's coining of the word, scientist, was roughly contemporary with the founding of the British Association for the Advancement of Science in 1831, and his publication of *History of the Inductive Sciences* in 1837 and *Philosophy of the Inductive Sciences* in 1840. George Levine, "Defining Knowledge: An Introduction," in *Victorian Science in Context,* ed. Bernard Lightman (Chicago: University of Chicago Press, 1997), 16.

35. USCC, *International Exhibition,* 1:634–35.

36. Daniel Brewer, "The Work of the Image: The Plates of the *Encyclopédie,*" *Stanford French Review* 8 (Fall 1984): 235, in Jay, *Downcast Eyes,* 98.

37. USCC, *International Exhibition,* 9:41.

38. Ibid., 9:51–52, 54.

39. Rydell, *All the World's a Fair,* 21–22.

40. See Marvin Harris, "Rise of Racial Determinism," in *The Rise of Anthropological Theory: A History of Theories of Culture* (New York: Thomas Y. Crowell, 1968).

41. *Webster's New Collegiate Dictionary* (1973), s.v. "race."

42. Rydell, *All the World's a Fair,* 4. The reference is to Robert H. Wiebe, *The Search for Order, 1877–1920* (New York: Hill and Wang, 1967).

43. Albert Boime, *The Magisterial Gaze: Manifest Destiny and American Landscape Painting c. 1830–1865* (Washington, D.C.: Smithsonian Institution Press, 1991), 79.

44. These include the 1893 Chicago, 1898 Omaha, 1904 St. Louis, 1915 San Francisco, and 1933 Chicago fairs. Burton Benedict, "The Anthropology of World's Fairs," in Burton Benedict et al., *The Anthropology of World's Fairs: San Francisco's Panama Pacific International Exposition of 1915* (Berkeley, Calif.: Scolar Press, 1983), 49–52.

45. Rydell, *All the World's a Fair,* 24–25; Robert A. Trennert Jr., "A Grand Failure: The Centennial Indian Exhibition of 1876," *Prologue* 6 (June 1974): 118, 127.

46. William Dean Howells, "A Sennight of the Centennial," *Atlantic Monthly* 38 (July 1876): 103.

47. "Characteristics of the International Fair," pt. 4, *Atlantic Monthly* 38 (Oct. 1876): 496.

48. "Characteristics of the International Fair," pt. 5, *Atlantic Monthly* 38 (Dec. 1876): 736.

49. USCC, *International Exhibition,* 1:38, 41–43, 48.

50. Ibid., 1:44, 47, 118, 120.

51. Ibid., 1:64.

52. Jay, *Downcast Eyes,* 116; Shierry M. Weber, "Walter Benjamin: Commodity

Fetishism, the Modern, and the Experience of History," in *The Unknown Dimension: European Marxism since Lenin,* ed. Dick Howard and Karl E. Klare (New York: Basic Books, 1972), 261 ff. Cf. chap. 4, no. 61.

53. Jay, *Downcast Eyes,* 52–53, 57, 69. Locke adopted a similar position. Jonathan Crary, *Techniques of the Observer: On Vision and Modernity in the Nineteenth Century* (Cambridge: MIT Press, 1992), 41–43.

54. Bill Brown, "Science Fiction, the Worlds Fair, and the Prosthetics of Empire," in *Cultures of United States Imperialism,* ed. Amy Kaplan and Donald Pease (Durham, N.C.: Duke University Press, 1993), 342; Crary, *Techniques,* 48, 50; Jay, *Downcast Eyes,* 70, 75–76, 81.

55. Jay, *Downcast Eyes,* 56.

56. USCC, *International Exhibition,* 1:48–50. The installation of Machinery Hall was similarly marked out.

57. Francis A. Walker, "The Philadelphia Exhibition," pt. 1, *International Review* 4 (May 1877): 367.

58. USCC, *International Exhibition,* 1:50, 52–53.

59. Ibid., 1:53; USCC, Executive Committee, *Report of the Executive Committee of the United States Centennial Commission* (Philadelphia, 1876), 28, booklet bound in USCC, *Journals and Reports of the United States Centennial Commission, Philadelphia, 1872-76,* Historical Society of Pennsylvania, Philadelphia. In the last twenty-four hours, janitors removed an estimated seventy-five tons of refuse from the Main Building. Walker, "Philadelphia Exhibition," pt. 1, 367.

60. Howells, "Sennight," 92.

61. "Characteristics of the International Fair," pt. 1, *Atlantic Monthly* 38 (July 1876): 90.

62. "The United States International Exhibition of 1876," *Journal of the Franklin Institute* 101 (June 1876): 364.

63. USCC, *International Exhibition,* 1:59.

64. Ibid., 1:59–61, 65, 124.

CHAPTER 4

1. Benedict, "Anthropology," 7–12.

2. [Marietta Holley], *Josiah Allen's Wife as a P.A. and P.I. Samantha at the Centennial* (Hartford, Conn.: American Publishing, 1878), 411.

3. *Dictionary of American Biography* (Detroit: Gale Research, 1982), s.v. "Marietta Holley," 11:207.

4. Howells, "Sennight," 98; "Characteristics of the International Fair," pt. 4, 494.

5. Wilson, *Masterpieces,* 3:cxxv.

6. Cf. Susan Buck-Morss, *Dialectics of Seeing: Walter Benjamin and the Arcades Project* (Cambridge: MIT Press, 1989), 81–82: "Everything desirable, from sex to social status, could be transformed into commodities as fetishes-on-display that held the crowd enthralled even when personal possession was far beyond reach."

7. Lewis Mumford, *The Brown Decades: A Study of the Arts in America, 1865–1895* (New York: Dover, 1955), 139, in Larry D. Lutchmansingh, "Commodity Exhibitionism at the London Great Exhibition of 1851," *Annals of Scholarship* 7 (1990): 206.

8. Lutchmansingh, "Commodity Exhibitionism," 203.

9. Cf. ibid., 206: "The organized abstraction of these vistas produced their own

kind of irrationality, and while they served to stun and dominate the spectator, the regularity of their organization gave the impression of law and inevitability."

10. Frederick A. Tozier, "Centennial Record," diary, 1876, 29, Manuscripts and Archives Department, Historical Society of Pennsylvania, Philadelphia.

11. Howells, "Sennight," 93, 101–2. Cf. "Characteristics of the International Fair," pt. 5, 734, for corroboration.

12. Ingram, *Centennial Exposition*, 455, 530. Cf. "Characteristics of the International Fair," pt. 2, *Atlantic Monthly* 38 (Aug. 1876): 238, on the French: "These people possess the secret of taste, and it adorns whatever they attempt, outside the realm of art, where the higher laws prevail."

13. Cf. "Characteristics of the International Fair," pt. 5, 734: "It is curious to see how much sameness there is in the productions of these out-of-the-way places of creation. . . . Feather and shell flowers, straw work, simple woolen, cotton, hempen, or linen fabrics with bright stripes and borders, rude weapons and utensils, coral, strange roots and fruits, formed the aboriginal staples of them all."

14. George E. Thomas, Jeffrey A. Cohen, and Michael J. Lewis, *Frank Furness: The Complete Works*, rev. ed. (New York: Princeton Architectural Press, 1996), 196.

15. Brazil was a major presence at the Centennial; in addition to the section in the Main Building, the country had substantial exhibits in Agricultural Hall, Machinery Hall, the Art Gallery, and the Women's Pavilion, as well as a Brazilian villa at the top of Lansdowne Ravine. Ingram, *Centennial Exposition*, 500–502.

16. USCC, *International Exhibition*, 9:42.

17. The elevator is not by itself significant; the first had appeared in the Haughwout Building of New York in 1857. Roth, *Concise History*, 121.

18. USCC, *International Exhibition*, 1:103.

19. Émile Bellier de la Chavignerie and Louis Auvray, *Dictionnaire général des artistes de l'École française* (New York: Garland, 1979), s.v. "Piton, Camille."

20. Henry Pettit, *International Exhibition, Philadelphia, 1876. Specifications for International Trophies, Designed by Camille Piton, Artist, for Central Pavilion, Main Exhibition Building* (Philadelphia, 1875), 1–4, Historical Society of Pennsylvania, Philadelphia.

21. Bruce, *Century*, 68.

22. Unbuilt examples include the three-hundred-foot observation tower that James Bogardus had proposed as part of his design for the New York Crystal Palace, and the one-thousand-foot tower that the Phoenix Iron Company had proposed to build at the Centennial. Condit, *American Building Art*, 2:71–72.

23. Roland Barthes, "The Eiffel Tower," in *Rethinking Architecture: A Reader in Cultural Theory*, ed. Neil Leach (London: Routledge, 1997), 177.

24. USCC, *International Exhibition*, 1:121–22.

25. Cf. "Characteristics of the International Fair," pt. 2, 238, on displays in the French department: "There are singularly few things in the department which one covets or would care to own; . . . but the arrangement is so attractive, the simple show-cases of black wood and thin, clear glass, with their plain, slim, gold lettering, have such a native elegance, that the eye ranges or rests among them with pleasure and contentment."

26. Ingram, *Centennial Exposition*, 432–33.

27. Cf. Bennett, "Exhibitionary Complex," 94: "After 1851, world fairs were to function less as vehicles for the technical education of the working classes than as instruments for their stupefaction before the reified products of their own labor, 'places of pilgrimage,' as Benjamin put it, 'to the fetish Commodity.'"

28. Brook Hindle and Steven Lubar, *Engines of Change: The American Industrial Revolution, 1790–1860* (Washington, D.C.: Smithsonian Institution Press, 1986), 194, 233.

29. "Characteristics of the International Fair," pt. 4, 498–99.

30. Simon J. Bronner, introduction to *Consuming Visions: Accumulation and Display of Goods in America, 1880–1920*, ed. Simon J. Bronner. (New York: W.W. Norton for the Henry Francis du Pont Winterthur Museum, 1989), 8–9.

31. Cf. David Nye, *American Technological Sublime* (Cambridge: MIT Press, 1994), 120–23, for a discussion of the Corliss engine. Cf. "Characteristics of the International Fair," pt. 3, *Atlantic Monthly* 38 (Sept. 1876): 350, on Machinery Hall: "The place makes an extraordinary impression upon everybody. . . . Nowhere else are the triumphs of ingenuity, the marvels of skill, so displayed and demonstrated; there is something at once sublime and infernal in the spectacle."

32. Originally: "The price makes the commodity identical to all those which are sold at the same price." Walter Benjamin, 3 Feb. 1939, *Briefe*, 2:805–9, in Weber, "Walter Benjamin," 267.

33. Crary, *Techniques*, 11.

34. Jean Baudrillard, *L'Échange symbolique et la mort* (Paris: Gallimard, 1976), 86, in Crary, *Techniques*, 12.

35. Crary, *Techniques*, 70.

36. Katherine C. Grier, *Culture and Comfort: People, Parlors and Upholstery, 1850–1930* (Amherst: University of Massachusetts Press, 1988), 49.

37. Artur Hazelius used period rooms in his new Museum of Scandinavian Ethnography, established in 1873 in Stockholm. Edward P. Alexander, *Museum Masters: Their Museums and Their Influence* (Nashville: American Association for State and Local History, 1983), 8; Steven Conn, *Museums and American Intellectual Life, 1876–1926* (Chicago: University of Chicago Press, 1998), 226.

38. "Characteristics of the International Fair," pt. 4, 496.

39. Ingram, *Centennial Exposition*, 528.

40. Alexander, *Museum Masters*, 245–47. The painting was *The Little Girl's Last Bed* by Amalia Lindegren.

41. Ibid., 8, 279–80; Ingram, *Centennial Exposition*, 146–47.

42. See Ritvo, "Zoological Nomenclature," 334–53.

43. In a series of articles about the Centennial Photographic Company, John L. Gihon recalled, "I am telling the truth . . . , when I relate to you how a photographer from the suburban districts, after examining a handsome stereoscopic picture of the lady's specimens, with herself occupying a prominent position in the centre, asked me confidentially if the woman was not stuffed as well as the rest of the animals." John L. Gihon, "Rambling Remarks Resumed," *Philadelphia Photographer* 14 (Mar. 1877): 71.

44. Crary, *Techniques*, 69–70.

45. Guy Debord, *The Society of the Spectacle* (Detroit, Mich.: Black & Red, 1983), chap. 1, art. 34. Cf. Allan Pred, "Spectacular Articulations of Modernity: The Stockholm Exhibition of 1897," *Geografiska Annaler, Series B, Human Geography* 73 (1991): 48.

46. Crary, *Techniques*, 100–105.

47. USCC, *International Exhibition*, 1:55.

48. "Notes and Clippings," *American Architect and Building News* 1 (13 May 1876): 159.

49. About the smells, cf. "Characteristics of the International Fair," pt. 5, 734: "The Eastern courts exhaled delicious whiffs of attar of roses, scented woods and clays, and

that strange sweet, stimulating perfume which must be the breath of Orient." About the music, cf. Jackson, *American Space*, 236–37: "The atmosphere in the large Main Building and in the Agricultural Building was that of a county fair. . . . There was a continuous background of music."

50. USCC, *International Exhibition*, 1:96–100.

51. "Characteristics of the International Fair," pt. 2, 234; pt. 4, 494. Cf. Holley, *Josiah Allen's Wife*, 450–51. Samantha says, "But now, havin' gone the rounds of the Nations . . . I told Josiah that I must git out in the open air and rest off the eyes of my spectacles a little, or I didn't know what the result would be."

52. USCC, *International Exhibition*, 1:99. Cf. "Characteristics of the International Fair," pt. 2, 234: "All around are fellow countryfolk from every part of our wide land, some looking at particular things, others at things in general, a great number only at the people." Cf. Philadelphia, *Vienna Exposition*, 15, on the necessity of providing cheap and attractive transportation to the Centennial: "No one will walk to see it a second time, as the fatigue of going through and examining a large exposition, is sufficiently exhausting." Cf. Walker, "Philadelphia Exhibition," pt. 1, 378–79, on the Centennial Commission's decision to abandon its original intention to install the exhibition in a single fifty-acre building: "I can entertain no doubt that the millions of visitors enjoyed the display of products better by reason of their division among half a score of considerable buildings, found rest to body and mind in the transition, got closer to things, and brought away clearer images and more of them, than if every thing had found a place in the Main Building."

53. Cf. Walter Benjamin, "On Some Motifs in Baudelaire," in *Illuminations*, ed. Hannah Arendt (New York: Schocken Books, 1968), 166–74. Benjamin describes the crowd in nineteenth-century literature as jostling, bustling, rushing, streaming, speeding, thronging, surging, rushing, whirling, swarming.

54. Cf. Rydell, *All the World's a Fair*, 2–3: "World's fairs performed a hegemonic function precisely because they propagated the ideas and values of the country's political, financial, corporate, and intellectual leaders."

55. This is the basic premise of Mary Douglas and Baron Isherwood, *The World of Goods* (New York: Basic Books, 1979).

56. Cf. Bennett, "Exhibitionary Complex," 81–82: "The exhibitionary complex . . . perfected a system of looks in which the subject and object positions can be exchanged."

CHAPTER 5

1. "The United States International Exhibition of 1876," *Journal of the Franklin Institute* 102 (Dec. 1876): 364.

2. USCC, *International Exhibition*, 9:140.

3. Cf. Schlereth, "Material Universe": "World's fairs especially served the middle-class penchant for the associative life."

4. Julius Bien, *1776–1876: Album of the International Exhibition at Philadelphia to Commemorate the Centennial of the United States of America* (New York: Bien, 1875), n.p.; USCC, *International Exhibition*, 2:79; 9:139–40.

5. Patrick Geddes, *Industrial Exhibitions and Modern Progress* (Edinburgh: David Douglas, 1887), 37.

6. USCC, *International Exhibition*, 1:564; vol. 2, app., 68.

7. Ibid., vol. 2, app., 68; Walker, "Philadelphia Exhibition," pt. 1, 390.

8. It recalled the charter of the American Philosophical Society, the Philadelphia-based institution founded in 1769 "for promoting useful knowledge." Daniel Boorstin, *The Lost World of Thomas Jefferson* (Chicago: University of Chicago Press, 1981), 10.

9. *National Cyclopaedia of American Biography* (1897), s.v. "Walker, Francis A."; USCC, *Journal of the Proceedings of the United States Centennial Commission at Philadelphia. [Eighth Session: May, 1876]* (n.p., [1876?]), 27, booklet bound in USCC, *Journals and Reports.* Historical Society of Pennsylvania, Philadelphia. The Bureau of Awards was an executive department of the Centennial Commission; its responsibilities included representing the commission to the judges, editing the judges' reports, and expediting their work. USCC, *International Exhibition,* 1:24.

10. Walker, "Philadelphia Exhibition," pt. 1, 387–88.

11. In a speech to the ninth and final session of the Centennial Commission, Joseph Hawley concluded that, "to use a commercial expression, we [Americans] have been exceedingly well advertised." USCC, *International Exhibition,* 1:149.

12. I must thank architect Barbara Judy for bringing this to my attention.

13. Jürgen Habermas, "Modernity—An Incomplete Project," in *Postmodernism: A Reader,* ed. Thomas Docherty (New York: Columbia, 1993), 103.

14. USCC, *Journal of the Proceedings of the United States Centennial Commission at Philadelphia. Sixth Session: May, 1875, (n.p., [1875?]),* booklet bound in *Journals and Reports of the United States Centennial Commission, 1872-76,* Historical Society of Pennsylvania, Philadelphia, app., 39.

15. USCC, *International Exhibition,* 1:10–11.

16. Ibid., 1:564.

17. Ibid., vol. 2, app., 56.

18. Ibid., vol. 2, app., 69.

19. Ibid., 1:565.

20. USCC, Executive Committee, *Report of the Executive Committee,* 62–63. Because some judges declined to serve or resigned their positions, or because some countries neglected to appoint representatives, the final number was 233—115 American and 118 foreign, according to USCC, *International Exhibition,* 1:567.

21. USCC, *International Exhibition,* vol. 2, app., 56.

22. Ibid., vol. 2, app., 15; James D. McCabe, *The Illustrated History of the Centennial Exhibition* (Philadelphia: National Publishing, 1876), 843–45.

23. USCC, *International Exhibition,* 1:566.

24. McCabe, *Illustrated History,* 906–7.

25. USCC, *Journal* (1875), 6.

26. USCC, *International Exhibition,* 1:12.

27. USCC, *Journal* (1876), 27.

28. USCC, *International Exhibition,* 7:161. The derivation of the term, American System of Manufactures, is discussed in Eugene S. Ferguson, "History and Historiography," in *Yankee Enterprise: The Rise of the American System of Manufactures,* ed. Otto Mayr and Robert C. Post (Washington, D.C.: Smithsonian Institution Press, 1981), 15n. 1; in Merrit Roe Smith, "Military Entrepreneurship," in *Yankee Enterprise,* 95–96n. 3.

29. Hindle and Lubar, *Engines of Change,* 218; L. Simonin, *A French View of the Grand International Exposition of 1876* (Philadelphia: Claxton, Remsen & Happelfinger, 1877), 19.

30. USCC, *International Exhibition,* 1:635.

31. Walker, "Philadelphia Exhibition," pt. 1, 377.

32. USCC, *International Exhibition*, 1:562–64.

33. Geddes, *Industrial Exhibitions*, 20.

34. USCC, *International Exhibition*, 1:563.

35. Ibid., 1:575.

36. Ibid., 2:79–80.

37. Ibid., 1:570, 576; 3:iv; George Ward Nichols, "Correspondence: The Centennial Painting Awards," *Nation* 23, no. 589 (12 Oct. 1876): 227.

38. Nichols, an art critic for the *New York Times*, was the husband of Maria Longworth, founder of Rookwood Pottery, and the author of two books, *Art Education Applied to Industry* (1877) and *Pottery: How It Is Made, Its Shape and Decoration* (1878). Diana Korzenik, *Drawn to Art: A Nineteenth-Century American Dream* (Hanover, N.H.: University Press of New England, 1985), 228; Jessie Poesch, *Newcomb Pottery: An Enterprise for Southern Women, 1895–1940* (Exton, Pa.: Schiffer Publishing, 1984), 11.

39. "The Awards at the Centennial Exhibition," *Nation* 23, no. 595 (23 Nov. 1876): 310.

40. Nichols, "Correspondence," 227.

41. Frank Hill Smith, "Correspondence: The Centennial Art Awards," *Nation* 23, no. 597 (7 Dec. 1876): 340.

42. George Ward Nichols, "Correspondence. The Fine Arts Group at the Centennial Exhibition," *Nation* 25, no. 652 (27 Dec. 1877), 393; and Francis A. Walker, "Correspondence. The Fine Arts Group at the Centennial Exhibition," *Nation* 25, no. 652 (27 Dec. 1877), 393.

43. Walter Benjamin, "The Work of Art in the Age of Mechanical Reproduction," in *Illuminations*, ed. Hannah Arendt (New York: Schocken Books, 1968), 220–21.

44. The original members included Congressman Daniel J. Morrell of Pennsylvania and industrialist George H. Corliss of Rhode Island. USCC, Committee on Appeals, [*Report to the United States Centennial Commission*], pamphlet, 1876, 1, Historical Society of Pennsylvania, Philadelphia.

45. "Awards," 310.

46. The appointees included Prof. Spencer F. Baird of the Smithsonian Institution. USCC, Committee on Appeals, [*Report*], 2.

47. Ibid., 2–3.

48. USCC, *International Exhibition*, 1:571.

49. Walker, "Philadelphia Exhibition," pt. 1, 394–95.

50. The exact number of awards was 13,104, with American exhibitors taking home 5,302. USCC, *International Exhibition*, 1:569–70; Coleman Sellers, "System of Awards at the United States International Exhibition of 1876," *Journal of the Franklin Institute* 103, no. 1 (Jan. 1877): 14.

51. Walker, "Philadelphia Exhibition," pt. 1, 393; USCC, *International Exhibition*, 1:569–70.

52. USCC, "Reports of the Judges of Awards," form, 1877, Philadelphia City Archives.

53. J. Stuart Freeman Jr., *Toward a Third Century of Excellence: An Informal History of the J.B. Lippincott Company on the Occasion of Its 200th Anniversary* (Philadelphia: J.B. Lippincott, 1992), vii.

54. USCC, *International Exhibition*, 1:568; "United States International Exhibition," 363. The *Journal* later went on to state that the Centennial Commission had made a mistake "in attempting to substitute for the prizes for prominent or acknowledged

excellence, usually distributed at the great Exhibitions, a system of awards, founded upon some universal standard of mediocrity . . . , judiciously qualified by numerous adjectives." "Motive Power of the International Exposition," *Journal of the Franklin Institute* 103, no. 1 (Jan. 1877): 1.

55. United States, World's Columbian Commission [H. N. Higinbotham], *Report of the President to the Board of Directors of the World's Columbian Exposition* (Chicago: Rand, McNally, 1898), 105; United States, World's Columbian Commission, *Final Report of the Executive Committee of Awards* (Washington, D.C.: John F. Sheiry, 1895), 17, 20, 33–34.

56. The countries that originally withdrew their exhibits were Austria, Belgium, Brazil, British Guiana, Denmark, France, Germany, Great Britain, Italy, Japan, Norway, Portugal, Russia, Siam, Spain, Sweden, and Switzerland. United States, World's Columbian Commission, *Final Report,* 24, 36–38.

57. United States, World's Columbian Commission, *Report of the President,* 295.

58. A Century of Progress, *Official Book of the Fair, Giving Pre-Exposition Information, 1932-33, of a Century of Progress International Exposition, Chicago, 1933* (Chicago: A Century of Progress, 1932), 5.

59. A Century of Progress [Rufus C. Dawes], *Report of the President of a Century of Progress to the Board of Trustees* ([Chicago?]: [A Century of Progress?], 1936), 35, 72.

60. See Umberto Eco, "A Theory of Expositions," in *Travels in Hyper Reality: Essays,* trans. William Weaver (San Diego: A Helen and Kurt Wolff Book, Harcourt Brace Jovanovich, 1983), 291–307.

61. Sellers, "System of Awards," 16.

62. Cf. Benjamin, 3 Feb. 1939, *Briefe,* 2:805–9, in Weber, "Walter Benjamin," 267: "The price makes the commodity identical to all those which are sold at the same price." Also Lutchmansingh, "Commodity Exhibitionism," 208: "It was, therefore, their constitution as commodities in an expanding world market that disabled the differences between otherwise radically unrelated objects in the interest of an abstract and universal law of exchange. In the milieu of the international exhibition, differences of ethnic and artistic character, tradition and custom, function, skill, and conditions of production were converted by the sorcery of the international market into a new kind of commensurability. This, as Marx pointed out, is the disguise of the *fetish.*"

63. See chap. 2, n. 99.

64. Francis A. Walker, "The Philadelphia Exhibition," pt. 3, *International Review* 4 (Sept. 1877): 685.

65. George F. Kunz referred to the "vital initiative given [by the Centennial] to art study and art collection in the United States," and he claimed that the exhibition had contributed to an "art movement of national proportions," which resulted in the creation of public museums and private collections. Kunz, "Management and Uses of Expositions," *North American Review* 175 (Sept. 1902): 411, 417. Cf. Allwood, *Great Exhibitions,* 56; Reid Badger, *The Great American Fair: The World's Columbian Exposition and American Culture* (Chicago: Nelson-Hall, 1970), 17–18; Beers, "Centennial City," 417; Holger Cahill, introduction to *The Index of American Design,* by Erwin O. Christensen (New York: Macmillan, 1950), ix; J. Edward Clarke to Dalton Dorr, 17 Feb. 1880, Philadelphia Museum of Art Archives, Dorr Collection, Letterbook 4, letter 206, in Conn, *Museums,* 202; Laurence Vail Coleman, *The Museum in America: A Critical Study* (Washington, D.C.: American Association of Museums, 1939), 32–33, in Christine Hunter Donaldson, "The Centennial of 1876: The Exposition, and Culture for

America" (Ph.D. diss., Yale University, 1948), 124; Talbot F. Hamlin, *The American Spirit in Architecture* (New Haven, Conn.: Yale University Press, 1926), in Maass, *Glorious Enterprise,* 84; Korzenik, *Drawn to Art,* 221, 226–28; Luckhurst, *Story of Exhibitions,* 52; Russell Lynes, *The Art-Makers: An Informal History of Painting, Sculpture and Architecture in 19th Century America* (New York: Dover, 1982), 278; Poesch, *Newcomb Pottery,* 11–12; George B. Tatum, *Penn's Great Town* (Philadelphia: University of Pennsylvania Press, 1961), 102; H. Barbara Weinberg, introduction to *Our American Artists,* by Samuel G.W. Benjamin (New York: Garland Publishing, 1977), 2–3, 9.

66. Cf. Donaldson, "Centennial of 1876," 122: "Where there had been nothing at the War's end, the nation saw within a dozen years the firm establishment of the Corcoran Gallery in Washington [1874], the expansion of both the National Academy of Design in New York (1865). and the Academy of Fine Arts in Philadelphia (1876) into new buildings, the founding of the Crocker Art Gallery in Sacramento [as a private collection, donated in 1885], Memorial Hall (of Centennial fame) in Philadelphia, and most important of all, the great public museums of New York and Boston, the Metropolitan Museum in New York and the Boston Museum of Fine Arts, both officially established about 1870."

67. On anxiety, cf. T.J. Jackson Lears, "Beyond Veblen: Rethinking Consumer Culture in America," in Bronner, *Consuming Visions,* 83–84: "Fashion ideologues constantly emphasized the control and care with which clothes and other goods should be presented to the world. The meanings associated with goods, especially fashionable or luxury goods, were always shifting, unstable, and perhaps even dangerous. . . . Madness, the literature implied, bubbled just beneath the surface of select society, so there was a constant need to organize the meanings attached to consumption—to domesticate and moralize them." Lears goes on to explain that this concern was rooted in the very real "insecurities of everyday life in an expanding market society."

CHAPTER 6

1. Geddes, *Industrial Exhibitions,* 2, 25, 38.

2. *Oxford English Dictionary,* 2d ed., s.v. "bazaar."

3. http://www.dictionary.com, s.v. "fancy goods," (16 Feb. 2002).

4. William Phipps Blake, "Report of the Executive Commissioner," in USCC, *Journal* (1872), app., 93–94.

5. Pennsylvania Board, *Pennsylvania and the Centennial Exposition,* vol. 1, pt. 1, 249.

6. Benedict, "Anthropology," 2. Cf. Korzenik, *Drawn to Art,* 225: "Despite all its apparent concern with art, the Centennial was a massive blitz to create new appetites, to increase American spending."

7. "Correspondence," *American Architect and Building News* 1 (23 Dec. 1876): 413–14.

8. "Characteristics of the International Fair," pt. 4, 498.

9. International Exhibition Company [IEC], *Official Bulletin of the International Exhibition,* no. 4 (May 1877): 14.

10. Great Exhibition, *First Report of the Commissioners,* xliii.

11. Allwood, *Great Exhibitions,* 35.

12. U.S. Commission to the Vienna Exhibition, *Reports,* 1:61.

13. Francis A. Walker, "The Philadelphia Exhibition," pt. 2, *International Review* 4 (July 1877): 501–2.

14. Anna K. Baker, diary, 1874–76, entries dated 7 June and 19 June 1876, Historical Society of Pennsylvania, Philadelphia.

15. McCabe, *Illustrated History,* 688–90. These were the Bethlehem and Jerusalem Bazaars and the building of the Sponge Fishers of Turkey. Pennsylvania Board, *Pennsylvania and the Centennial Exposition,* vol. 1, pt. 1, 137 ff.

16. Baker diary, 8 Sept. 1876.

17. *Atlantic Monthly* 39 (Jan. 1876): 99. In Donaldson, "Centennial of 1876," 105.

18. USCC, *International Exhibition,* 1:337–40, 417–19, 421–23; Walker, "Philadelphia Exhibition," pt. 2, 500.

19. Nicolai, *Centennial Philadelphia,* 93. Cf. Maass, *Glorious Enterprise,* 125.

20. Ingram, *Centennial Exposition,* 31.

21. Patrick Geddes went so far as to argue that, not only the museum, but the entire system of public art education, including the network of design schools in British manufacturing centers, owed its existence specifically to the object lesson provided by the French exhibits at the Great Exhibition. Geddes, *Industrial Exhibitions,* 42.

22. Ferguson, "Technical Museums," 30; Robert W. Rydell, "The Culture of Imperial Abundance: World's Fairs in the Making of American Culture," in Bronner, *Consuming Visions,* 210–11; Simon J. Bronner, "Object Lessons," in Bronner, *Consuming Visions,* 236; Kunz, "Management and Uses," 420.

23. *American Architect and Building News* 1 (4 Nov. 1876): 356, in Donaldson, "Centennial of 1876," 124.

24. United States, Centennial Board of Finance, *Third Annual Report of the Centennial Board of Finance to the Stockholders* (Philadelphia: J.B. Lippincott, 1876), 6.

25. *Philadelphia Press,* 9 Nov. 1876, p. 4, in Donaldson, "Centennial of 1876," 96.

26. Blake, "Report to the United States Centennial Commission," 276.

27. Bennett, "Exhibitionary Complex," 73–74.

28. David R. Brigham, *Public Culture in the Early Republic: Peale's Museum and Its Audience* (Washington, D.C.: Smithsonian Institution Press, 1995), 18; Ferguson, "Technical Museums," 33.

29. Brigham, *Public Culture,* 45–46; Charles Coleman Sellers, *Mr. Peale's Museum: Charles Willson Peale and the First Popular Museum of Natural Science and Art* (New York: W.W. Norton, 1980), 52.

30. Morris J. Vogel, *Cultural Connections: Museums and Libraries of Philadelphia and the Delaware Valley* (Philadelphia: Temple University Press, 1991), 215; Academy of Natural Sciences, "The Academy of Natural Sciences," 1998-2002, www.acnatsci.org. (16 Feb. 2002).

31. Ferguson, "Technical Museums," 34.

32. Vogel, *Cultural Connections,* 60, 226; Wagner Free Institute of Science. *Annual Announcement of Lecture Courses and Programs for Session of 1998–99,* pamphlet (Philadelphia: Wagner Free Institute of Science, 1998), 1–2.

33. Edwin Wolf II, *Philadelphia: Portrait of an American City* (Harrisburg, Pa.: Stackpole Books, 1975), 219; Academy of Natrual Sciences, "Academy."

34. *Magee's Illustrated Guide of Philadelphia and the Centennial Exhibition* (Philadelphia: Richard Magee, 1876), 5, 39, 51, 159.

35. Beers, "Centennial City," 449; *Magee's Illustrated Guide,* 20.

36. USCC, *International Exhibition,* vol. 2, app., 15.

37. These are the buildings that survived into the twentieth century. The English commissioner's building was razed in 1961. Horticultural Hall was demolished in 1955, after being damaged by a storm. Esther M. Klein, *Fairmount Park: A History and a Guidebook* (Bryn Mawr, Pa.: Harcum Junior College Press, 1974), 32; Maass, *Glorious Enterprise,* 70; Nicolai, *Centennial Philadelphia,* 94–95.

38. "Notes and Clippings," *American Architect and Building News* 1 (9 Dec. 1876): 400; "Correspondence," *American Architect and Building News* 1 (23 Dec. 1876): 414.

39. "Summary," *American Architect and Building News* 1 (23 Sept. 1876): 305.

40. John William Wallace, *Upon the Origin and Objects of the International Exhibition Company,* pamphlet, 1880, 2, Centennial Collection, Historical Society of Pennsylvania, Philadelphia.

41. Ibid., 2; McCabe, *Illustrated History,* 910. Clement Biddle, a member of the Centennial Board of Finance, became IEC president; Thomas Cochran and John Wanamaker, also members of the Board of Finance, served as IEC directors; Henry Pettit took charge of the IEC's Bureau of Management; John Sartain, formally chief of the Centennial Commission's Bureau of Art, became head of the IEC Fine Art Department.

42. McCabe, *Illustrated History,* 910.

43. IEC, *Official Bulletin,* no. 4 (May 1877): 18.

44. Thomas Prasch, "The Invention of the Theme Park: Crystal Palace—Sydenham" (paper presented at the annual meeting of the Nineteenth-Century Studies Association, Philadelphia, 18–20 Mar. 1999).

45. "Notes and Clippings" (9 Dec. 1876): 400.

46. "The Philadelphia Fair," *New York Times,* 11 May 1877, p. 2.

47. Philadelphia, Commissioners of Fairmount Park, *License granted by the Commissioners of Fairmount Park to the International Exhibition Company* (1876), 1–2, Historical Society of Pennsylvania, Philadelphia.

48. McCabe, *Illustrated History,* 910; "Correspondence," *American Architect and Building News* 2 (5 May 1877): 143.

49. "Summary:—The Permanent Exhibition at Philadelphia," *American Architect and Building News* 2, no. 69 (21 Apr. 1877): 121.

50. "Philadelphia's New Exhibition," *Harper's Weekly* 21 (26 May 1877): 414; IEC, *Opening Ceremonies, May 10th, 1877,* program, [1877], Athenaeum, Philadelphia.

51. IEC, *Official Bulletin,* no. 3 (Mar. 1877): 16; no. 4 (May 1877): 22-25. See chap. 3, no. 12.

52. Ibid., no. 4 (May 1877): 30.

53. Ibid.

54. Ibid., no. 4 (May 1877):14, 32; no. 5 (Apr. 1879): 10.

55. John W. Forney, *Oration by Mr. John W. Forney, at the 101st Celebration of American Independence: July 4, 1877, in the International Exhibition Building, Fairmount Park, by Invitation of the Board of Managers* (Philadelphia: Vallette, Haslam, 1877), 13.

56. IEC, *Official Bulletin,* no. 2 (Feb. 1877): 8.

57. *National Cyclopaedia of American Biography* (1932), s.v. "Biddle, Clement Miller."

58. Wallace, *Upon the Origin and Objects,* 6.

59. IEC, *Official Bulletin,* no. 4 (May 1877):16.

60. "Summary:—The Permanent Exhibition," 121.

61. IEC, *Official Bulletin,* no. 2 (Feb. 1877): 4; no. 5 (Apr. 1879): 9.

62. "A thousand little pebbles are in some instances required in the formation of a single flower." Ibid., no. 4 (May 1877): 31, 35, 37, 41.

63. Committee of the Fifth of July, *Ceremonies in Commemoration of the 104th Anniversary of American Independence, in the International Exhibition Building, Philadelphia, July 5th, 1880,* program (Philadelphia: Times Printing House, 1880), n.p., Historical Society of Pennsylvania, Philadelphia.

64. "General Notes," *New York Times,* 2 Aug. 1877, p. 4.

65. "The Permanent Exhibition's Trials," *New York Times,* 22 Dec. 1877, p. 1.

66. "The Permanent Exhibition," *New York Times,* 15 Mar. 1878, p. 1; IEC, Board of Managers, report to the stockholders (Philadelphia, ca. 1877), n.p.

67. "Continuing the Philadelphia Exhibition," *New York Times,* 21 Jan. 1879, p. 2; "The Permanent Exhibition," *New York Times,* 15 Mar. 1878, p. 1.

68. "End of the Permanent Exhibition," *New York Times,* 3 Aug. 1879, p. 7.

69. "The Permanent Exhibition," *New York Times,* 11 Apr. 1880, p. 7.

70. Wallace, *Upon the Origin and Objects,* 3–6.

71. "The Permanent Exhibition," *New York Times,* 15 Jan. 1881, p. 2.

72. "End of the Permanent Exhibition," *New York Times,* 3 Nov. 1881, p. 1; "General Notes," *New York Times,* 19 Dec. 1881, p. 4.

73. "Profits of an Exhibition," *New York Times,* 17 Jan. 1882, p. 5.

74. "The Permanent Exhibition Company," *New York Times,* 29 Mar. 1883, p. 5.

75. Maass claimed that the design was based on an unpremiated project for the French Prix de Rome, that it was the first Beaux Arts–style art museum in the United States, and that it influenced the design of the Reichstag in Berlin. Maass, *Glorious Enterprise,* 50 ff.

76. For a summary of other responses, see Donaldson, "Centennial of 1876," 54–55; Hicks, "United States Centennial Exhibition," 182; and Maass, *Glorious Enterprise,* 47–48.

77. Howells, "Sennight," 93.

78. James Douglas Jr., "The Centennial Exhibition," *Canadian Monthly* 9 (June 1876): 542.

79. "Correspondence," *American Architect and Building News* 2 (17 Feb. 1877): 54. An earlier account was equally critical: *American Architect and Building News* 1 (3 June 1876): 179, in Donaldson, "Centennial of 1876," 54.

80. USCC, *International Exhibition,* vol. 2, app., 204, 242.

81. Provisional Committee, *Report of the Provisional Commmittee to a Meeting of Citizens, Held November 19th, 1875,* pamphlet, [1875?], 1–2, Pennsylvania Museum of Art; "The Pennsylvania Museum and School of Industrial Art," *Bulletin of the Pennsylvania Museum,* Apr. 1905, 17.

82. Provisional Committee, *Report,* app. C, 1–2.

83. Pennsylvania Museum, 1876 charter, art. 2.

84. "Summary:—Effect of the Centennial upon Our Industrial Arts," *American Architect and Building News* 2 (28 July 1877): 237.

85. Provisional Committee, *Report,* app. A, 1; Pennsylvania Museum and School of Industrial Art, Board of Trustees, *First and Second Reports of the Board of Trustees* (Philadelphia: Review Printing House, 1878), 7.

86. Blake, "Report of the Executive Commissioner," 95–96.

87. Walter Smith, Boston, to the Provisional Committee on the Organization of a Museum of Art in Philadelphia, 25 Sept. 1875, in Provisional Committee, *Report,* app. B, 3.

88. Ibid., 1; Pennsylvania Museum, *First and Second Reports,* 7–8.

89. "Summary," *American Architect and Building News* 2 (15 Dec. 1877): 398.

90. Pennsylvania Museum, *First and Second Reports,* 8.

91. Maass, *Glorious Enterprise,* 48–49.

92. Pennsylvania Museum, *First and Second Reports,* 8–12.

93. Ibid., 12.

94. Conn, *Museums,* 207–8, 216, 218.

95. Helen W. Henderson, *The Pennsylvania Academy of the Fine Arts and Other Collections of Philadelphia* (Boston: L.C. Page, 1911), 223–24.

96. Conn, *Museums,* 226.

97. David B. Brownlee, *Making a Modern Classic: The Architecture of the Philadelphia Museum of Art* (Philadelphia: Philadelphia Museum of Art, 1977), 99.

98. Pennsylvania Museum, *First and Second Reports,* 11.

99. Ibid.

100. Conn, *Museums,* 209, 213.

101. Ibid., 210, 214–15, 219; Brownlee, *Making a Modern Classic,* 55–57.

102. Brownlee, *Making a Modern Classic,* 99–102; Conn, *Museums,* 224–27, 229.

103. Conn, *Museums,* 10–12.

104. Foucault, *Order of Things,* 219–21, 367–73.

105. John Wanamaker, *Golden Book of the Wanamaker Stores. Jubilee Year, 1861–1911* ([Philadelphia]: John Wanamaker, 1911), 26–34.

106. Herbert A. Gibbons, *John Wanamaker* (New York: Harper & Brothers, 1926), 1:111, 113.

107. Ibid., 1:112, 115.

108. Joseph H. Appel, *John Wanamaker: A Study* ([Camden, N.J.]: n.p., 1927), 77; Gibbons, *Wanamaker,* 1:130; John Wanamaker, *Golden Book,* 35–36, 38–42.

109. John Wanamaker, *Golden Book,* 43–45.

110. Joseph H. Appel, *The Business Biography of John Wanamaker, Founder and Builder: America's Merchant Pioneer from 1861 to 1922* (New York: Macmillan, 1930), 98.

111. John Wanamaker, *Golden Book,* 47–49.

112. Wanamaker Papers, box 3-A, file 9, Historical Society of Pennsylvania, Philadelphia.

113. John Wanamaker, *Golden Book,* 53–54. Cf. Gibbons, *John Wanamaker,* 1:114 on similar practices at the Chestnut Street store.

114. Appel, *Business Biography,* 100.

115. Ibid., 92.

116. *Magee's Illustrated Guide,* 60–61.

117. Thomas A. Markus, *Buildings and Power: Freedom and Control in the Origin of Modern Building Types* (London: Routledge, 1993), 177–78.

118. Michel Foucault, *Discipline and Punish: The Birth of the Prison,* trans. Alan Sheridan (New York: Vintage Books, 1979), 200–202.

119. John Wanamaker, *Golden Book,* 53, 73.

120. Ibid., 51.

121. Ibid., 65, 71.

122. Gibbons, *John Wanamaker,* 1:79; Appel, *Business Biography,* 78. In 1916, he is reputed to have made the original proposal for the 1926 Sesquicentennial International Exposition in Philadelphia, but he died in 1922 before it could take place. Conn, *Museums,* 233.

123. Wanamaker Papers, box 3, file 9.

124. John Wanamaker, *Golden Book,* 67.

125. There were supposed to be thirty-five thousand invited guests. John Wanamaker,

A Friendly Guide to Philadelphia and the Wanamaker Store (Philadelphia: John Wanamaker, 1926), 43.

126. Hines, *Burnham of Chicago*, 288–92, 303; John Andrew Gallery, ed., *Philadelphia Architecture: A Guide to the City,* 2d ed. (Philadelphia: Foundation for Architecture, 1994), 85; John Wanamaker, *Friendly Guide*, 61.

127. John Wanamaker, *Friendly Guide,* 43, 45, 47.

128. Appel, *Business Biography,* 404; Bronner, "Object Lessons," 233–34, 236–37.

129. John Wanamaker, *Golden Book,* 73–74.

130. John Wanamaker, *Friendly Guide,* 50, 52–53.

131. Appel, *Wanamaker,* 92.

132. Stewart, *On Longing,* 152.

SELECT BIBLIOGRAPHY

Alex, William. *Calvert Vaux: Architect and Planner.* New York: Ink, 1994.

Alexander, Edward P. *Museum Masters: Their Museums and Their Influence.* Nashville: American Association for State and Local History, 1983.

Allwood, John. *The Great Exhibitions.* London: Studio Vista, 1977.

Appel, Joseph H. *The Business Biography of John Wanamaker, Founder and Builder: America's Merchant Pioneer from 1861 to 1922.* New York: Macmillan, 1930.

———. *John Wanamaker: A Study.* [Camden, N.J.], 1927.

"The Arrangement of Great Exhibitions." *Nation* 21, no. 543 (25 Nov. 1875): 336–37.

"The Awards at the Centennial Exhibition." *Nation* 23, no. 595 (23 Nov. 1876): 310–11.

Badger, Reid. *The Great American Fair: The World's Columbian Exposition and American Culture.* Chicago: Nelson-Hall, 1970.

Baker, Anna K. Diary. 1874–76. Manuscript and Archives Department. Historical Society of Pennsylvania, Philadelphia.

Barthes, Roland. "The Eiffel Tower." In *Rethinking Architecture: A Reader in Cultural Theory,* ed. Neil Leach, 172–80. London: Routledge, 1997.

———. "The Plates of the *Encyclopedia.*" In *New Critical Essays,* trans. Richard Howard, 23–39. New York: Hill & Wang, 1980.

Bassin, Joan. *Architectural Competitions in Nineteenth-Century England,* Studies in the Fine Arts: Architecture, no. 6. Ann Arbor: UMI Research Press, 1984.

Beers, Dorothy Gondos. "The Centennial City, 1865–1876." In *Philadelphia: A 300-Year History,* ed. Russell F. Weigley, 417–70. New York: W.W. Norton, 1982.

Bellier de la Chavignerie, Émile, and Louis Auvray. *Dictionnaire général des artistes de l'École française.* 5 vols. New York: Garland, 1979.

Benedict, Burton. "The Anthropology of World's Fairs." In *The Anthropology of World's Fairs: San Francisco's Panama Pacific International Exposition of 1915,* by Burton Benedict et al., 1–65. Berkeley, Calif.: Scolar Press, 1983.

Benjamin, Walter. "On Some Motifs in Baudelaire." In *Illuminations,* ed. Hannah Arendt, 155–200. New York: Schocken Books, 1968.

———. "Unpacking My Library: A Talk About Book Collecting." In *Illuminations,* ed. Hannah Arendt, 59–67. New York: Schocken Books, 1968.

————. "The Work of Art in the Age of Mechanical Reproduction." In *Illuminations,* ed. Hannah Arendt, 217–51. New York: Schocken Books, 1968.

Bennett, Tony. "The Exhibitionary Complex." *New Formations* 4 (1988): 73–102.

Bennitt, Mark, ed. *History of the Louisiana Purchase Exposition.* St. Louis: Universal Exposition Publishing, 1905.

Bien, Julius. *1776–1876: Album of the International Exhibition at Philadelphia to Commemorate the Centennial of the United States of America.* New York: Julius Bien, 1875.

Blake, William P. "Appendix C. Report to the United States Centennial Commission, upon the Organization, Administration, and Results of the Vienna International Exhibition, 1873, by William P. Blake, Member and Agent of the United States Centennial Commission." In U.S. Congress, Senate, *National Centennial,* 109–278.

————. "Previous International Expositions." In United States Centennial Commission, *Journal of the Proceedings* (1872), 53–66.

————. "Report of the Executive Commissioner." In United States Centennial Commission, *Journal of the Proceedings* (1872), app. no. 3, 54–107.

Boime, Albert. *The Magisterial Gaze: Manifest Destiny and American Landscape Painting c. 1830–1865.* Washington, D.C.: Smithsonian Institution Press, 1991.

Boorstin, Daniel. *The Lost World of Thomas Jefferson.* Chicago: University of Chicago Press, 1981.

Brigham, David R. *Public Culture in the Early Republic: Peale's Museum and Its Audience.* Washington, D.C.: Smithsonian Institution Press, 1995.

Bronner, Simon J. "Object Lessons: The Work of Ethnological Museums and Collections." In *Consuming Visions,* ed. Simon J. Bronner, 217–54.

Bronner, Simon J., ed. *Consuming Visions: Accumulation and Display of Goods in America, 1880–1920.* New York: W.W. Norton for the Winterthur Museum, 1989.

Brown, Bill. "Science Fiction, the Worlds Fair, and the Prosthetics of Empire." In *Cultures of United States Imperialism,* eds. Amy Kaplan and Donald Pease, 129–63. Durham, N.C.: Duke University Press, 1993.

Brownlee, David B. *Making a Modern Classic: The Architecture of the Philadelphia Museum of Art.* Philadelphia: Philadelphia Museum of Art, 1977.

Bruce, Edward C. *The Century: Its Fruits and Its Festival.* Philadelphia: J.B. Lippincott, 1877.

Buck-Morss, Susan. *Dialectics of Seeing: Walter Benjamin and the Arcades Project.* Cambridge: MIT Press, 1989.

Burat, Jules. *Exposition de l'industrie française année 1844.* Paris: Challamel, [1844].

Cahill, Holger. Introduction to Erwin O. Christensen, *The Index of American Design,* ix–xviii. New York: Macmillan; Washington, D.C.: National Gallery of Art, 1950.

Carpenter, Kenneth E. "European Industrial Exhibitions Before 1851 and Their Publications." *Technology and Culture* 13 (July 1972): 465–86.

Centennial Guide to the Exposition and Philadelphia. Philadelphia: Richard Magee & Son, 1876.

Centennial Photographic Company. *Catalog of the Centennial Photographic Company's Views of the International Exhibition, 1876.* Philadelphia: Sherman for the Centennial Photographic Company, 1876.

Century of Progress International Exposition (1933–34: Chicago, Ill.). *Official Book of the Fair, Giving Pre-Exposition Information, 1932–33, of a Century of Progress International Exposition, Chicago, 1933.* Chicago: Century of Progress, 1932.

Century of Progress International Exposition [Dawes, Rufus C.]. *Report of the President of a Century of Progress to the Board of Trustees.* [Chicago?]: [A Century of Progress?], 1936.

"Characteristics of the International Fair." *Atlantic Monthly* 38 (July 1876): 85–91; (Aug. 1876): 233–39; (Sept. 1876): 350–59; (Oct. 1876): 492–501; (Dec. 1876): 732–40; 39 (Jan. 1877): 94–100.

Cole, Henry. "Report on the Management of the British Portion of the Paris Universal Exhibition." In Great Britain, Royal Commission to the Paris Exposition, *Reports on the Paris Universal Exhibition,* 17–51. London: Eyre & Spottiswoode, 1856.

Collins, [Edward], and [Charles M.] Autenrieth. *Proposed Centennial Buildings.* Pamphlet. [1873]. Centennial Collection, Historical Society of Pennsylvania, Philadelphia.

Colmont, A. de. *Histoire des expositions des produits de l'industrie française.* Paris, 1855.

Committee of the Fifth of July. *Ceremonies in Commemoration of the 104th Anniversary of American Independence, in the International Exhibition Building, Philadelphia, July 5th, 1880.* Program. Philadelphia: Times Printing House, 1880. Historical Society of Pennsylvania, Philadelphia.

Condit, Carl W. *American Building Art.* 2 vols. New York: Oxford University Press, 1960.

———. *American Building: Materials and Techniques from the First Colonial Settlements to the Present.* Chicago: University of Chicago Press, 1968.

Conn, Steven. *Museums and American Intellectual Life, 1876–1926.* Chicago: University of Chicago Press, 1998.

"Continuing the Philadelphia Exhibition." *New York Times,* 21 Jan. 1879, p. 2.

Cordato, Mary F. "Representing the Expansion of Woman's Sphere: Women's Work and Culture at the World's Fairs of 1876, 1893, and 1904." Ph.D. diss., New York University, 1989.

"Correspondence." *American Architect and Building News* 1 (23 Dec. 1876): 413–14.

"Correspondence." *American Architect and Building News* 2 (17 Feb. 1877): 54–55.

"Correspondence." *American Architect and Building News* 2 (5 May 1877): 143.

Crary, Jonathan. *Techniques of the Observer: On Vision and Modernity in the Nineteenth Century.* Cambridge: MIT Press, 1992.

Cummings, Charles A., William R. Ware, and Samuel F. Thayer. *Suggestions of Architects of Boston to Committee on Plans and Architecture of Centennial Commission.* Reprint of letter to Henry Probasco, 21 Mar. 1872. Pamphlet. [1872]. In United States Centennial Commission, "Documentary Record of the Centennial," 1:89. Centennial Collection, Historical Society of Pennsylvania, Philadelphia.

Debord, Guy. *The Society of the Spectacle.* Detroit: Black & Red, 1983.

Ditter, Dorothy E.C. "The Cultural Climate of the Centennial City: Philadelphia, 1875–76." Ph.D. diss., University of Pennsylvania, 1947.

Donaldson, Christine Hunter. "The Centennial of 1876: The Exposition, and Culture for America." Ph.D. diss., Yale University, 1948.

Douglas, James. "The Centennial Exhibition." *Canadian Monthly* 9 (June 1876): 535–43.

Douglas, Mary, and Baron Isherwood. *The World of Goods.* New York: Basic Books, 1979.

Eco, Umberto. "A Theory of Expositions." In *Travels in Hyper Reality: Essays,* trans. William Weaver, 291–307. San Diego: A Helen and Kurt Wolff Book, Harcourt Brace Jovanovich, 1983.

"End of the Permanent Exhibition." *New York Times,* 3 Aug. 1879, p. 7.

"End of the Permanent Exhibition." *New York Times,* 3 Nov. 1881, p. 1.

The Exhibition of Art-Industry in Paris, 1855. Paris: Stassin & Xavier; London: Virtue, [ca. 1855].

Exposition des produits de l'industrie française, 1819 (Paris, France). Jury central. *Rapport du Jury central sur les produits de l'industrie française,* ed. Costaz. Paris: Imprimerie royale, 1819.

Exposition des produits de l'industrie française, 1823 (Paris). Jury central. *Rapport sur les produits de l'industrie française . . .,* ed. Héricart de Thury and Migneron. Paris: Imprimerie royale, 1824.

Exposition des produits de l'industrie française, 1834 (Paris). Jury central. *Rapport du Jury central sur les produits de l'industrie française exposé en 1834,* ed. Charles Dupin. Paris: Imprimerie royale, 1836.

Exposition universelle, 1855 (Paris). [Commission impériale]. *Exposition des produits de l'industrie de toutes les nations, 1855. Catalog officiel publié par ordre de la Commission impériale,* 2d ed. Paris: E. Panis, [1855].

Exposition universelle, 1855 (Paris). Commission impériale. *Rapport sur l'Exposition universelle de 1855 présenté à l'empereur par S.A.I. le prince Napoléon, president de la commission.* Paris: Imprimerie impériale, 1857.

Exposition universelle, 1867 (Paris). Commission impériale. *Rapport sur l'Exposition universelle de 1867, à Paris.* Paris: Imprimerie impériale, 1869.

Fairfax, J[oseph] S. *Proposed Centennial Buildings.* Pamphlet. [1873]. Centennial Collection, Historical Society of Pennsylvania, Philadelphia.

Ferguson, Eugene S. "History and Historiography." In *Yankee Enterprise: The Rise of the American System of Manufactures,* eds. Otto Mayr and Robert C. Post, 1–23. Washington, D.C.: Smithsonian Institution Press, 1981.

———. "Technical Museums and International Exhibitions." *Technology and Culture* 6, no. 1 (Dec. 1965): 30–46.

Findling, John E. *Chicago's Great World's Fairs.* Manchester: Manchester University Press, 1995.

———, ed. *Historical Dictionary of World's Fairs and Expositions, 1851–1988.* New York: Greenwood Press, 1990.

Forney, John W. *Oration by Mr. John W. Forney, at the 101st Celebration of American Independence: July 4, 1877, in the International Exhibition Building, Fairmount Park, by Invitation of the Board of Managers.* Philadelphia: Vallette, Haslam, 1877. Historical Society of Pennsylvania, Philadelphia.

Foster, Hal, ed. *Vision and Visuality.* Dia Art Foundation/Discussions in Contemporary Culture. Seattle: Bay Press, 1988.

Foucault, Michel. *Discipline and Punish: The Birth of the Prison.* Trans. Alan Sheridan. New York: Vintage Books, 1979.

———. *The Order of Things: An Archaeology of the Human Sciences.* World of Man series, ed. R.D. Laing. New York: Vintage Books, 1973.

Francis, David R. *The Universal Exposition of 1904.* 2 vols. St. Louis: Louisiana Purchase Exposition, 1913.

Freeman, J. Stuart, Jr. *Toward a Third Century of Excellence: An Informal History of the J.B. Lippincott Company on the Occasion of Its 200th Anniversary.* Philadelphia: J.B. Lippincott, 1992.

Gallery, John Andrew, ed. *Philadelphia Architecture: A Guide to the City.* 2d ed. Philadelphia: Foundation for Architecture, 1994.

Gatchel, Francis R., and Stephen Rush Jr. *Proposed Centennial Buildings.* Pamphlet. [1873]. Centennial Collection, Historical Society of Pennsylvania, Philadelphia.

Gates, Barbara T. "Ordering Nature: Revisioning Victorian Science Culture." In *Victorian Science in Context,* ed. Bernard Lightman, 179–86. Chicago: University of Chicago Press, 1997.

Geddes, Patrick. *Industrial Exhibitions and Modern Progress.* Edinburgh: David Douglas, 1887.

"General Notes." *New York Times,* 2 Aug. 1877, p. 4.

"General Notes." *New York Times,* 19 Dec. 1881, p. 4.

Gibbons, Herbert A. *John Wanamaker.* New York: Harper & Brothers, 1926.

Giedion, Sigfried. *Space, Time and Architecture: The Growth of a New Tradition.* Cambridge: Harvard University Press, 1976.

Gihon, John L. "Rambling Remarks Resumed." *Philadelphia Photographer* 14 (Jan. 1877): 3–7; (Feb. 1877): 38–42; (Mar. 1877): 70–74.

Gillette, Howard, Jr. "The Emergence of the Modern Metropolis: Philadelphia in the Age of Its Consolidation." In *The Divided Metropolis: Social and Spatial Dimensions of Philadelphia, 1800–1975,* eds. William W. Cutler III and Howard Gillette Jr., 3–25. Contributions in American History series, vol. 85. Westport Conn.: Greenwood Press, 1980.

Great Exhibition of the Works of Industry of All Nations (1851: London, England). *First Report of the Commissioners for the Exhibition of 1851.* London: W. Clowes, 1851.

———. *Official Descriptive and Illustrated Catalogue of the Great Exhibition of the Works of Industry of All Nations, 1851.* London: Spicer Brothers and W. Clowes, 1851.

———. *Reports by the Juries on the Subjects in the Thirty Classes into Which the Exhibition Was Divided.* London: Spicer Brothers, 1852.

———. *[Reports of the Juries of the Exhibition of Works of Industry of All Nations].* London: William Clowes, 1852.

Greenhalgh, Paul. *Ephemeral Vistas: The Expositions Universelles, Great Exhibitions and World's Fairs, 1851–1939.* Studies in Imperialism series. Manchester: Manchester University Press, 1988.

Grier, Katherine C. *Culture and Comfort: People, Parlors and Upholstery, 1850–1930.* Amherst: University of Massachusetts Press, 1988.

Haan, Hilde de, and Ids Haagsma. *Architects in Competition.* New York: Thames and Hudson, 1988.

Habermas, Jürgen. "Modernity—An Incomplete Project." In *Postmodernism: A Reader,* ed. Thomas Docherty, 98–109. New York: Columbia University Press, 1993.

Harris, Marvin. *The Rise of Anthropological Theory: A History of Theories of Culture.* New York: Thomas Y. Crowell, 1968.

Harris, Neil. "American Fairs and Civic Identity." In *Civic Visions, World's Fairs,* 7–11. Montreal: Canadian Centre for Architecture, 1993.

Henderson, Helen W. *The Pennsylvania Academy of the Fine Arts and Other Collections of Philadelphia.* Boston: L.C. Page, 1911.

Hicks, John Henry. "The United States Centennial Exhibition of 1876." Ph.D. diss., University of Georgia, 1972.

Hindle, Brook, and Steven Lubar. *Engines of Change: The American Industrial Revolution, 1790–1860.* Washington, D.C.: Smithsonian Institution Press, 1986.

Hines, Thomas S. *Burnham of Chicago: Architect and Planner.* Chicago: University of Chicago Press, 1979.

Hitchcock, Henry-Russell. *Architecture: Nineteenth and Twentieth Centuries.* 3d ed. Baltimore: Penguin Books, 1969.

[Holley, Marietta]. *Josiah Allen's Wife as a P.A. and P.I.: Samantha at the Centennial.* Hartford, Conn.: American Publishing, 1878.

Hornung, Clarence P., and Fridolf Johnson. *Two Hundred Years of American Graphic Art: A Retrospective Survey of the Printing Arts and Advertising since the Colonial Period.* New York: George Braziller, 1976.

Howells, William Dean. "A Sennight of the Centennial." *Atlantic Monthly* 38 (July 1876): 92–107.

Hudson, Derek, and Kenneth W. Luckhurst. *The Royal Society of Arts, 1754–1954.* London: Murray, 1954.

Ingram, J.S. *The Centennial Exposition, Described and Illustrated.* Philadelphia: Hubbard Brothers, 1876.

International Exhibition Company. *Official Bulletin of the International Exhibition.* Philadelphia, 1877–79.

———. *Opening Ceremonies, May 10th, 1877.* Program. [1877]. Athenaeum, Philadelphia.

International Exhibition Company. Board of Managers. Report to the stockholders. Philadelphia, ca. 1877.

Jackson, James B. *American Space: The Centennial Years, 1865–1876.* New York: W.W. Norton, 1972.

Jay, Martin. *Downcast Eyes: The Denigration of Vision in Twentieth-Century French Thought.* Berkeley: University of California Press, 1994.

Jay, Robert. *The Trade Card in Nineteenth-Century America.* Columbia: University of Missouri Press, 1987.

Jayne, Thomas Gordon. "The New York Crystal Palace: An International Exhibition of Goods and Ideas." Master's thesis, University of Delaware, 1990.

John Wanamaker. *A Friendly Guide to Philadelphia and the Wanamaker Store,* Philadelphia: John Wanamaker, 1926.

———. *Golden Book of the Wanamaker Stores. Jubilee Year, 1861–1911.* [Philadelphia]: John Wanamaker, 1911.

Kervick, Francis W. *Architects in America of Catholic Tradition.* Rutland, Vt.: Charles E. Tuttle, 1962.

Knight, David. *Ordering the World: A History of Classifying Man.* London: Burnett Books with Andre Deutsch, 1981.

Korzenik, Diana. *Drawn to Art: A Nineteenth-Century American Dream.* Hanover, N.H.: University Press of New England, 1985.

Kowsky, Francis R. *Country, Park, and City: The Architecture and Life of Calvert Vaux.* New York: Oxford University Press, 1998.

Kunz, George F. "Management and Uses of Expositions." *North American Review* 175 (Sept. 1902): 409–22.

Kusamitsu, Toshio. "Great Exhibitions before 1851." *History Workshop Journal,* no. 9 (Mar. 1980): 70–89.

Landau, Sarah Bradford. "Coming to Terms: Architecture Competitions in America and the Emerging Professions." In *The Experimental Tradition: Essays on Competitions in Architecture,* ed. Hélène Lipstadt, 53–78. New York: Princeton Architectural Press for the Architectural League of New York, 1989.

Lathrop, J.C. "The Philadelphia Centennial Exhibition of 1876." Master's thesis, Rutgers University, 1936.

Leach, William. "Strategists of Display and the Production of Desire." In *Consuming Visions,* ed. Simon J. Bronner, 99–132.

Lears, T.J. Jackson. "Beyond Veblen: Rethinking Consumer Culture in America." In *Consuming Visions,* ed. Simon J. Bronner, 73–97.

Le Corbusier. *Towards a New Architecture.* Trans. Frederick Etchells. New York: Praeger, 1960.

Lee, Antoinette J. *Architects to the Nation: The Rise and Decline of the Supervising Architect's Office.* New York: Oxford University Press, 2000.

Levine, George. "Defining Knowledge: An Introduction." In *Victorian Science in Context,* ed. Bernard Lightman, 15–23. Chicago: University of Chicago Press, 1997.

Levy, Richard Michael. "The Professionalization of American Architects and Civil Engineers, 1865–1917." Ph.D. diss., University of California, Berkeley, 1980.

Louisiana Purchase Exposition (1904: Saint Louis, Mo.). *Official Guide to the Louisiana Purchase Exposition*, St. Louis: Official Guide Co., 1904.

Luckhurst, Kenneth W. *The Story of Exhibitions.* London: Studio Publications, 1951.

Lutchmansingh, Larry D. "Commodity Exhibitionism at the London Great Exhibition of 1851." *Annals of Scholarship* 7 (1990): 203–16.

Lynes, Russell. *The Art-Makers: An Informal History of Painting, Sculpture and Architecture in 19th Century America.* New York: Dover, 1982.

Maass, John. *The Glorious Enterprise: The Centennial Exhibition of 1876 and H.J. Schwarzmann, Architect-in-Chief.* Watkins Glen, N.Y.: American Life Foundation, 1973.

———. "Who Invented Dewey's Classification?" *Wilson Library Bulletin* 47 (Dec. 1972): 335–41.

Magee's Illustrated Guide of Philadelphia and the Centennial Exhibition: A Guide and Description to All Places of Interest In or About Philadelphia, to the Centennial Grounds and Buildings, and Fairmount Park. Philadelphia: Richard Magee, 1876.

Mainardi, Patricia. *Art and Politics of the Second Empire: The Universal Expositions of 1855 and 1867.* New Haven, Conn.: Yale, 1987.

Marchand, Roland. "Corporate Imagery and Popular Education: World's Fairs and Expositions in the United States, 1893–1940." In *Consumption and American Culture,* eds. David E. Nye and Carl Pedersen, 18–33. Amsterdam: Vu University Press, 1991.

Markus, Thomas A. *Buildings and Power: Freedom and Control in the Origin of Modern Building Types.* London: Routledge, 1993.

Mathews, Arthur F. "House Decoration in San Francisco: First Paper." *Mark Hopkins Institute Review of Art: An Illustrated Quarterly Magazine Published by the San Francisco Art Association* 1, no. 4 (Dec. 1901): 9–17.

McArthur, John, Jr., and Joseph M. Wilson. *Revised Design in Competition for Proposed Centennial Exhibition Building, for Exposition of Industry of All Nations, to Be Held in Philadelphia in 1876.* Pamphlet. Philadelphia: King & Baird, 1873. Centennial Collection, Historical Society of Pennsylvania, Philadelphia.

McCabe, James D. *The Illustrated History of the Centennial Exhibition.* Philadelphia: National Publishing, 1876.

McIntyre, Philip W., and William F. Blanding, eds. *Men of Progress: Biographical Sketches and Portraits of Leaders in Business and Professional Life in and of the State of Maine,* comp. Richard Herndon. Boston: New Eng-land Magazine, 1897. S.v. "Nye, Joshua."

Meeks, Carroll L.V. *The Railroad Station: An Architectural History.* New Haven, Conn.: Yale University Press, 1956.

Merquior, J.G. *Foucault.* London: Fontana Press/Collins, 1985.

Morford, Henry. *Paris in '67, or, The Great Exposition, Its Side-Shows and Excursions.* New York: G.W. Carleton, 1867. In *Library of American Civilization.* Chicago: Library Resources, 1970. Microfiche 11799.

"Motive Power of the International Exposition." *Journal of the Franklin Institute* 103, no. 1 (Jan. 1877): 1–7.

New York Historical Society. *Dictionary of Artists in America.* New Haven, Conn.: Yale University Press, 1957. S.v. "Blake, William."

Nichols, George Ward. "Correspondence. The Centennial Painting Awards." *Nation* 23, no. 589 (12 Oct. 1876): 227–28.

———. "Correspondence. The Fine Arts Group at the Centennial Exhibition." *Nation* 25, no. 652 (27 Dec. 1877): 393.

Nicolai, Richard R. *Centennial Philadelphia.* Bryn Mawr, Pa.: Bryn Mawr Press, 1976.

Norton, Frank H. *Illustrated Historical Register of the Centennial Exhibition, Philadelphia, 1876, and of the Exposition Universelle, Paris, 1878.* New York: American News, 1879.

"Notes and Clippings." *American Architect and Building News* 1 (13 May 1876): 159.

"Notes and Clippings." *American Architect and Building News* 1 (9 Dec. 1876): 400.

Nye, David. *American Technological Sublime.* Cambridge: MIT Press, 1994.

O'Gorman, James F., et al. *Drawing Toward Building: Philadelphia Architectural Graphics, 1732-1986.* Philadelphia: University of Pennsylvania Press for Pennsylvania Academy of the Fine Arts, 1986.

Panama-Pacific International Exposition (1915: San Francisco, Calif.). *Official Catalogue of Exhibitors.* San Francisco: Wahlgreen, 1915.

Pan-American Exposition (1901: Buffalo, N.Y.). *Official Catalogue and Guide Book to the Pan-American Exposition.* Buffalo: Charles Ahrhart, 1901.

The Paris Exhibition of Industrial Art. N.p., 1855.

Pennsylvania Board of Centennial Managers. *Pennsylvania and the Centennial Exposition: Comprising the Preliminary and Final Reports of the Pennsylvania Board of Centennial Managers.* 2 vols. 3 pts. Philadelphia: Gillin & Nagle, 1878.

"The Pennsylvania Museum and School of Industrial Art." *Bulletin of the Pennsylvania Museum,* Apr. 1905, 17–23.

Pennsylvania Museum and School of Industrial Art. Charter. 1876. Philadelphia Museum of Art.

Pennsylvania Museum and School of Industrial Art. Board of Trustees. *First and Second Reports of the Board of Trustees.* Philadelphia: Review Printing House, 1878.

"The Permanent Exhibition." *New York Times,* 15 Mar. 1878, p. 1.

"The Permanent Exhibition." *New York Times,* 11 Apr. 1880, p. 2.

"The Permanent Exhibition." *New York Times,* 15 Jan. 1881, p. 2.

"The Permanent Exhibition Company." *New York Times,* 29 Mar. 1883, p. 5.

"The Permanent Exhibition's Trials." *New York Times,* 22 Dec. 1877, p. 1.

Peters, Tom F. *Building the Nineteenth Century.* Cambridge: MIT Press, 1996.

Pettit, Henry. "Appendix D. Report of Mr. Henry Pettit, Civil Engineer, Special Agent to the Vienna Exhibition." In U.S. Congress, Senate, *National Centennial,* 279–320.

———. "Centennial Exhibition." Scrapbooks. 2 vols. 1878. Athenaeum, Philadelphia.

————. *Final Report to the U.S. Centennial Commission on the Structures Erected for the Vienna Universal Exhibition, 1873, and Previous Exhibitions in London and Paris.* Philadelphia, 1873. Centennial Collection, Historical Society of Pennsylvania, Philadelphia.

————. *International Exhibition, Philadelphia, 1875. Specifications for International Trophies, Designed by Camille Piton, Artist, for Central Pavilion, Main Exhibition Building.* Philadelphia, 1875. Historical Society of Pennsylvania, Philadelphia.

————. "Obituary Notices of Members Deceased. Joseph Miller Wilson, A. M., C. E." *Proceedings of the American Philosophical Society* 42, no. 173 (Apr. 1903): i-vi.

————. "Report of Henry Pettit, Consulting Engineer." In United States Centennial Commission, *Journal of the Proceedings of the United States Centennial Commission at Philadelphia: May, 1874,* app. no. 1, 20-23. N.p. [1874?]. Booklet bound in United States Centennial Commission, *Journals and Reports of the United States Centennial Commission, Philadelphia, 1872-76.* Historical Society of Pennsylvania, Philadelphia.

Pettit, Henry, and Joseph M. Wilson. *International Exhibition, Philadelphia, 1876. Specifications for the Construction, Erection and Finishing of the Main Exhibition Building.* Philadelphia: J.B. Lippincott, 1874.

Pevsner, Nikolaus. *A History of Building Types.* Princeton, N.J.: Princeton University Press, 1976.

Philadelphia and Its Environs. Philadelphia: J.B. Lippincott, 1875.

Philadelphia Architects. "Instructions to Architects Competing for Plans for the Centennial Anniversary Building," Pamphlet. [1872]. In United States Centennial Commission, "Documentary Record of the Centennial," 1:87. Centennial Collection, Historical Society of Pennsylvania, Philadelphia.

Philadelphia. Commissioners of Fairmount Park. *License granted by the Commissioners of Fairmount Park to the International Exhibition Company.* 1876. Historical Society of Pennsylvania, Philadelphia.

Philadelphia. Commission to Vienna. *The Vienna Exposition.* Philadelphia: King & Baird, 1873.

"The Philadelphia Fair." *New York Times,* 11 May 1877, p. 2.

"Philadelphia's New Exhibition." *Harper's Weekly* 21, no. 1065 (26 May 1877): 414.

Plowman, Thomas M., and B[artholomew] Oertly. *Proposed Centennial Buildings.* Pamphlet. [1873]. Centennial Collection, Historical Society of Pennsylvania, Philadelphia.

Poesch, Jessie. *Newcomb Pottery: An Enterprise for Southern Women, 1895–1940.* Exton, Pa.: Schiffer Publishing, 1984.

Post, Robert C., ed. *1876: A Centennial Exhibition.* Washington, D.C.: Smithsonian Institution Press, 1976.

Prasch, Thomas. "The Invention of the Theme Park: Crystal Palace—Sydenham." Paper presented at the annual meeting of the Nineteenth-Century Studies Association, Philadelphia, 18–20 Mar. 1999.

Pred, Allan. "Spectacular Articulations of Modernity: The Stockholm Exhibition of 1897." *Geografiska Annaler, Series B, Human Geography* 73 (1991): 45–84.

"Profits of an Exhibition." *New York Times,* 17 Jan. 1882, p. 5.

Provisional Committee. *Report of the Provisional Committee to a Meeting of Citizens, Held November 19th, 1875.* Pamphlet. [1875?]. Philadelphia Museum of Art.

Pulos, Arthur J. *American Design Ethic: A History of Industrial Design.* Cambridge: MIT Press, 1986.

Rittel, Horst W. J., and Melvin M. Webber. "Dilemmas in a General Theory of Planning." *DMG-DRS Journal* 8, no. 1 (1974): 219–33.

Ritvo, Harriet. "Zoological Nomenclature and the Empire of Victorian Science." In *Victorian Science in Context,* ed. Bernard Lightman, 334–53. Chicago: University of Chicago Press, 1997.

Roth, Leland M. *A Concise History of American Architecture.* New York: Harper & Rowe, 1980.

Rydell, Robert W. *All the World's a Fair: Visions of Empire at American International Expositions, 1876–1916.* Chicago: University of Chicago Press, 1984.

———. "The Culture of Imperial Abundance: World's Fairs in the Making of American Culture." In *Consuming Visions,* ed. Simon J. Bronner, 191–216.

Schlereth, Thomas J. "The Material Universe of American World Expositions, 1876–1915." In *Cultural History and Material Culture: Everyday Life, Landscapes, Museums,* by Thomas J. Schlereth, 265–99. American Material Culture and Folklife series, ed. Simon J. Bronner. Ann Arbor: UMI Research Press, 1990.

Schön, Donald A. *The Reflective Practitioner: How Professionals Think in Action.* New York: Basic Books, 1983.

Schroeder-Gudehus, Brigitte, and Anne Rasmussen. *Les fastes du progrès: le guide des Expositions universelles, 1851–1992.* Paris: Flammarion, 1992.

Sellers, Charles Coleman. *Mr. Peale's Museum: Charles Willson Peale and the First Popular Museum of Natural Science and Art.* New York: W.W. Norton, 1980.

Sellers, Coleman. "System of Awards at the United States International Exhibition of 1876." *Journal of the Franklin Institute* 103, no. 1 (Jan. 1877): 14–16.

Sidney, James C. *Proposed Centennial Buildings.* Pamphlet. [1873]. Centennial Collection, Historical Society of Pennsylvania, Philadelphia.

Simonin, L[ouis Laurent]. *A French View of the Grand International Exposition of 1876.* Philadelphia: Claxton, Remsen & Happelfinger, 1877.

Sims, H[enry] A., and J[ames] P. Sims. *Proposed Centennial Buildings.* Pamphlet. [1873]. Centennial Collection, Historical Society of Pennsylvania, Philadelphia.

Sloan, Samuel. *Description of Design and Drawings for the Proposed Centennial Buildings, to Be Erected in Fairmount Park.* Pamphlet. Philadelphia: King & Baird, 1873. Centennial Collection, Historical Society of Pennsylvania, Philadelphia.

Smith, Frank Hill. "Correspondence. The Centennial Art Awards." *The Nation* 23, no. 597 (7 Dec. 1876): 340.

Smith, Merrit Roe. "Military Entrepreneurship." In *Yankee Enterprise: The Rise of the American System of Manufactures,* eds. Otto Mayr and Robert C. Post, 63–102. Washington, D.C.: Smithsonian Institution Press, 1981.

Solà-Morales Rubió, Ignasi de. "Weak Architecture." In *Differences: Topographies of Contemporary Architecture,* trans. Graham Thompson, ed. Sarah Whiting, 57–70. Cambridge: MIT Press, 1997.

Stewart, Susan. *On Longing: Narratives of the Miniature, the Gigantic, the Souvenir, the Collection.* Durham, N.C.: Duke University Press, 1993.

Suggestions of Architects of New York City. Pamphlet. [1872]. In United States Centennial Commission, "Documentary Record of the Centennial," 1:91. Centennial Collection, Historical Society of Pennsylvania, Philadelphia.

"Summary." *American Architect and Building News* 1 (23 Sept. 1876): 305–6.

"Summary." *American Architect and Building News* 2 (15 Dec. 1877): 397–98.

"Summary:—Effect of the Centennial upon Our Industrial Arts." *American Architect and Building News* 2 (28 July 1877): 237–38.

"Summary:—The Permanent Exhibition at Philadelphia." *American Architect and Building News* 2, no. 69 (21 Apr. 1877): 121.

Tatman, Sandra L., and Roger W. Moss. *Biographical Dictionary of Philadelphia Architects: 1700–1930.* Boston: G.K. Hall, 1985.

Tatum, George B. *Penn's Great Town.* Philadelphia: University of Pennsylvania Press, 1961.

Tenkotte, Paul A. "Kaleidoscopes of the World: International Exhibitions and the Concept of Culture-Place, 1851–1915." *American Studies* 28 (Mar. 1987): 5–29.

Todd, Frank Morton. *The Story of the Exposition.* 5 vols. New York: G.P. Putnam's Sons, 1921.

Tozier, Frederick A. "Centennial Record." Diary. 1876. Manuscript and Archives Department, Historical Society of Pennsylvania, Philadelphia.

Trachtenberg, Alan. *The Incorporation of America: Culture and Society in the Gilded Age.* New York: Hill and Wang, 1982.

Trennert, Robert A., Jr. "A Grand Failure: The Centennial Indian Exhibition of 1876." *Prologue* 6 (June 1974): 118–29.

United States. Centennial Board of Finance. *Second Annual Report.* N.p., 1875.

———. *Third Annual Report of the Centennial Board of Finance to the Stockholders.* Philadelphia: J.B. Lippincott, 1876

United States Centennial Commission. "Documentary Record of the Centennial." Scrapbooks. 31 vols., plus 9 boxes. 1876-79. Centennial Collection, Historical Society of Pennsylvania, Philadelphia.

———. *Grouping for the Judges' Work.* Philadelphia, 1876.

———. *International Exhibition, 1876.* Reports. 11 vols. Washington, D.C.: GPO, 1880–84.

———. *International Exhibition. 1876. Official Catalogue.* 2d ed. 4 pts. Philadelphia: John R. Nagle, 1876.

————. *International Exhibition, Philadelphia. 1876. System of Classification.* Philadelphia, 1874.

————. *Journal of the Proceedings of the United States Centennial Commission, at Philadelphia, 1872.* 1st, 2d, and 3d sessions. Philadelphia: E.C. Markley, 1872.

————. *Journal of the Proceedings of the United States Centennial Commission at Philadelphia. [Eighth Session: May, 1876].* N.p., [1876?]. Booklet bound in United States Centennial Commission, *Journals and Reports of the United States Centennial Commission, Philadelphia, 1872–76.* Historical Society of Pennsylvania, Philadelphia.

————. *Journal of the Proceedings of the United States Centennial Commission at Philadelphia. Sixth Session: May 1875.* N.p., [1875?]. Booklet bound in United States Centennial Commission, *Journals and Reports of the United States Centennial Commission.* Historical Society of Pennsylvania, Philadelphia.

————. "Reports of the Judges of Awards." Form. 10 Nov. 1877. Philadelphia City Archives.

United States Centennial Commission. Committee on Appeals. *[Report to the United States Centennial Commission].* Pamphlet. 1876. Historical Society of Pennsylvania, Philadelphia.

United States Centennial Commission. Committee on Classification. "Report on the Classification." In United States Centennial Commission, *Journal of the Proceedings of the United States Centennial Commission at Philadelphia. Fifth Session: May, 1874,* app. no. 3, 31–47. N.p., [1874?]. Booklet bound in United States Centennial Commission, *Journals and Reports of the United States Centennial Commission.* Historical Society of Pennsylvania, Philadelphia.

————. *System of Classification.* Philadelphia, 1874.

United States Centennial Commission. Committee on Plans and Architecture. Photographs of plans for Centennial Exhibition buildings. 3 vols. 1873. Free Library of Philadelphia. Copy at Historical Society of Pennsylvania, Philadelphia.

————. *Report of the Committee on Plans and Architecture, to the U.S. Centennial Commission.* Nov. 1, 1873. Philadelphia: J.B. Lippincott, [1873].

United States Centennial Commission. Executive Committee. *Report of the Executive Committee of the United States Centennial Commission.* Philadelphia, 1876. Booklet bound in United States Centennial Commission, *Journals and Reports of the United States Centennial Commission, Philadelphia, 1872-76..* Historical Society of Pennsylvania, Philadelphia.

United States, Commission to the Paris Exposition, 1867. *Reports of the United States Commissioners to the Paris Universal Exposition, 1867,* ed. William P. Blake. 6 vols. Washington, D.C.: GPO, 1870.

United States, Commission to the Paris Exposition, 1900 [Ferdinand W. Peck]. *Report of the Commissioner-General for the United States to the International Exposition at Paris 1900,* 6 vols. Washington, D.C.: GPO, 1901.

United States, Commission to the Vienna Exhibition, 1873. *Reports of the Commissioners of the United States to the International Exhibition Held at Vienna, 1873,* ed. Robert H. Thurston. 4 vols. Washington, D.C.: GPO, 1876.

"The United States International Exhibition of 1876." *Journal of the Franklin Institute* 101 (June 1876): 361–66; 102 (Dec. 1876): 361–64.

United States Patent Office. *Classified Index of Subjects of Invention Adopted in the U.S. Patent Office.* Washington, D.C.: GPO, 1872.

United States. World's Columbian Commission. *A Plan for the Organization of a Bureau of Awards for the World's Columbian Exposition.* Washington, D.C.: Judd & Detweiler, 1890.

———. *Report of the Committee on Awards.* Washinton, D.C.: GPO, 1901.

———. *Final Report of Executive Committee of Awards.* Washington, D.C.: John F. Sheiry Printer, 1895.

———. [Higinbotham, H.N.]. *Report of the President to the Board of Directors of the World's Columbian Exposition.* Chicago: Rand, McNally, 1898.

University of Arizona. *The Published Writings of William Phipps Blake.* Introduction by Kendric Charles Babcock. N.p., 1910.

Upton, Dell. "Another City: The Changing Urban Landscape of Early Republican America." Paper presented at the "Everyday Life in the Early Republic, 1789–1828" conference. Winterthur Museum, Winterthur, Del., 3–4 Nov. 1988.

U.S. Congress. House. *The National Celebration of the Centennial Anniversary of the Independence of the United States by an International Universal Exhibition, to be Held in Philadelphia in the Year 1876.* Report to Congress by the United States Centennial Commission, ed. Henry D.J. Pratt. 42d Cong., 3d sess. H. misc. doc. 99. Serial 1572. Washington, D.C.: GPO, 1873.

U.S. Congress. Senate. *Final Report of the Louisiana Purchase Exposition Commission.* Washington, D.C.: GPO, 1906.

———. *The National Centennial. The International Exhibition of 1876. Message of the President of the United States to Congress, Transmitting the Third Report of the United States Centennial Commission. . . .* 43d Cong., 1st sess. S. ex. doc. 30. Serial 1580. Washington, D.C.: GPO, 1874.

Vaux, Calvert, and George Kent Radford. "Designs for the Proposed Centennial Exposition Building." *New-York Sketch-Book of Architecture* 1 (Sept. 1874): 2.

———. *Proposed Centennial Buildings.* Pamphlet. [1873]. Centennial Collection, Historical Society of Pennsylvania, Philadelphia.

Visitor's Guide to the Centennial Exhibition and Philadelphia. Philadelphia: J.B. Lippincott, 1876.

Vogel, Morris J. *Cultural Connections: Museums and Libraries of Philadelphia and the Delaware Valley.* Philadelphia: Temple University Press, 1991.

[Vrydagh, Josse A.]. *Proposed Centennial Buildings.* Pamphlet. [1873]. Centennial Collection, Historical Society of Pennsylvania, Philadelphia. The name on the pamphlet is erroneously printed as "J.A.V. Rydagh."

Wagner Free Institute of Science. *Annual Announcement of Lecture Courses and Programs for Session of 1998–99.* Pamphlet. Philadelphia: Wagner Free Institute of Science, 1998.

Walker, Francis A. "Correspondence. The Fine Arts Group at the Centennial Exhibition." *Nation* 25, no. 652 (27 Dec. 1877): 393–94.

———. "The Philadelphia Exhibition." *International Review* 4 (1877): 363–96, 497–513, 673–85.

Wallace, John William. *Upon the Origin and Objects of the International Exhibition Company.* Pamphlet. 1880. Centennial Collection, Historical Society of Pennsylvania, Philadelphia.

Wanamaker Papers. Four series: Personal Records; Store Records; Miscellaneous Publications; Prints and Photos. 295 boxes plus Gibbons card files. Historical Society of Pennsylvania, Philadelphia.

Weber, Shierry M. "Walter Benjamin: Commodity Fetishism, the Modern, and the Experience of History." In *The Unknown Dimension: European Marxism since Lenin,* eds. Dick Howard and Karl E. Klare, 249–75. New York: Basic Books, 1972.

Weigley, Russell F. "The Border City in Civil War, 1854–1865." In *Philadelphia: A 300-Year History,* ed. Russell F. Weigley, 363–416. New York: W.W. Norton, 1982.

Weinberg, H. Barbara. Introduction to *Our American Artists* (1879), by Samuel G.W. Benjamin, 1–13. The Art Experience in Late Nineteen-Century America series, ed. H. Barbara Weinberg. New York: Garland Publishing, 1977.

Whewell, William. "The General Bearing of the Great Exhibition on the Progress of Art and Science." In *Lectures on the Results of the Exhibition, Delivered before the Society of Arts, Manufactures, and Commerce, at the Suggestion of H.R.H. Prince Albert, President of the Society,* 1–25. London: D. Bogue. Philadelphia: reprinted by A. Hart, 1852.

White, Theo B., ed. *Philadelphia Architecture in the Nineteenth Century.* Philadelphia: Art Alliance Press, 1973.

Wilson Brothers and Company. *Catalogue of Work Executed.* Philadelphia: J.B. Lippincott, 1885.

———. *Wilson Brothers & Co.* [Philadelphia]: [Armstrong & Fears], 1897.

Wilson, Joseph M. *The Masterpieces of the Centennial International Exhibition.* Vol. 3, *History, Mechanics, Science.* Philadelphia: Gebbie & Barrie, 1876.

Withey, Henry F., and Elsie Rathburn Withey. *Biographical Dictionary of American Architects (Deceased).* Detroit: Omnigraphics, 1996.

Wolf, Edwin II. *Philadelphia: Portrait of an American City.* Harrisburg, Pa.: Stackpole Books, 1975.

INDEX

CPSIA information can be obtained
at www.ICGtesting.com
Printed in the USA
BVHW03s0319140218
508041BV00001B/126/P